CW01512506

ONENESS PENTECOSTALISM

STUDIES IN THE HOLINESS AND PENTECOSTAL MOVEMENTS

Editors

DAVID BUNDY, *Manchester Wesley Research Centre*

GEORDAN HAMMOND, *Manchester Wesley Research Centre* AND *Nazarene Theological College*

DAVID SANG-EHIL HAN, *Pentecostal Theological Seminary*

The Holiness and Pentecostal movements have influenced most Christian churches since the 1830s and have been a central force in the global spread of Christianity. The histories and theologies of the Holiness, Pentecostal, Charismatic, and related movements are intertwined. Yet, they are often studied as distinct movements in relative isolation from each other.

Studies in the Holiness and Pentecostal Movements seeks to enhance our understanding of both traditions by examining the two movements, and their complex relationship, through multidisciplinary approaches. Bringing these traditions into critical comparison and dialogue opens up extensive possibilities for scholarly research. The series publishes original work from a variety of scholarly disciplines and geographical perspectives.

Advisory Board

DANIEL ÁLVAREZ, *Pentecostal Theological Seminary, US*

KWABENA ASAMOAH-GYADU, *Trinity Theological Seminary, Ghana*

CANDY GUNTHER BROWN, *Indiana University, US*

DALE M. COULTER, *Pentecostal Theological Seminary, US*

NAOMI HAYNES, *University of Edinburgh, UK*

MARK HUTCHINSON, *Alphacrucis College, Australia*

MELISSA WEI-TSING INOUYE, *University of Auckland, New Zealand*

GIANCARLO RINALDI, *University of Naples, Italy*

CHERYL J. SANDERS, *Howard University School of Divinity, US*

ELIZABETH SALAZAR SANZANA, *Comunidad Teológica Evangélica de Chile*

For more information about the series, please visit https://www.psupress.org/books/series/book _SeriesStudiesInHolinessAndPentecostalMovements.html.

ONENESS PENTECOSTALISM

Race, Gender, and Culture

EDITED BY LLOYD D. BARBA,
ANDREA SHAN JOHNSON, AND DANIEL RAMÍREZ

WITH A FOREWORD BY GRANT WACKER

The Pennsylvania State University Press | *University Park, Pennsylvania*

Library of Congress Cataloging-in-Publication Data

Names: Barba, Lloyd Daniel, editor. | Johnson, Andrea Shan, editor. | Ramirez, Daniel, 1958– editor.
Title: Oneness Pentecostalism : race, gender, and culture / edited by Lloyd D. Barba, Andrea Shan
    Johnson, and Daniel Ramírez ; with a foreword by Grant Wacker.
Other titles: Studies in the Holiness and Pentecostal movements.
Description: University Park, Pennsylvania : The Pennsylvania State University Press, [2023] | Series:
    Studies in the Holiness and Pentecostal movements | Includes bibliographical references and index.
Summary: "A collection of essays exploring Oneness Pentecostal history, theology, and culture in North
    America"—Provided by publisher.
Identifiers: LCCN 2022046257 | ISBN 9780271094557 (paperback)
Subjects: LCSH: Oneness Pentecostal churches—North America. | Oneness doctrine (Pentecostal-
    ism) | LCGFT: Essays.
Classification: LCC BX8763 .O54 2023 | DDC 289.9/4097—dc23/eng/20221118
LC record available at https://lccn.loc.gov/2022046257

Copyright © 2023 The Pennsylvania State University
All rights reserved
Printed in the United States of America
Published by The Pennsylvania State University Press,
University Park, PA 16802–1003

The Pennsylvania State University Press is a member of the Association of University Presses.

It is the policy of The Pennsylvania State University Press to use acid-free paper. Publications on
uncoated stock satisfy the minimum requirements of American National Standard for Information
Sciences—Permanence of Paper for Printed Library Material, ANSI Z39.48–1992.

CONTENTS

ILLUSTRATIONS

"Four score and seven years ago"—or so it now seems—I wrote a long essay on "Bibliography and Historiography" for the landmark *Dictionary of Pentecostal and Charismatic Movements* (1988). For a young historian wading into uncharted waters, it was, I hope, a useful effort. Yet looking at that essay today, I am shocked—though not really surprised—by the topics that I shortchanged. The most notable was Oneness Pentecostalism.

In my defense, at that point, there was not much to go on. For one thing, the major survey textbooks of American religious history had virtually ignored the Oneness Movement. Take Sydney Ahlstrom's field-defining tome, *A Religious History of the American People* (1972). Though weighing in at 1,158 pages, and blessed with exquisite detail about countless traditions, living and dead, Oneness Pentecostalism won a grand total of 4.5 lines in one footnote. Other standard textbooks of that era, such as Winthrop Hudson's *Religion in America* (1965) and Edwin Scott Gaustad's *A Religious History of America* (1966) did not mention the movement at all. More recent and otherwise superb survey textbooks, such as Catherine Albanese's *America: Religions and Religion* (1981), Peter Williams's *America's Religions* (1990), and Edwin Gaustad and Leigh E. Schmidt's *The Religious History of America* (2002), also failed to mention it at all.

General early academic studies of Pentecostal history did not offer much help, either. In Klaude Kendrick's *The Promise Fulfilled* (1961) and John Thomas Nichol's *Pentecostalism* (1966), which grew from doctoral dissertations at the University of Texas and Boston University, respectively, the Oneness tradition scored only a few pages. Walter Hollenweger's *The Pentecostals* (1972), the first global history of the movement, gave it less than one page.[1] Carl Brumback's *Suddenly . . . from Heaven* (1961), did allot a full chapter to Oneness origins within the Assemblies of God, but framed them as a grievously heterodox deviation from orthodox Trinitarian Pentecostalism.[2]

Historical studies focused on the origins and development of Oneness Pentecostalism also left much to be desired. Virtually all of them were written by white men who had grown up in the movement, self-published, or published by in-house denominational presses. Though they contained a wealth of hard-to-find primary data, they did not consistently reflect the standards of fairness, contextualization, and self-critical reliability that we have come to expect of serious religious historians.

In the past forty years, however, the academic study of Oneness has witnessed dramatic improvement. Monographs by Robert Mapes Anderson, Edith Blumhofer, Douglas Jacobson, Roger Robins, Vinson Synan, and myself, among others, began to give Oneness the attention it deserved. Soon insiders started writing first-rate doctoral dissertations and turning them into first-rate books. David Reed's *In Jesus' Name: The History and Beliefs of Oneness Pentecostals* (2008), Daniel Ramirez's *Migrating Faith* (2015), and Lloyd Barba's *Sowing the Sacred* (2022) represent pioneering studies that reflect deep research, polished prose, and self-critical analysis. This volume furthers their (and others') work in extraordinarily helpful ways. It constitutes a gold standard by which new studies of Oneness Pentecostalism will be measured.

This is not the place to try to preview the riches that lie ahead in an extended way. The authors, who reflect a variety of academic "social locations," have spoken for themselves with clarity and force. In time, reviewers will pick up the threads and weave them into interpretive responses of their own. But it may be helpful at least to intimate the insights that these scholars project.

Viewed whole, I see those insights as a tapestry consisting of three distinct bands. The first is indicators of the sheer numerical size of the Oneness movement; second, the threads that have held it together; and third, the internal diversity that makes it a coat of many colors.

First, then, the size. Today, religious demographers find at least fifteen, and perhaps as many as thirty, million partisans worldwide, with roughly two million residing in the United States and Canada. They have gathered themselves into more than four hundred denominations worldwide, and more than twenty-five in the United States and Canada. The Apostolic Church of the Faith in Christ Jesus, centered in Mexico, and predominantly middle class, forms the oldest Pentecostal denomination in that country, with churches in more places than any other. Oneness folk constitute the largest Protestant denomination (under native leadership) in Colombia, they are becoming the largest denomination in Nicaragua, and the majority in many towns in Mexico. One particularly conspicuous strand in the tapestry, La Luz del Mundo, boasts more than four million zealots, living mostly but by no means entirely in Mexico.

The point is this. A century ago, journalists could dismiss Oneness as inconsequential, a sect of a sect. But no more. Any movement that commands the loyalties of millions of earnest Christians around the globe merits sustained scrutiny by historians, theologians, and social scientists.

Second, what holds the movement together? What makes it possible to talk about it within the covers of a single book? The chapters ahead make clear that Oneness is not like contemporary evangelicalism, where the borders are shaggy, entwined with the borders of other traditions, and subject to constant dispute. Rather from the beginning in the early twentieth century until the present, Oneness has borne markers that firmly hold it together and, at the same time, set it apart from other Pentecostals and certainly from other conservative Christians.

Members themselves undoubtedly would begin with doctrinal assertions. They are Oneness because they *believe* certain things that distinguish them on the Christian/Protestant/Evangelical/Pentecostal landscape. As fits the name, Oneness folk have held to a One-Person God who manifests the divine self in three ways, commonly called Father, Son, and Holy Ghost, or by functional synonyms such as Creator, Redeemer, and Sustainer.

This conviction grew from two fundamental sources. The first was the centuries-long tradition of Jesu-centrism that defined the entire Pietist tradition. The latter birthed the Holiness and Pentecostal movements, which in turn birthed the Oneness movement. The second was the ubiquity of biblical literalism. The Bible implies but never explicitly speaks of a Trinity. And the New Testament offers straight-up affirmations of God's oneness, unfolded in Jesus, such as Colossians 2:9: "In Christ all the fullness of the deity lives in bodily form."

A second doctrinal assertion has centered on the necessity of baptizing converts in water in the name of Jesus alone, as detailed in Acts 2:38. The focus on Jesus' name is important, echoing the proper use of the name of "Yahweh" in the Old Testament. In the early days the movement often went by the label "Jesus' name" Pentecostals. Indeed, mainstream (Trinitarian) Pentecostals sought to combat the perceived danger in their midst by diminishing them with a put-down: "Jesus Only."

Other unifying bonds grew from the dense weaving of daily life. Most conspicuous perhaps was a "holy" lifestyle. That meant abjuring the allurements of secular culture, especially for women—cosmetics, short hair, smoking, drinking, gambling, cussing, immodest dress, and flirtatious deportment. Sexual morality was simply presupposed. Boundaries counted.

And then there was the commonality of worship practices. The oral, energetic preaching, and the aural, animated music, and the testimonial, heartfelt affirmations of the Lord's work in one's life formed the baseline. No one mistook a Oneness revival meeting for an Episcopal Eucharist service.

And women? To be sure, their roles evolved, they sometimes challenged male control of the pulpit, and they enjoyed opportunities on the mission field not available at home. Women also exercised power in less visible though forceful ways behind the scenes. No male pastor proceeded without first checking with the "Mothers" of the church. Even so, overall, women were excluded (and sometimes excluded themselves) from the highly symbolic sacerdotal functions of preaching, teaching men, presiding over the Lord's supper, and rendering the final word on church finances.

These considerations bring us to the third major strand in the tapestry: diversity. After all, by some measures, at the turn of the twenty-first century, the movement was 40 percent Black, 30 percent Asian, 20 percent Hispanic, and 9 percent white.

The most obvious source of diversity was the perennial wall, especially in the continental United States and Canada, between Black and white denominational bodies. That wall was best (or perhaps we should say worst) represented by the multiple barriers that divided the overwhelmingly Black Pentecostal Assemblies of the World, headquartered in Indianapolis, from the overwhelmingly white United Pentecostal Church, headquartered near St. Louis. Mexican Oneness Pentecostalism stood on the far side of another wall, separating those who worshipped in Spanish from those who did not.

Though the Oneness Movement's theological formulations varied little, the salience that different groups assigned to them varied over time and from place to place. Viewed from afar, US-based groups, both Black and white, articulated their theological claims more precisely and deployed them more rigorously, as behavioral codes and boundary markers, than their counterparts in Mexico, who looked more to the testimony of a Spirit-filled life.

The rainbow of diverse colors took additional forms. Though music enlivened and toughened the sinews of all Pentecostal bodies (for that matter, all Christian bodies), it likely played a larger role as a vehicle of theological expression and corporate solidarity among Mexican partisans. Then too the latter policed women's roles more austerely than their US/Canadian counterparts. The list of differences could be extended at length. But by now it should be evident that Oneness did not always mean oneness.

The danger of the foregoing analysis is that it threatens to reduce the Oneness aspiration to its trees while failing to see the forest. As with humor, or joy, dissection destroys. And so it is that we need to back up and see the entire movement; see the fundamental impulse that created and sustained it.

The following lines come from O. K. Bouwsma, a Christian philosopher who taught at the University of Nebraska and at the University of Texas from 1928 to 1977. They ring true for all believers.

> But what then is Christianity? Christianity is a faith. . . . It is also a Hope. . . . It is a light shining in the darkness. It is a knock at the door. It is a guest at supper. It is coals of fire. . . . It is reconciliation. It is hearing the voice of the shepherd. It is new wine to drink. It is madness. It is a house built on a rock. It is the truth walking. It is the eternal and rags. It is the lily of the valley. . . . It is the black sheep found. It is the ratio on a ruler. . . . It is the widows' mite. . . . It is . . . "a brand plucked out of the fire."[3]

At the end of the day, Oneness Pentecostalism, like all forms of Pentecostalism—indeed, like all forms of heartfelt Christianity—eludes simple definition. But this much we know. The movement offers its partisans a taste of God's goodness, and that is a faith worth living for. The chapters in this book show us why.

GRANT WACKER
Gilbert T. Rowe Distinguished Professor
Emeritus of Christian History
Duke Divinity School
January 2022

NOTES

1. Kendrick, *The Promise Fulfilled*, 171–75; Nichol, *Pentecostalism*, 116–11, 89–91; Hollenweger, *The Pentecostals*, 31. To be fair, several of Hollenweger's students, such as Roswith Gerloff and Kenneth A. Gill, later studied Oneness traditions in other parts of the world. I wish to thank Wayne Warner, of the Flower Pentecostal Heritage Center, and Cecil M. Robeck, of Fuller Theological Seminary, for providing me with these citations, as well as Brumback below.

2. Brumback, *Suddenly . . . from Heaven*, 191–210. These words, which constitute the third paragraph, represent the line of interpretation that pervades the whole chapter. "Unfortunately, that which should have been a most edifying study of the Word of God was diverted by the enemy into a distressing error which almost ruined the work of God. Satan, realizing what a disaster would befall his kingdom if the people of God were really to grasp the power in the precious name of Jesus, adroitly maneuvered these sincere souls into heresy and fanaticism" (pp. 192–202). It is telling that *Suddenly . . . from Heaven: A History of the Assemblies of God*, was released by the Gospel Publishing House, the official publication arm of the largest Pentecostal denomination in the United States.

3. Bouwsma, "Faith, Evidence, and Proof," 21. I owe this marvelous quotation to James K. A. Smith of Calvin Theological Seminary.

BIBLIOGRAPHY

Bouwsma, O. K. "Faith, Evidence, and Proof." In *Without Proof or Evidence: Essays of O. K. Bouwsma*, edited by J. L. Craft and Ronald E. Hustwit, 1–25. Lincoln: University of Nebraska Press, 1984.
Brumback, Carl. *Suddenly . . . from Heaven: A History of the Assemblies of God*. Springfield, MO: Gospel Publishing House, 1961.
Hollenweger, Walter. *The Pentecostals*. Minneapolis, MN: Augsburg Publishing House, 1972.
Kendrick, Klaude. *The Promise Fulfilled: A History of the Modern Pentecostal Movement*. Springfield, MO: Gospel Publishing House, 1961.
Nichol, John Thomas. *Pentecostalism*. New York: Harper and Row, 1966.

ACKNOWLEDGMENTS

Any edited volume is a collaborative effort. First and foremost, we thank the contributors, without whom this volume would not have been written. We drafted a proposal just before the pandemic, and little did we know then that the whole world would slow down a bit. Nevertheless, the contributors kept their commitments. Second, we would like to thank Penn State University Press and our editor Kathryn Bourque Yahner, editorial assistant Maddie Caso, and the series editors for agreeing to take on this volume just as the pandemic began, a decision that no doubt came with some risk.

Discussions about this volume began with colleagues at the Society for Pentecostal Studies annual conference in Hyattsville, Maryland. In the earliest stages Jeff Brickle lent strong support as did many colleagues from the Society: Felipe Agredano, Estrelda Alexander, Kimberly Ervin Alexander, Sammy Alfaro, Linda Ambrose, David Bernard, Roy Fisher, Kenneth Gill, Robin Johnston, Jorge Montes, Leah Payne, Joey Peyton, Johnnie Peyton, Erica Ramirez, Mel Robuck, Alexander Stewart, and Ekaputra Tupamahu, to name a few.

Without the preservations of church archivists and chroniclers, we would have very little to write about. Thanks to the efforts of past and present individuals such as Benjamín Cantú, Ismael Martín del Campo, Milca Montañez-Vizcarra, José Ortega, Benjamín Ortega, Felipe Rangel, and Abraham Ruiz of the Apostolic Assembly of the Faith in Christ Jesus; Maclovio Gaxiola, Manuel Gaxiola, and Domingo Torres of the Iglesia Apostólica de la Fe en Cristo Jesús; Sherry Sherrod DuPree and Alexander Stewart of the Church of Our Lord Jesus Christ; Morris Golder and James Tyson of the Pentecostal Assemblies of the World; Robin Johnston, Crystal Napier, and Fred Foster of the United Pentecostal Church International and the Center for the Study of Oneness Pentecostalism; archivists at the Flower Pentecostal Heritage Center and the David Allan Hubbard Library at Fuller Theological Seminary. In addition, there are countless authors and collectors of Pentecostal history whose files have been shared for use outside of church archives, including David Bundy, Nancy Glower, Adam Gossman, and Juan Martínez, all of whom assisted in establishing the Manuel J. Gaxiola and Manuel Vizcarra collections at Fuller Theological Seminary. The Papers of Patricia Pickard, also at Fuller Theological Seminary, proved indispensable for chapter 8. Finally, we thank the indefatigable primary source collector Herminia "Minnie" Martinez and pastor Ramón Rentería who provided musical scores from the Iglesia Apostólica's newly scored hymnal.

Daniel blesses the memory of Manuel Gaxiola, José Ortega, Ernesto Cantú, Felipe Rangel, and Isaac Cota, solicitous custodians and protagonists of Apostolic history in the United States and Mexico. María Mendoza Ramírez, pioneer member of the Apostolic Church of Solana Beach, California, bequeathed her considerable musical gifts to her sons Eliseo, Tomás, Luis, and Roberto, and they in turn passed them to the following generations. Luis and Roberto preserved their gifts for posterity on vinyl LPs. Luis's wife Margarita, a convert, transmitted her love of the (for her) new hymnody during long hymn-singing sessions in the family living room. As Daniel made his way into the religious studies guild, Rudy Busto, Arlene Sanchez Walsh, Grant Wacker, Mark Noll, Russ Richey, Louise Meintjeis, Edith Blumhofer, Cecil "Mel" Robeck, David Bundy, David Daniels, Otto Maduro, Daisy Machado, Justo González, Luis Rivera Pagán, Paul Barton, Juan Martínez, Anthea Butler, Timothy Matovina, Gastón Espinosa, Alan Anderson, and others did not dissuade him from singing, and encouraged his transdisciplinary move through the ethnomusicological window. Patient and supportive colleagues in the Red de Investigadores del Fenómeno Religioso de México and in the Comisión para el Estudio de la Historia de la Iglesia Latinoamericana (CEHILA) orbit have also welcomed the move, as have generous colleagues in the Society for the Scientific Study of Religion, the American Academy of Religion, the American Society of Church History, the Hispanic Theological Initiative, and, especially, the Society for Pentecostal Studies (SPS). Chapter 3 represents a developed version of a plenary address delivered to the SPS's 2014 meeting at Evangel University. On that memorable occasion, the Urshan College Choir, led by Sharla Bender, moved the audience with inspired (bilingual) renditions of the songs under discussion. All lecturers should be so blessed! Finally, Daniel thanks colleagues and students at Claremont Graduate University for their collegial respect and support.

Andrea would like to extend thanks to her department and college at California State University, Dominguez Hills, for their support of the research related to this project. In particular Kate Fawver, Chris Monty, and Laura Talamante have taught her much about maintaining a research agenda at a teaching institution. Bianca Murillo, Joshua Jeffers, and Kerry Shannon have been a joy to have as colleagues, and their willingness to pull together as a department has made completing this work possible. Thanks also to those who have served as writing group partners during parts of this project, including Kirstin Ellsworth, Jenn Stacy, Leah Payne, Saili Kulkarni, and Linda Ambrose, and thanks to Debbie Best for the early pandemic parking lot meet-up to witness her signing the contract for this book. Andrea also gratefully acknowledges the contributions of her parents Douglas and Kandas, without whose support her educational and career path would not have been possible and the legacy of family members, particularly her grandmother Jane, whose lived experiences contributed to a deeper understanding of this topic.

Lloyd would like to offer a special thanks for the unending support of his colleagues in the religion department at Amherst College: Andrew Dole, Rebecca Falcasantos, Maria Heim, Tariq Jaffer, and Susan Niditch. He also thanks Laurie Canter for helping organize our editorial meeting at Amherst College in December 2021. He expresses special gratitude to his various conversation partners, who all in various ways have sharpened his analysis: Arlis Barba, Morgan "Ted" Cassady, Priscilla Cortez, James Cisneros, Ruth Leon Barba, Seth Ortiz, Jerry Powell, CaVar Reid, Santino Simental, and Don Whitt. Finally, he owes his deepest gratitude to his family: Ruth, Arlis, Fatima, and, finally, Daniel, who kept threatening to climb out of his playpen during our editorial meeting.

Introduction
Remapping the History of North American Oneness Pentecostalism

Lloyd D. Barba, Andrea Shan Johnson, and Daniel Ramírez

There was an inaudible shudder that swept the preachers on the platform
and the people in the vast arena.
—FRANK EWART

On August 24, 2013, a group of Pentecostals gathered in Hermon Park in the
Arroyo Seco area of Los Angeles. There to commemorate the centennial of the
modern revelation of Jesus' name baptism, attendees were treated to a reen-
actment of R. E. McAlister's 1913 sermon calling for the use of the recovered
baptismal formula, and were invited to witness the baptisms of new converts.
They also partook in the dedication of a permanent park bench to commemorate the historic events at Maria Woodworth-Etter's 1913 camp meeting.[1] Less
formal than the Azusa Street Revival 2006 centennial, the commemoration was
a reminder that a heterodox theology challenging accepted Trinitarian views of
the godhead had emerged during the Progressive Era, had survived two world
wars and the Great Depression, and now projected significant influence in the
global Pentecostal Movement.

In 1913, the land that is now Hermon Park lay between the rapidly growing
cities of Los Angeles and Pasadena. Electric rail lines would have facilitated
attendance from within the two cities' region. It was a good choice of location

for a revival. However, Los Angeles was host to many religious spectacles, a phenomenon that muckraking novelist Upton Sinclair would complain about in his 1917 work *The Profits of Religion*. It is likely that the camp meeting, like so many others held in the region, would have faded from historical memory were it not for the controversy that arose there concerning the proper mode of baptism.

The best eyewitness account of the revival came from Frank Ewart, an Australian immigrant who had recently begun pastoring the late William Durham's Upper Room Mission in Los Angeles. Amid the emerging controversy, he spread the Jesus' name message in his periodical *Meat in Due Season* (see fig. I.1). Ewart's 1947 *The Phenomenon of Pentecost: A History of the Latter Rain*, is the earliest known insider history of the Oneness Movement and of the catalytic moment at Arroyo Seco. Ewart recalled, "There was an inaudible shudder that swept the preachers on the platform and the people in the vast arena," when Canadian evangelist R. E. McAlister proclaimed that the Apostles baptized in the "Name of Jesus Christ" rather than with the titles of Father, Son, and Holy Ghost. Ewart remembered that Frank Denny, a missionary to China, immediately went to McAlister and told him to cease, lest the revival be associated with a Dr. Sykes.[2] While Ewart was mistaken about the doctoral honorific, Denny had identified a serious concern. Joshua Sykes, one of the region's many revivalists, had arrived in California around the time of the Azusa Street Revival and established himself as a religious upstart. His Apostolic Church (later called the Church of the Living God) practiced baptism "in the name of Christ," spoke in tongues, believed in visions as answers to prayer, made improbable claims to the miraculous, and had a suspect sense of morality. In May 1914, Sykes, facing legal troubles in Los Angeles, would deem it necessary to decamp with his extensive congregation to the San Francisco Bay Area, where his troublesome reputation continued to grow. If a shudder swept through the ministers on the platform that day, it is likely that the inspiration (or specter) was Sykes rather than the Holy Spirit.[3]

The Pentecostal Movement would soon have a greater problem than association with the controversial Sykes. The recovery of the proper baptismal formula led to a reexamination of ideas about the godhead. As primitivists, Oneness adherents pointed to scriptural examples such as Acts 2:38, 4:12, 10:44–48, and 19:1–6 to argue that the name of Jesus should be proclaimed over the baptized. They argued that the godhead was not a Trinity with three distinct persons, but rather that Father, Son, and Holy Spirit were manifestations of one God. The "New Issue" prompted mutual epithets and charges: "Jesus Only" and tritheism. As the debate heated up in 1914, its expansion coincided with the

MEAT IN DUE SEASON

Vol. 1, No. 9   Los Angeles, Cal., December, 1915   Circulation Free

WHY I WAS RE-BAPTIZED, IN THE NAME OF JESUS CHRIST

I have been requested to give a condensed statement of my reason for being baptized again, this time in the name of Jesus Christ. It would be a satisfaction to go into detail in the matter, but unfortunately space forbids. I must condense. I may say I never had much sympathy with this sort of matter. Like many others obedience to outward ceremony did not seem very important to me. I was ignorant as to the real object of baptism. But I have found that obedience, even in the smallest detail, means something. There

water baptism meant that I had never had before. When I was baptized over twenty years ago my whole thought was to confess Christ. I was fully converted. But now I seemed to see a real death with Jesus, separation from the world, and from Pentecostal gainsayers even, such as I had never dreamed of before. It was real death. Romans 6:3 was made very plain to me. I can truly say that I have never known such content and willingness and glory in being dead to praise and blame, to the opinions of the people, and to everything but the will of God, as I do today. I praise Him! Separated unto God.

THE REVELATION OF GOD IN OUR LORD JESUS CHRIST

Evangelist I. C. Hall

Which God?

Jesus said: "Hear, O Israel: the Lord our God is one Lord." Mark 12:29. This He said was the first commandment.

Moses said: "Thou shalt have no other gods beside me." Not us.

Isaiah said: "Thus saith the Lord, the King of Israel, and His redeemer the Lord of Hosts; I am the first and I am the last; and beside me there is no God." Is. 44:6.

How much the following sounds like

mediate between God and man, in each of which the divine fulness was abridged and the divine glory shaded in proportion to the remoteness from God in successive emanation.

Thank God for the scales that are falling from the believers' eyes when this fulness of the Godhead is revealed in Him, where "Dwells all the fulness of the Godhead bodily."

"O wondrous sight, a blissful sight Of our Almighty's throne! There sits the Saviour, crowned with light, Clothed in a body like our own.

Fig. I.1. Frank Ewart's periodical *Meat in Due Season* reached all corners of the Pentecostal Movement, advancing the Jesus' name message to missionaries, who in turn, submitted reports about their revivals abroad. Photo courtesy of Flower Pentecostal Heritage Center.

attempt by several Pentecostal groups to merge under a single umbrella. The nascent Assemblies of God (AG) would spend the first two years of its existence trying to unify the two factions until 1916, when its leaders issued a sixteen-point "Statement of Fundamental Truths" that flatly rejected Oneness theology as heresy.[4]

Many Oneness Pentecostals who left the AG found a ready home in the already-existing Pentecostal Assemblies of the World (PAW). Since large portions of the African American Pentecostal Movement embraced the Oneness doctrine, the PAW became not only the premier Oneness group but also one of the more integrated denominations in the United States. Other ministers had met in Arkansas in 1917 and formed the General Assembly of Apostolic Assemblies (GAAA), but this group merged with the PAW soon thereafter, driven in part by the need to use the established PAW name to guarantee exemption from World War I military service for their largely pacifist membership. This short-lived experiment in interracial cooperation stands out against the national backdrop of the time. Nevertheless, as with American Protestantism generally, the prophetic light would soon be eclipsed in the encroaching shadow of Jim Crow.

Oneness adherents from historically Black and white denominations would recognize this origin story. Those from Spanish-speaking churches might not. The US-based Apostolic Assembly of the Faith in Christ Jesus (AAFCJ) and its sister Iglesia Apostólica de la Fe en Cristo Jesús (IAFCJ) of Mexico date their practice of Jesus' name baptism to as early as 1909, predating the events of 1913 at Arroyo Seco.[5] The differing origin narratives have resulted in different heroes and heroines of the faith as well, with each denomination centering its histories around a variety of figures. For the predominantly white churches, men like Andrew Urshan (the Persian Evangelist) and Howard Goss (the Texas revivalist) take center stage. In the now mostly Black PAW and its daughter denominations, founders G. T. Haywood and Robert C. Lawson are accorded pride of place. For churches with shared origins in the borderlands, figures like Francisco Llorente and Antonio Nava, founders of the AAFCJ, and Romana Carbajal de Valenzuela, founding matriarch of the IAFCJ, are commemorated.

These different origin stories help to explain the current diversity within the Oneness Pentecostal Movement. This volume offers readers the chance to develop an understanding of the ways in which race, gender, and sometimes class impacted the growth of the movement. Oneness Pentecostals were not and are not a homogeneous group. The experiences of any particular member of the ministry or laity could be influenced by their social status, race, sex, location/setting, or a combination of such factors. The chapters of this volume explore these themes and identify further areas of investigation; *Oneness Pentecostalism: Race, Gender, and Culture* can be considered, then, as an initial overdue foray into this topic in the broader fields of Pentecostal studies and North American religious history.

The color line was washed away in the blood of Christ.[6]

If our Lord would return to the earth again in the flesh,
and would go down South incognito, he would be jim-crowed and segregated.[7]

Foremost among the themes of these chapters is the issue of race and ethnicity; the church was not exempt from conflict along these lines. The church leaders of the 1920s and 1930s found themselves constantly revisiting conflicts over race. In his 1925 retrospective, Azusa Street eyewitness and chronicler Frank Bartleman penned one of the most famous proclamations concerning the Revival: "The color line was washed away in the blood of Christ" (a riposte to W. E. B. Du Bois's dismal 1903 prophecy on race relations in the looming twentieth century).[8] In that same year, Church of Our Lord Jesus Christ (COOLJC) founder (and PAW dissident) Robert C. Lawson offered a much less triumphant take on the state of race relations in American Christianity generally and in Oneness Pentecostalism in particular: "If our Lord would return to the earth again in the flesh, and would go down South incognito, he would be jim-crowed and segregated."[9] While Bartleman nostalgically celebrated Azusa's interracial harmony, Lawson lamented its decline. The 1920s concluded the "golden age" of Pentecostalism, a time of theological and social breakups, on the one hand, and an era of denomination-building, on the other.[10]

Despite Pentecostals' best efforts, by the 1920s the color line had been restitched across Pentecostalism's social fabric. Although at moments between the 1910s and the 1930s, the PAW would be the most racially integrated Pentecostal denomination, racial harmony over the long term proved difficult to sustain.[11] If the 1910s figured as an era of doctrinal definition, the following two decades prefigured subsequent and distinct social trajectories. And no social issue tested Oneness Pentecostals more than race. The legion withstood exorcism, however, owing to white Southern ministers' sensibilities and actions.

The PAW entered the 1920s with a racially integrated leadership board as a result of mergers from 1918 and 1919. The interracial board, however, proved a short-lived endeavor. In 1924 Southern ministers broke with the racially integrated PAW, inflicting damage by (1) holding their own segregated conferences in 1923 and 1924, (2) clamoring for the annual convention to be held in the South, where Blacks would be excluded under Jim Crow laws, (3) refusing credentials signed by African American executive board member G. T. Haywood, and (4) promoting a name change to the PAW and advocating for segregated branches within the organization. And although it is difficult to ascertain its impact, others objected to interracial marriages such as the one conducted by William Booth-Clibborn in St. Paul, Minnesota.[12] White Pentecostals not only chose to break with the interracial efforts, but some also wished to maintain the segregated order of the day. To suggest that the division was merely utilitarian because segregation posed barriers to effective evangelism and growth obscures the racial dynamics at play within the movement at that time.

Over the next two decades, independent white coreligionists joined the defecting Southern ministers in a course chartering new organizations and mergers. By the end of 1924, the PAW's ministerial roster was only about 20 percent white. In 1931 Haywood would lead the PAW in a final effort toward racial reconciliation, forming the Pentecostal Assemblies of Jesus Christ (PAJC) with white ministers. Haywood died that year, but the fellowship continued until 1937, when the PAJC held its annual convention in Tulsa and informed its African American constituency and leaders that they had made no accommodations for them. Fortunately for the PAW, Samuel Grimes, a protégé of Haywood, had possessed the foresight to renew the PAW charter in 1931 after Haywood vacated it.[13] This allowed Black ministers—and some white allies—to regroup under the PAW banner.

While the exclusionary subterfuge did not provoke a full-frontal critique from PAW quarters, one prophetic voice had emerged by 1925: that of Robert C. Lawson. The Haywood protégé had parted ways with his mentor in 1919 and headed east from Ohio to Harlem. His Refuge Temple represented one of the most successful Oneness Pentecostal ministries in the country and garnered the esteem of both the Harlem community and the larger African American uplift movement. Lawson's 1925 *An Anthropology of Jesus Christ Our Kinsman* offered a robust, scripturally based critique lambasting the Jim Crow inhospitality of both American society and white Pentecostals.[14]

Several scholars have noted that Oneness Pentecostals have historically been "more characteristically Pentecostal than their Trinitarian counterparts."[15] The movement was more steadfast in its retention of some of Pentecostalism's core spiritual practices and incubated an environment that has been "more compatible with an Afro-centric worldview than with that of non-Pentecostal white evangelicals."[16] In a similar vein, James Tinney argued that Oneness Pentecostalism represents "the survival and renewal of African impulses," and that its "New Issue" heterodoxy exemplified a "rejection of white attempts to harness and define the Pentecostal work of the Spirit." Tinney characterized this as a "counter reformation."[17] Another scholar, Joseph Howell, notes how Oneness Pentecostals engendered a "counter reformation of the Azusa revival" in its fourfold goal to recapture the early revival's vitality; thwart the theologizing experience; reaffirm the eschatological zeal; and revive interracial fellowship.[18] In the decades after the exodus from the AG, Oneness Pentecostalism would grow disproportionately among African Americans and Latinos; at times, the separate subaltern trajectories converged, especially in musical expressions and borrowings.

While racial tensions embroiled Black and white Pentecostalism, another stream of the movement emerged from the Azusa Street Revival. Mexican Oneness Pentecostals (Apostólicos) forged a different trajectory as they ministered primarily to Spanish-speakers. Apostólico patriarchs Francisco Llorente, Marcial de la Cruz, and Antonio Nava, among others, received ministerial credentials from the PAW (so did several women as deaconesses). In 1925, while still under PAW auspices, they formed their own smaller unofficial fellowship: Iglesia de la Fe Apostólica Pentecostés. The delegates from over two dozen churches gathered in San Bernardino, California, and continued to meet annually at different sites, including one across the border in the Colonia Zaragoza agrarian commune in Mexicali, Baja California. In 1929, they decided to formally seek their own charter and in the following year formed the Apostolic Assembly of the Faith in Christ Jesus (AAFCJ). Nava, the leader, helped unify the denomination's counterpart in Mexico in 1933, bringing together the discrete and regionally scattered workers and congregations in Mexico. Concerned over the distracting divisions between his Black and white Anglophone counterparts, Nava separated from the regionally distant PAW and fastened ties with more proximate—geographically and culturally—coreligionists.[19]

Nevertheless, doctrinal disputes and competing charisma threatened the unity of Mexican Pentecostals both north and south of the border at the same time that Black and white Oneness Pentecostals faced their own internal conflicts. In Mexico, relatives and converts of Romana Carbajal de Valenzuela augmented the movement in the decade following her arrival, but beginning in 1925 the movement suffered several schisms. Notably, Francisco Borrego launched the Iglesia Evangélica del Consejo Espiritual Mexicano, maintaining a close affiliation with two self-styled prophets, Saúl and Silas, who split several Jesus' name churches. Likely influenced by spiritualist teachings popular in Mexico at that time, they, along with Borrego, emphasized dreams and visions, often above scripture. Their most famous convert, Eusebio Joaquín, would also assume a prophetic mantle and rechristen himself in 1926 as the Apostle Aarón, charged to restore the primitive church. Unlike Saúl and Silas, who fell into historical obscurity, Joaquín realized great success with his new denomination, Iglesia del Dios Vivo Columna y Apoyo de la Verdad, La Luz del Mundo, known more colloquially as La Luz del Mundo (Light of the world).[20]

Set against the backdrop of centrifugal dynamics, many early leaders evinced a sentiment for unity in spirit while awaiting unity in belief. In one such fraught moment, pioneer Marcial de la Cruz's was reported to retreat in prayer and returned to a ministerial conclave with a moving anthem, "La Iglesia el Cuerpo de Cristo" (The Church the Body of Christ):

> *Somos un cuerpo en Cristo, con diferente don. . . .*
> *Y si en acuerdo vamos, crece la caridad.*
> *(We are one body in Christ, with different gifts. . . .*
> *And if we proceed in unity, love will grow.)*[21]

In the face of threatened fragmentation and implosion, some Apostólicos discovered the strength of transnational solidarity, exchanging personnel and material in a process that tied sister flagship denominations: the AAFCJ of the United States and the Iglesia Apostólica de la Fe en Cristo Jesús (IAFCJ) of Mexico. The exchange was unwittingly prompted, in part, by American xenophobia.

As US elites cast about for scapegoats to blame for the Great Depression, they settled on perennial ones: Mexicans. A concerted campaign between all levels of government and charitable agencies successfully pushed about one out of every three of the 1.3 million Mexicans residing in the country back to Mexico. The Great Repatriation (1929–39) also uprooted scores of thousands of US-born children and about the same ratio of Apostólicos. This is not surprising, as Pentecostals occupied the same humble strata as their vulnerable countrymen. What is remarkable, though, is their intrepid response. Rather than lament their circumstances, believers purposely set about evangelizing villages, towns, and agrarian communes in their native states, consolidated the movement in Mexico, and fastened fraternal bonds in the form of formal cross-border ecclesial accords in 1944–45: a joint Constitution and Treaty of Unification. The timely accords reinforced a practice of solidarity during subsequent periods of labor and family migration (e.g., the guest-worker Bracero Program, 1942–64) and missionary expansion (supported by the newly formed United Pentecostal Church) to Central America (1948) and the Southern Cone (1951). The first missionary expansion was fired by evangelistic reports from World War II Mexican American soldiers evangelizing in the Philippines and among Spanish refugees in France and facilitated by the bilingual gifts of a young leader, Isidro Pérez, who had been caught up in the Great Repatriation as a child and later studied at Apostolic Bible Institute, a UPC-endorsed Bible college in Tulsa, Oklahoma. Missionary endeavors in the Southern Cone began in response to a Macedonian call for help from diasporic Soviet Apostolics in Paraguay and Argentina (the religious progeny of Andrew D. Urshan). Notably, as Apostolicism inserted itself into a Mexican landscape beset by Herculean struggle between an ascendant liberal and revolutionary regime and a recalcitrant Catholic church (e.g., the Cristero War, 1926–29), believers affirmed historical ties and created defensive alliances with other beleaguered *evangélicos*. The shared circumstances attenuated the usual combative introversion of Oneness Pentecostalism at least in Mexico. The more peaceable spirit resulted in national leadership opportunities, including IAFCJ presiding bishop Manuel Gaxiola's presidency of the Mexican Bible Society and Adoniram Gaxiola's interlocution between the Carlos Salinas administration and Protestant churches during the historical 1992 constitutional reforms over religion.

The comparative analytical possibilities concerning the variables of migration and diaspora in different historical and social settings are promising. The Great Repatriation transpired, not coincidentally, at a time when California witnessed an influx of the so-called Okie migrants (to join the large Mexican agricultural labor force) from the states impacted by the Dust Bowl of the late 1920s and 1930s. The Dust Bowl, an American saga popularized by John Steinbeck's 1939 novel *The Grapes of Wrath*, stirred up a long-term change in the religious and political ethos in California, with the lower counties of the San Joaquin Valley undergoing the most extensive southernization. Pentecostalism boomed in California in large part due to migration from the South (including Arkansas and Texas) and developed a staunch religiously conservative culture that persists to this day.[22] White Pentecostal migrants, however, were not the only ones to introduce a new ethos and practice to migration destinations. Black Pentecostal Southerners, too, transformed the environments they entered, as made especially evident during the Great Migration. Pentecostals introduced a "new sacred order," challenging the existing culture of worship, music, preaching, and social concern.[23] An uptick in migration from Black, brown, and white migrants, thus, spread and transformed Oneness Pentecostalism. Discrete regional differences within denominations attest to legacies of migration and the social adaptability migration engenders. The analytical possibilities are promising. For example, the earlier migratory trajectories of celebrated pioneers like Frank Ewart and Andrew D. Urshan await critical study that can nuance the discussion of their theological contributions.

This long-overdue exploration of the movement's variegated origin points and streams expands the number of variables to consider. In the case of the three racial/ethnic groups under study, proletarian migration and racial or ethnic resistance can be added to the analytical mix. In the case of Mexico and the US Southwest, xenophobic persecution, religious intolerance, and transnational agency are also evident. Throughout, questions of gender and musical culture beg further exploration and analysis.

BOOK ROADMAP

Oneness Pentecostalism: Race, Gender, and Culture approaches North American Oneness Pentecostalism through an interdisciplinary lens. The reader will find chapters from the disciplines of history, anthropology, theology, and even architectural studies. Such interdisciplinary approaches are valuable because they provide the reader with multiple ways to understand the movement. For example, historians are able to look back and acknowledge the long-term impact of events, while sociologists tend to document life as it happens but are limited to the immediate moment. These varied disciplines all are key to understanding the movement.

The volume begins by paying tribute to the work of historical theologian Manuel Gaxiola (d. 2014) with the inclusion of his essay, "The Unresolved Issue: A Third-World Perspective on the Oneness Question" as chapter 1. The meditation, delivered to the 1987 meeting of the Society for Pentecostal Studies, and prior to that to a 1984 Harvard Divinity School symposium, laid out some of the important ambiguities and unfinished tasks addressed in this volume. A veteran executive and presiding bishop of the IAFCJ of Mexico, Gaxiola was among the first Latin American Pentecostals to earn a doctoral degree (with Walter Hollenweger at the University of Birmingham, 1989, and after master's studies with church growth theorist Donald McGavran at Fuller Theological Seminary). His is accorded pride of place as an important academic and theological voice from the Pentecostal global South. A participant at such gatherings as the World Council of Church's 1973 meeting in Bangkok, the 1974 Lausanne Conference, and observer of the International Roman Catholic–Pentecostal Dialogue (1972–82), Gaxiola urgently sought the theological maturation of the Apostolic Pentecostal Movement. He noted the significant global growth of the movement and predicted that it could no longer be ignored or dismissed by other Pentecostals, especially in countries like Mexico, Nicaragua, and Colombia, where they represented flagship *evangélico* denominations. Yet, with growth and maturity came an urgent task of clearer self-understanding.

The next three chapters of the volume focus on the theology of the movement and its earliest expressions from its theologians to its more popular form in music. In chapter 2, historical theologian David Reed traces the development of Oneness Pentecostal theology through its connections to prior evangelical movements and practices. He concludes that a robust Christology, emphasis on the name of God, and publications of the day provided the foundations of their Jesus' name heterodoxy, which challenged the Trinitarian view of the godhead that dominates North American Protestantism. Historian Daniel Ramírez furthers this work in chapter 3, as he examines early Oneness hymnody to demonstrate the more popular expressions of this theology. Songs were often shared across denominations and languages as a way to resist a Trinitarian-leaning Protestant orthodoxy and hegemonic Catholicism, and to catechize converts. In chapter 4, historical theologian Daniel Segraves provides readers with a detailed exploration of pioneer Andrew D. Urshan's theological trajectory in order to understand more fully the noted Persian Evangelist's conversance with Middle Eastern theological categories as he fashioned a Oneness Christology. In this section, the contributions of immigrants to the development of Oneness theology in America is emphasized over the traditional story of theological development rooted solely in William Durham's Finished Work salvation schema.

The remainder of the volume continues to build on the diverse origins and developments of the movement. In the fifth and sixth chapters, the authors explore the ways in which migratory movements of the 1920s and 1930s led to churches with distinct attributes that reflected their settlement and development in various regions. In chapter 5, historian Lloyd D. Barba examines how migrants from the "Dust Bowl" area of the Western South overwhelmed and ultimately transformed the earlier, more cosmopolitan generation of Pentecostals in California. Specifically, in the Central Valley, migrants from the Western South brought with them a no-compromise hard-liner strain of Pentecostalism that centered on ideas of being tough on doctrine and fashioned or reinforced strict holiness standards of dress. This transplanted ethos took deep root among the valley's booming population of Okies, Arkies, and Texans. While the groups (collectively lumped together as "Okies") developed a hard-liner, conservative strain of Pentecostalism during their migratory journey, African American Oneness Pentecostals uprooted by the Great Migration developed a social justice ethos driven by their faith. Scholar Rosa Sailes in chapter 6 tracks how three generations of the Brazier family in Chicago utilized their pastoral platform to bring about change for the African American community. The Braziers arrived as one of millions of families in the Great Migration who made their way from the rural South into urban areas of the North. Each generation of Braziers was deeply invested in the struggle for dignity and justice, culminating in the celebrated Woodlawn Organization. These chapters serve as examples of the ways in which different Oneness groups, built on congregations formed by and straddling migratory movements, diverged to arrive at different political and social commitments.

Sailes's chapter also demonstrates the importance of gender in the development of the movement. Her chapter details the struggles and triumphs of Geneva Brazier and serves as a reminder that Black women in ministry have consistently found themselves limited by both their race and gender. In the seventh chapter, historian Dara Coleby Delgado continues this theme by examining how the roles of women have changed within the predominantly African American PAW. From debates over women in the pulpit to the more recent elevation of women to the bishopric, Coleby Delgado argues that increased gender equality has its limitations, and that PAW women challenge the notion that only the male body can truly represent Christ. In chapter 8, historian Andrea Shan Johnson extends this volume's analysis of women in the ministry as she explores the ways in which predominantly white female ministers in the early years of the movement carved out a ministerial niche even while facing barriers put in place by male leaders. She finds that they often turned to pulpits in smaller congregations or to work on the mission field as a way to carry out their calling. They were circumspect in challenging gender norms of the day, but this circumspection came at a cost. Her work calls for further consideration of how women in ministry are presented in the broader historical narrative. These chapters collectively remind the reader of the ways that race and gender often intersect to enhance or limit the opportunities available to women seeking to exercise their gifts in the pulpit.

With the work of anthropologist Patricia Fortuny in chapter 9, the volume shifts the focus from the pulpit to the pews. Using the ethnographic tools of anthropology, Fortuny reflects on her years of association with female members of La Luz del Mundo, a denomination that has experienced recent considerable growth on both sides of the Mexican and American border. Adherents of Oneness Pentecostalism are often noted for their strict holiness dress codes and behavior, and these women clearly articulate the value that they find in living this distinctive sectarian life. Fortuny, however, explains that these women uniquely apply ostensibly standard church teachings and practices in pursuit of personal life projects and goals. In chapter 10, the volume offers readers an architectural analysis of the physical spaces that worshippers construct and inhabit. Historical theologian Daniel Chiquete's chapter on the spatial and architectural dimensions of Apostolic temples in Sinaloa, Mexico, considers how space, liturgy, aesthetics, and design influence the aspects of worship but also reflect regional influences. This northwestern state was among the very earliest regions evangelized by pioneer ministers, beginning with repatriated ones in the 1930s. Today it represents one of Apostolicism's strongest redoubts in that country, with considerable influence in the US Southwest through migration. The inevitable Charismatic and Neo-Pentecostal spin-offs have intensified the historical cross-fertilization with broader *evangélico* movements, especially Trinitarian ones, and especially in the area of worship and liturgy. These two chapters also remind us of how the movement successfully rode the ebbs and flows of twentieth-century globalization.

PAST SCHOLARSHIP AND FUTURE DIRECTIONS

This volume represents the first academic interdisciplinary book on Oneness Pentecostalism. Accordingly, these chapters open up the study of Oneness

Pentecostalism in North America, reveal the diversity of the movement, and point to the significance of that diversity. Early academic scholarship showed promise but failed to produce fruit in 1984 when Harvard Divinity School hosted the First Occasional Symposium on Aspects of the Oneness Pentecostal Movement. The papers presented at the symposium were compiled by Jeffery Gill of Harvard Divinity School but remain stored in select seminary archives with only limited accessibility to the public.

Most book-length histories of the movement have been published through church presses or independent religious publishing houses, with the Word Aflame Press offering valuable reprints of early volumes. These chronicles represent the earnest efforts to document the origins and development of the movement, but these works have largely been written for a church readership. Some of these published books attempt to tell the history of particular denominations while others chronicle the movement more broadly. Such broad histories include, among others: Frank Ewart's *The Phenomenon of Pentecost* (1947), Maclovio Gaxiola's *Historia de la Iglesia Apostólica de la Fe en Cristo Jesús de México* [History of the Apostolic Church of the Faith in Christ Jesus] (1964), the AAFCJ's semicentennial volume, *La Historia de la Asamblea Apostólica de la Fe en Cristo Jesús* [The History of the Apostolic Assembly of the Faith in Christ Jesus] (1966), Arthur Clanton's *United We Stand* (1970), and Morris Golder's *History of the Pentecostal Assemblies of the World* (1973).[24] Some more recent works represent a return to the biography format favored by early chroniclers. These include Daniel L. Segraves's *Andrew D. Urshan: A Theological Biography* (2017), published by an academic religious press, and historical theologian Robin Johnston's *Howard Goss: A Pentecostal Life* (2010), published by the academic imprint of the United Pentecostal Church International's (UPCI) Word Aflame Press.[25] Notably, several books, such as Manuel Gaxiola's *La Serpiente y La Paloma: Análisis del Crecimeinto de la Iglesia Apostólica de la Fe en Cristo Jesús de México* [The Serpent and the Dove: Analysis of the Growth of the Apostolic Church of the Faith in Christ Jesus in Mexico] (1970) and historian Talmadge French's *Our God Is One* (1999), began as master's theses and later enjoyed a wide readership within Oneness Pentecostal circles when they were published by religious and missionary presses.[26] One notable denominational effort was undertaken by the IAFCJ to commemorate its 2014 centenary.[27] A crowd-sourced WikiHistoria platform commissioned by the Comisión de Investigación Histórica [Historical Research Commission] and populated with individual congregations' historical projects from around the country provided a wealth of material that allowed a team helmed by Domingo Torres to produce a volume of essays on several themes (history, missions, music, women, Christian education, etc.).[28] Critical scholarly examinations of the origins and development of key Oneness doctrines have been taken up extensively by historian Thomas Fudge in *Christianity Without a Cross: A History of Salvation in Oneness Pentecostalism* (2003) and Douglas Jacobsen in *Thinking in the Spirit: Theologies of the Early Pentecostal Movement* (2003), as well as by David Reed, who turned his 1978 dissertation into the book *"In Jesus' Name": The History and Beliefs of Oneness Pentecostals* (2008).[29]

Other notable academic monographs closely examine aspects of the movement through a more intimate ethnographic or historical lens. Elaine Lawless's 1988 and 2005 books on women in independent Oneness Pentecostal churches in the Midwest and the US South, and Felicitas Goodman's study of glossolalia and related phenomena among Yucatec Mayan Apostolic women in Mexico focus on limited geographic and ethnic populations.[30] Historians Robert Mapes Anderson and Grant Wacker folded Oneness protagonists into their histories of early US Pentecostals, but did not focus necessarily on doctrinal and other distinctives.[31] Talmadge French's *Early Interracial Oneness Pentecostalism* (2014) revisits the origins of the Pentecostal Assemblies of the World and the shifts in interracial leadership by examining numerous primary sources. Daniel Ramírez's *Migrating Faith: Pentecostalism in the United States and Mexico in the Twentieth Century* (2015) examines the long history of the Apostolic Movement in the US and Mexico and the shared borderlands, recovering history through music and migration flows. The Luz del Mundo's notoriety has created a virtual (and critical) academic cottage industry in Mexico.[32] Judith Casselberry's *The Labor of Faith: Gender and Power in Black Apostolic Pentecostalism* (2017) discusses the various kinds of labor women of the Church of Our Lord Jesus Christ (COOLJC) undertake to advance their causes and work around patriarchal church structures. Most recently, Lloyd D. Barba's *Sowing the Sacred: Mexican Pentecostal Farmworkers in California* (2022) demonstrates how Mexican Pentecostal farmworkers claimed space and carved out a sense of personhood in the punishing world of industrial agriculture. These rigorous assessments of the movement showcase important theological, historical, gender, and anthropological dimensions of the movement. They signal an academic turn in the study of Oneness Pentecostalism.

The above-mentioned publications, in addition to sundry articles and stand-alone chapters, attest to the cultural vibrancy of the Oneness Pentecostal Movement.[33] But much work remains. One auspicious and recent endeavor came to fruition in the 2013 inauguration of the Manuel Gaxiola and Manuel Vizcarra collections at the David Allan Hubbard Library of Fuller Theological Seminary. The UPCI's recent opening of the Center for the Study of Oneness Pentecostalism also bodes well for the historical preservation of the movement. Efforts by Alexander Stewart and Sherry Sherrod Dupree to compile bibliographies of the Black Oneness Pentecostal Movements and leaders and to archive material in such places as Harlem's Arthur Schomburg Library further enhance our knowledge of the movement's origins and developments. Numerous grassroots efforts have aimed at preserving music and photographs on social media sites and YouTube. We encourage those with relevant materials to seek out trustworthy archivists such as those noted above. The work of historians can only be as good as the material available. The preserved past determines the stories we tell.

Finally, it is tempting to refract the history of Oneness Pentecostalism in North America through the aspirational lens of current attempts to unify the movement around a common "Apostolic Identity." This would be anachronistic; the aspirations are too often tied to national political agendas of the late twentieth and early twenty-first centuries. This volume offers a sobering reminder that disparate, discreet, and often conflictive origins made for distinct trajectories over the course of a century in a single continent. The work of reconstructing those trajectories, including in wider hemispheric and global dimensions, has only begun. The half has not yet been told.

NOTES

1. Johnston, "Pictorial Essay," 42–43.

2. Ewart, *Phenomenon*, 76–77; Synan, *Holiness-Pentecostal Tradition*, 156. We have chosen to utilize the spelling "Jesus' name" in keeping with scholarship on the movement.

3. Johnson, "Shudder Swept."

4. Barba and Johnson, "New Issue." According to Grant Wacker, the success of Pentecostalism lay within believer's ability to hold primitivist and pragmatic impulses in productive tension; see Wacker, *Heaven Below*, 10.

5. Barba and Johnson, "New Issue"; these origin stories are also complicated globally. Russian Pentecostals, for example, trace their Oneness origins to the missionary journeys of Andrew D. Urshan, who baptized in Jesus' name

as early as 1910. See Fletcher, *Soviet Charismatics*.

6. Bartleman, *Azusa Street*, 51.

7. Lawson, *Anthropology of Jesus Christ*, 32.

8. Bartleman, *Azusa Street*, 51. Du Bois famously declared that "the problem of the Twentieth Century is the problem of the color line," see Du Bois, *Souls*, 3.

9. On Lawson's views of race and the US church, see Barba, "Jesus Would Be Jim-Crowed."

10. Sánchez-Walsh, *Pentecostals in America*, xxi. By 1929, no fewer than thirty Oneness (including many African American) denominations populated the Pentecostal landscape. Most of these merged with others, but some persist to this day, such as the Birmingham-based

Apostolic Overcoming Holy Church of God. French, *Our God*, 85–125; Alexander, *Black Fire*, 206–48. Joe Creech and Alan Anderson's trenchant arguments for multipolar Pentecostal origins—national in the case of Creech and global in the case of Anderson—may ratchet down the Azusa Street Revival's primacy but not its significance for a critical historiography of race, ethnicity, and religion. Creech, "Visions of Glory"; Anderson, *To the Ends*, 17–18.

11. Ramírez, *Migrating Faith*, 35.

12. Brown, "Oneness Pentecostalism and Ethnicity," 131; French, *Early Interracial*, 146–51, 163–76; Tyson, *Early Pentecostal Revival*, 241–53; Reed, *In Jesus' Name*, 207–18; Golder, *History of the Pentecostal*, 82–83.

13. Reed, *In Jesus' Name*, 215–18.

14. Barba, "Jesus Would Be Jim-Crowed."

15. Ibid., 82; other earlier histories of the Pentecostal Movement agree with these historical qualities of Oneness Pentecostalism. See Blumhofer, *Restoring the Faith*, 187–93.

16. Reed, *In Jesus' Name*, 82.

17. Tinney, "Significance of Race," 56–57.

18. Howell, "People of the Name," 5.

19. Ramírez, *Migrating Faith*, 48; Gill, *Toward a Contextualized Theology*, 41–59. In 1946 the denomination in Mexico changed its name to Iglesia Apostólica de la Fe en Cristo Jesús to differentiate itself from its US counterpart.

20. Gill, *Toward a Contextualized Theology*, 41–59; Gaxiola, *La Serpiente y La Paloma*.

21. de la Cruz, "Iglesia."

22. Gregory, *American Exodus*; Dochuk, *From Bible Belt*.

23. Best, *Passionately Human*.

24. Ewart, *The Phenomenon*; Foster, *Think It Not Strange*; Gaxiola López, *Historia de la Iglesia*; Cantú et al., *Historia de la Asamblea*; Clanton, *United We Stand*; Golder, *History*; Tyson, *Early Pentecostal Revival*. See also the first five chapters of Bernard, *History of Christian Doctrine*.

25. Johnston, *Howard Goss*; Segraves, *Andrew D. Urshan*.

26. Gaxiola, *La Serpiente y la Paloma*; French, *Our God Is One*.

27. Torres Alvarado, *Cien Años*.

28. IAFCJ 2014 Comisión de Investigación Histórica, https://historia.iafcj.org/Bienvenidos, accessed March 17, 2020.

29. Fudge, *Christianity*; Reed, *In Jesus' Name*.

30. Goodman, *Speaking in Tongues*; Goodman, *Maya Apocalypse*; Lawless, *Handmaidens*; Lawless, *God's Peculiar People*; Ramírez, *Migrating Faith*; Casselberry, *Labor of Faith*; Barba, *Sowing the Sacred*.

31. Anderson, *Vision of the Disinherited*; Wacker, *Heaven Below*.

32. Masferrer, *Luz del Mundo*; de la Torre, *Hijos de la Luz*. On June 3, 2022, the Luz del Mundo's leader, Apostle Naasón Joaquín García, pleaded guilty in Los Angeles, California, to sexually abusing three girls, receiving a nearly seventeen-year sentence.

33. Barba and Johnson, "New Issue."

BIBLIOGRAPHY

Alexander, Estrelda. *Black Fire: One Hundred Years of African American Pentecostalism*. Downers Grove, IL: Intervarsity Press, 2011.

Anderson, Alan H. *To the Ends of the Earth: Pentecostalism and the Transformation of World Christianity*. Oxford: Oxford University Press, 2013.

Anderson, Robert Mapes. *Vision of the Disinherited*. New York: Oxford University Press, 1979.

Barba, Lloyd. "Jesus Would Be Jim Crowed: Bishop Robert Lawson on Race and Religion in the Harlem Renaissance." *Journal of Race, Ethnicity, and Religion* 6, no. 3 (2015): 1–32.

———. *Sowing the Sacred: Mexican Pentecostal Farmworkers in California*. New York: Oxford University Press, 2022.

Barba, Lloyd, and Andrea Shan Johnson. "The New Issue: Approaches to Oneness Pentecostalism in the United States." *Religion Compass* 12, no. 11 (2018).

Bartleman, Frank. *Azusa Street: An Eyewitness Account to the Birth of the Pentecostal Revival*. New Kensington, PA: Whitaker House, 1982. First privately printed 1925 (Los Angeles).

Bernard, David K. *A History of Christian Doctrine: The Twentieth Century*. Hazelwood, MO: Word Aflame Press, 2007.

Best, Wallace. *Passionately Human, No Less Divine: Religion and Culture in Black Chicago, 1915–1952*. Princeton: Princeton University Press, 2007.

Blumhofer, Edith. *Restoring the Faith: The Assemblies of God, Pentecostalism, and American Culture*. Urbana: University of Illinois Press, 1993.

Brown, Roderick R. "Oneness Pentecostalism and Ethnicity: A Decision out of Step." Master's thesis, University of South Dakota, 2005.

Cantú, Ernesto S., José A. Ortega, Isaac Cota, and Phillip Rangel. *Historia de La Asamblea Apostólica de la Fe en Cristo Jesús, 1916–1966* [History of the Apostolic Assembly of the Faith in Christ Jesus]. Mentone, CA: Sal's Printing Service, 1966.

Casselberry, Judith. *The Labor of Faith: Gender and Power in Black Apostolic Pentecostalism*. Durham: Duke University Press, 2017.

Clanton, Arthur L. *United We Stand—A History of Oneness Organizations*. Hazelwood, MO: Pentecostal Publishing House, 1970.

Creech, Joe. "Visions of Glory: The Place of the Azusa Street Revival in Pentecostal History." *Church History* 65, no. 3 (1996): 405–24.

Cruz, Marcial de la, composer. "La Iglesia, el Cuerpo de Cristo." No. 254 in *Himnario de suprema alabanza a Jesús*. 6th ed. Zapopan, Jalisco: Iglesia Apostólica de la Fe en Cristo Jesús, 1996.

Dochuk, Darren. *From Bible Belt to Sunbelt: Plain Folk Religion, Grassroots Politics, and the Rise of Evangelical Conservatism*. New York: W. W. Norton Press, 2011.

Du Bois, W. E. B. *The Souls of Black Folk*. 1903. Repr., New York: Fine Creative Media, 2003.

Ewart, Frank J. *Phenomenon of Pentecost: A History of the Latter Rain*. Houston, TX: Herald, 1947.

Fletcher, William. *Soviet Charismatics: The Pentecostals in the USSR*. New York: Peter Lang, 1985.

Foster, Fred J. *Think It Not Strange: A History of the Oneness Movement*. St. Louis: Pentecostal Publishing House, 1965.

French, Talmadge. *Early Interracial Oneness Pentecostalism: G. T. Haywood and the Pentecostal Assemblies of the World, 1901–1931*. Eugene, OR: Pickwick, 2014.

———. *Our God Is One: The Story of the Oneness Pentecostals*. Indianapolis: Voice and Vision, 1999.

Fudge, Thomas. *Christianity Without the Cross: A History of Salvation in Oneness Pentecostalism*. Parkland, FL: Universal Publishers, 2003.

Gaxiola Gaxiola, Manuel J. *La serpiente y la paloma: Análisis del crecimiento de la Iglesia Apostólica de la Fe en Cristo Jesús de México* [The Serpent and the Dove: Analysis of the Growth of the Apostolic Church of the Faith in Christ Jesus in Mexico]. South Pasadena, CA: William Carey Library, 1970.

———. *La serpiente y la paloma: Historia, teología y análisis de la Iglesia Apostólica de la Fe en Cristo Jesús, 1914–1994* [The Serpent and the Dove: History, Theology and Analysis of the Apostolic Church of the Faith in Christ Jesus, 1914–1994]. 2nd ed., corregida y aumentada. México, D.F.: Libros Pyros, 1994.

Gaxiola López, Maclovio. *Historia de La Iglesia Apostólica de la Fe en Cristo Jesús de México* [History of the Apostolic Church of the Faith in Christ Jesus of Mexico]. Mexico City: La Iglesia Apostólica de la Fe en Cristo Jesús, 1964.

Gill, Kenneth. *Toward a Contextualized Theology for the Third World: The Emergence and Development of Jesus' Name Pentecostalism in Mexico.* Bern, Switzerland: Peter Lang International, 1994.

Golder, Morris E. *History of the Pentecostal Assemblies of the World.* Indianapolis: Self-published, 1973.

Goodman, Felicitas. *Maya Apocalypse: Seventeen Years with the Women of a Yucatán Village.* Bloomington: Indiana University Press, 2001.

———. *Speaking in Tongues: A Cross-Cultural Study of Glossolalia.* Chicago: University of Chicago Press, 1972.

Gregory, James. *American Exodus: The Dust Bowl Migration and Okie Culture in California.* New York: Oxford University Press, 1989.

Howell, Joseph. "The People of the Name: Oneness Pentecostalism in the United States." PhD diss., Florida State University, 1985.

Jacobsen, Douglas. *Thinking in the Spirit: Theologies of the Early Pentecostal Movement.* Bloomington: Indiana University Press, 2003.

Johnson, Andrea Shan. "A Shudder Swept Through Them: An Identification of the Controversial Joshua Sykes." *Pneuma* 38, no. 3 (2016): 312–29.

Johnston, Robin. *Howard Goss: A Pentecostal Life.* Hazelwood, MO: Word Aflame Press Academic, 2010.

———. "A Pictorial Essay of the Centennial Celebration of the Arroyo Seco Campmeeting." *Pentecostal Herald,* November 2013.

Lawless, Elaine. *God's Peculiar People: Women's Voice and Folk Tradition in a Pentecostal Church.* Lexington: University Press of Kentucky, 2005.

———. *Handmaidens of the Lord: Pentecostal Women Preachers and Traditional Religion.* Philadelphia: University of Pennsylvania Press, 1988.

Lawson, Robert C. *The Anthropology of Jesus Christ Our Kinsman.* Piqua, OH: Ohio Ministries, 2000. First printed in 1925 (New York).

Masferrer, Elio. *La Luz del Mundo: Un análisis multidisciplinario de la controversia religiosa que ha impactado a nuestro país* [A Multidisciplinary Analysis of the Religious Controversy That Has Impacted Our Country]. Mexico City: Revista Académica para el Estudio de la Religiones, 1997.

Ramírez, Daniel. *Migrating Faith, Pentecostalism in the United States and Mexico.* Chapel Hill: University of North Carolina Press, 2015.

Reed, David. *In Jesus' Name: The History and Beliefs of Oneness Pentecostals.* Blandford Forum, UK: Deo, 2008.

Sánchez-Walsh, Arlene. *Pentecostals in America.* New York: Columbia University Press, 2018.

Segraves, Daniel. *Andrew D. Urshan: A Theological Biography.* Lexington, KY: Emeth Press, 2017.

Synan, Vinson. *The Holiness-Pentecostal Tradition: Charismatic Movements in the Twentieth Century*. Grand Rapids, MI: William B. Eerdmans, 1997.

Tinney, James S. "The Significance of Race in the Rise and Development of the Apostolic Pentecostal Movement." In *Papers Presented to the First Occasional Symposium on Aspects of the Oneness Pentecostal Movement*, 55–69. Cambridge: Harvard Divinity School, 1984.

Torre, Renée de la. *Los Hijos de la luz: Discurso, identidad y poder en La Luz del Mundo* [The Children of the Light: Discourse, Identity, and Power in the Light of the World]. Tlaquepaque, Jalisco, Mexico: Instituto Tecnológico de Estudios Superiores de Occidente, 2000.

Torres Alvarado, Domingo, ed. *Cien años de Pentecostés, desde la vivencia de la Iglesia Apostólica* [One Hundred Years of Pentecost in the Lived Experience of the Apostolic Church]. Zapopan, Mexico: Iglesia Apostólica de la Fe en Cristo Jesús, 2014.

Tyson, James. *The Early Pentecostal Revival: History of Twentieth-Century Pentecostals and the Pentecostal Assemblies of the World, 1901–1930*. Hazelwood, MO: Word Aflame Press, 1990.

Wacker, Grant. *Heaven Below: Early Pentecostals and American Culture*. Cambridge: Harvard University Press, 2001.

CHAPTER I

The Unresolved Issue
A Third-World Perspective on the Oneness Question

Manuel Gaxiola

Heretics are those who try to answer the questions that were left unanswered by other theologians.

—W. J. HOLLENWEGER

All of us would agree that the Pentecostal Movement as we know it today is very different from what began in Topeka, Kansas, in 1901 or from the Apostolic Faith Mission established in Los Angeles in 1906.[1] Although retaining, and in some cases emphasizing even more, their belief in glossolalia, divine healing, and other practices and beliefs that made them distinctive from other Christians since the beginning, they have overcome their original aversion to, among other things: organizational structures, secular and theological education, interchurch cooperation, contact with groups like the Roman Catholic Church, racism, "worldliness" as defined by certain types of attire for both men and women, the use of cosmetics and jewelry, radio and television, medicine, bishops, the ministry of women, etc. All of these, and many more, were at certain times "issues" that Pentecostals combatted or defended, Bible in hand, with the passion of which only they were capable, engaging in a thousand theological disputes, skirmishes, and struggles into which they put their whole heart. Only in the early days could a man use a double entendre to refute the Oneness position and, in the process, ridicule one of its staunchest defenders at the risk of provoking a melee.[2] Only Oliver Fauss could say that the Assemblies of God, by singing "Holy, Holy, Holy: Lord God Almighty," while the Oneness brethren abandoned the 1916 General Council, "forgot that they were fulfilling a Scripture to the dot of an 'i' and the cross of a 't,'" for Isaiah 66:5 said, "Your brethren that hated you, that cast you out for my name's sake . . ."[3] We, their heirs, by contrast, are too sophisticated, too expert in theological nuances, too eager for a compromise and, consequently, in danger of becoming spineless or of falling into an unfruitful relativism.

There is, however, an issue that has been present in Pentecostalism for more than seventy years and that cannot continue being faced in the same way that it was faced at the beginning (direct confrontation, excision, or mutual ridicule).[4] The Oneness Movement has grown to such an extent, and in practically every country where other Pentecostals have arrived, that it cannot simply be ignored. Witness the twenty-seven Oneness denominations listed by Arthur Piepkorn for the United States and Canada, which constitute a very small list (there are more than fifty Oneness denominations and groups affiliated with the Apostolic World Christian Fellowship led by Bishop A. G. Rowe, with headquarters in South Bend, Indiana).[5] We must also include the United Pentecostal Church International with an aggressive missionary program in many countries. Witness the Apostolic Assembly of Faith in Christ Jesus, my own denomination in the USA, born among the poorest city dwellers and migrant workers in California, with churches now in practically every state of the American union and missionary work in Central and South America, Italy, Spain, and even Pakistan.

Witness also my own denomination, the Apostolic Church of the Faith in Christ Jesus, in Mexico, the oldest Pentecostal denomination in the country, with more churches in more places than any other denomination, autochthonous since the beginning and with an economic puissance surpassed perhaps only by the Seventh-Day Adventist Church, a predominantly middle-class church that has been in Mexico for almost one hundred years. Notice in the same country the Light of the World Church (Luz del Mundo), now spread all over Latin America, the United States, and Europe, reputed to have between 600,000 and 700,000 members world-wide.[6] Bizarre even by Pentecostal standards, this group combines the iron rule of its prophet, Samuel, son of "Aaron" its founder; the practice of the Lord's Supper at one place only; its magnificent and huge headquarters church in Guadalajara; and the interesting way in which they have attained great political influence at local, state, and national levels.

According to the Mexico City daily *Excelsior* (August 19, 1987, p. 2), 100,000 of its members met in Guadalajara this year for the Lord's Supper and during their seven days of festivities, they spent the equivalent of about US$20 million. Many were housed in five special buildings owned by the Church; 6,000 were baptized and more than 2,500 weddings were celebrated. Whatever opinion we may hold of this group, it begs an in-depth study.[7]

Witness also the United Pentecostal Church in Colombia (under native leadership), the largest Protestant denomination in that South American country, with missions in other places of South America, the United States, Canada, and Spain, together with other groups of the same persuasion. Witness also the Apostolic Church in Nicaragua, which is not only thriving and becoming perhaps the largest denomination in that country but at the same time has learned to be the center of coexistence for Sandinistas and former *Somocistas* and is conducting its own foreign missionary program in Belize. The list of similar churches all over the world is endless.

The theological foundations and the world-wide growth of the Oneness Movement have not suffered from inadvertence in the scholarly field. Although at the beginning most references to the Oneness people and doctrines were of a passing, controversial, and partisan nature (to which the Oneness people responded in kind), beginning, perhaps, with David Reed's doctoral dissertation at the University of Boston, the treatment of the Oneness position becomes more serious and more equitably critical.[8] W. J. Hollenweger, at the University of Birmingham in England, has encouraged some of his students to analyze Oneness doctrines with more seriousness, and the results so far seem very encouraging. Roswith Gerloff, a German Lutheran pastor and doctoral candidate under Hollenweger, has become an expert on the Black Oneness churches in England and the West Indies.[9] Kenneth A. Gill, another doctoral candidate under Hollenweger, is writing on Spanish-speaking Oneness theology. Both are members of the Society for Pentecostal Studies.[10] Also important is the 1984 Harvard Symposium on Oneness Pentecostal Theology.[11] The fact that the SPS has now made it possible for Oneness scholars to be accepted as members is very encouraging, and much more if a paper like this can be presented at the meeting.

The sheer number of Oneness people in all the world, who by now are numbered in the millions and who have evolved, in some cases, into strong and solid organizational structures and have improved their education and theological understanding (something that also took place in other Pentecostal denominations), makes it imperative that we face the issues in a more serious way and open a fruitful dialogue with a view to a mutual edification and understanding. This paper is written with that purpose in mind and its main thesis is as follows: What came to be known as "The New Issue" has not been settled either by those who more than seventy years ago adopted the simple expedient of expelling the "Jesus' name" people or forcing them to abandon their ranks, or by those who even now deridingly dismiss the "Jesus' name" beliefs as "a rehash of heretical doctrines that were long ago condemned by the Church."[12] On the other hand, it could be that Oneness people themselves have not settled the "New Issue" that brought them into being, for they seem to lack even now a clear and concise definition of their doctrinal stand, ignoring some historical and theological factors that now force them to come to grips with some questions that have been neglected. Both sides, especially in the USA, look like they would rather forget that for almost fifteen years, at the beginning of this century, there was a close fellowship between those who baptized in the name of the Trinity, those who baptized in Jesus' name, and those who did not baptize anybody in water.

This paper is a modest and personal attempt at suggesting some of the components for a possible reinitiation of a long interrupted dialogue and, further down the road, a settling of the issue or at least a better mutual understanding between the two sides. Before we venture some possible solutions, it will be necessary to refer to some historical facts. The reader is asked to remember that this presentation comes from the Third World and does not necessarily represent the point of view of Oneness people in other countries. The reader is also asked to remember that most of this history that follows refers to a particular group of Spanish-speaking churches, although occasional references will be made to others in an effort to make us conscious of the need for further and more specific study, including of Black Oneness churches both inside and outside the USA.

SOME HISTORICAL FACTS

The Apostolic Faith Gospel Mission on Azusa Street, Los Angeles, California, was bound to attract some of the people who were part of the predominantly Mexican population in that city. Frank Bartleman makes a passing reference to them when he reports a sad incident that unfortunately he does not describe in detail: "The Spirit tried to work through some poor, illiterate Mexicans who had been saved and 'baptized' in the Spirit, but the leader deliberately refused to let them testify, crushing them ruthlessly. It was like murdering the Spirit of God."[13]

As early as October and November 1906, *The Apostolic Faith* mentions an evangelist couple, Abundio and Rosa López, who were being "used of God in street meetings and in helping Mexicans at the altar at Azusa Street" and later moved to San Diego.[14] In that city in 1909, a Luís López was baptized in Jesus' name. Others followed. (By contrast, the Assemblies of God work among Mexicans in California was begun by British missionary Alice E. Luce in 1918, although some Anglo-Saxon Pentecostals had also been making inroads among the Mexicans as early as 1917.)[15] This small band of believers eventually joined the Pentecostal Assemblies of the World (PAW), apparently as a matter of convenience, for they needed ministerial credentials of some kind. Since most of the Mexicans spoke Spanish only, all their contacts with the PAW were made through an English-speaking man from Acapulco, Mexico, who was the "Mexican Representative" for the PAW.

By the year 1914 there was a small network of house churches that met in Los Angeles, San Bernardino, and San Diego counties. Out of one of those house churches in Los Angeles a lady by the name of Romana Valenzuela obtained her husband's permission to visit her relatives in Mexico and tell them about the baptism of the Holy Spirit. She came to her hometown, Villa Aldama, Chihuahua, about two hundred miles south of El Paso, Texas, and after considerable opposition from her family, she was able to convince them that they should seek the baptism of the Holy Spirit. On November 1, 1914, twelve of those people spoke in other tongues, which as far as we know is the first time this ever happened in Mexico. Mrs. Valenzuela wanted to return to her home in Los Angeles, but she also wanted her relatives to be baptized and organized into a church, so she went to the capital city of Chihuahua, met with the pastor of a large Methodist church in that city, prayed with him until he also spoke in new tongues, and then took him to a Black Oneness church in El Paso, where he was baptized in Jesus' name and ordained into the ministry. The man then resigned his pastorate in the Methodist church, moved to Villa Aldama, baptized the original twelve believers, and became their pastor. This was the beginning of the Iglesia Apostólica de la Fe en Cristo Jesús, which is also this writer's denomination.

Returning to the believers in California whose pastors held ministerial licenses from the PAW, we can see that there was hardly any contact between these great men and the officials and other members of the PAW. This was due in great part to the language barrier and to the loose control that the PAW apparently exerted over those who carried its credentials. The main reason may be that Mexican people wanted to have an organization of their own that would address itself specifically to the Spanish-speaking people, of whom every city and village was full all the way from California to Texas and the rest of the territory that had once been half of Mexico's land and was then, and still is, in the hands of the Americans. Besides that, there was the difference in the kind of people that the Mexicans on one side and Blacks and Anglo-Saxons on the other were trying to reach.

The Mexicans were naturally interested in the great number of nominal Roman Catholics in the territory we have mentioned, while Blacks and Anglo-Saxons wanted to reach the English-speaking people. It is of special interest to mention that in contrast to the Assemblies of God, who as early as 1918 were doing missionary work among Mexicans on both sides of the border,[16] none of the Oneness organizations mentioned by Arthur Clanton opened an exclusively Spanish-speaking department until the United Pentecostal Church did so in the seventies.[17]

The missionary field of the Mexicans required other themes and other messages, very different from what the English-speaking people were preaching. Consequently, it would seem safe to say that these Oneness Mexicans were many times unaware of (because of the language barrier), and sometimes indifferent to, some of the great doctrinal controversies that were taking place among the English-speaking Oneness people, especially in regard to the New Birth. The Mexicans preached a very simple and practical message. They stressed belief in the Lord Jesus Christ, repentance, and water baptism in Jesus' name. After this it was expected that people would receive the baptism of the Spirit, but they never considered this baptism as something essential for salvation in the sense that no person was saved unless he spoke in new tongues. Their newborn experience was expressed in rather practical terms: a new family relationship, sexual morality, personal honesty, freedom from alcohol and other vices, the ability to win others to Christ by this new "testimony," etc.

Fred Foster, speaking mostly of white Anglo-Saxon Oneness people, tells us that the early discussions about water baptism centered on "who would make up the bride of Christ" or the accountability of a believer in proportion to the "light" he had received.[18] Foster, however, would seem to imply that the question of the New Birth arose in early Oneness circles only with respect to water baptism, but clearly this was not so. George Farrow wrote in 1930 that "being born of water and the Spirit and being baptized in water and with the Spirit mean one and the same thing. For if being baptized in water and the Spirit, as in Acts 2:38, is not the birth that Jesus referred to in the third chapter of St. John, then we will search the New Testament in vain for the description of one experience which is that."[19] The stance of another Oneness organization in regard to the New Birth is also typical: "Most of the ministers in the organization believed that water baptism in Jesus' name remitted sins and was the same as being born of water. They further believed that the receiving of the baptism of the Holy Ghost was synonymous with being born of the Spirit."[20] The authors quoted state quite well what could be the general stance of the American English-speaking Oneness churches, both Black and white, with respect to the New Birth, but the Mexican Oneness people, as we will see later, never took a radical stand on the question of the New Birth.

By 1925 the Mexican believers had established churches in nineteen cities scattered all the way from San Francisco to Lordsburg, New Mexico. Although they still considered themselves "subject" to the PAW, they decided to hold that year their first convention, which was attended by thirty-three ministers, most of whom had credentials with the PAW, although no leader from the PAW was present, except Francisco Llorente, the "Mexican Representative." At this meeting, held in San Bernardino, California, the delegates decided to organize themselves under the name of Iglesia de la Fe Apostólica Pentecostés. It is significant that no mention is made at all of the PAW in the minutes. Since they decided to issue their own ministerial credentials, it seems correct to assume that they considered themselves separated from the PAW.

It would not be farfetched to suppose that the Mexican people who came in contact with the PAW experienced a severe cultural shock, which would eventually trigger their withdrawal from the English-speaking group. They resented the fact that most of the white Pentecostal ladies did not cover their heads in the services. Although many of the Mexican ladies were pleased to see that the Black sisters did wear hats, and imitated this practice to the extent that they also wore hats instead of the traditional veil of the Catholics, the laymen and ministers seem to have felt very uncomfortable seeing how both Anglo-Saxon and Black churches had women preachers and allowed lay people of both sexes the use of the pulpit or the platform. This even now is not the practice of the Apostolic Assembly in the United States or the Apostolic Church in Mexico, although in both groups the role of women was prominent, and it is now even more so.

Perhaps the Mexican leaders felt their position within their own church was being threatened if they allowed their own women to see that other women did preach and speak from the pulpit. Consequently, they rejected the custom and justified their rejection on the traditional ideas [of] having women be silent in the congregation and not allowing them to usurp the men's authority. These men were not only reflecting the customary ideas on the role of women in their society but at the same time seem to have acted in accordance with a peculiar and unexplained condition: A great number of those leaders were unmarried.

It must also be remembered that many of those Mexicans were recent arrivals to the USA, for those days coincided with the Mexican Revolution, when many people from Mexico fled to the United States. This means that, at least initially, they had to react in a slightly different way to the kind of Pentecostal worship they observed in both Black and white churches. Although knowing that one is venturing into little-trodden territory, which is the territory of inhibitions and emotionalism, and that one is consequently exposing oneself to misunderstandings and criticism, one must, nevertheless, refer to marked differences of temperament in the Anglo-Saxon, the American Black, and the Mexican cultures. What to a Pentecostal Black or Anglo-Saxon Christian might look like ordinary and spontaneous behavior in church, to the Mexican might seem something that requires an exceptional amount of disinhibition. Instead of the epic triumphalism of the Anglo-Saxon, a Mexican might react with his tragic sense of life and his mysticism. Poetry would be more meaningful to him than an outburst of emotion, and he uses it in his services more than the average American Pentecostal.

The inevitable process of acculturation, however, was just beginning around 1915. The early contacts with the prevailing culture were broken in the religious sphere, and the Mexicans severed their ties with their Oneness counterparts on the Black and Anglo-Saxon sides, except for a few personal contacts. More than thirty years passed before formal relations were established between the Mexicans and one of the larger Anglo-Saxon Oneness organizations. By this time there was a considerable number of young Mexican pastors who had been born and raised in the USA and spoke good English and who began to attend Bible schools where all the teaching was done in that language. They were the ones who introduced features of the Anglo-Saxon and Black worship into their particular congregations and to some degree permeated the organization with some of those practices, expressions, and terms of the prevailing culture.

For many of these young men, the practical solution would be to go into an all-English type of service and organization, but this would be precluded by two practical considerations: first, the existence of churches and pastors who prefer the Spanish language and can hardly express themselves in English, and second, the fact that although the Apostolic Assembly is experiencing a commendable rate of biological growth, most of its new converts are people who only recently arrived in the USA, many of them undocumented and from other Spanish-speaking countries besides Mexico.[21]

THEOLOGICAL EXPRESSIONS

As we know, theology is not only done in the systematic ways used by those who have had formal theological training usually expressed in categories and with the help of philosophy, linguistics, history, etc. Theology is also done by simple people and is usually expressed in their hymnology and their poetry. In many cases, as happens in the case of the Apostolic Assembly in the USA and the Apostolic Church in Mexico, both groups who consider themselves one single church with two different organizations, have fortunately created since the beginning an invaluable musical lore that, among other things, reflects very clearly their doctrinal stance. We will offer but a few examples.

In regards to theological formulation, the following hymn offers a very good example of the orthodox way in which those early believers presented an ordered form of worship. For many years this was the song with which Apostolics opened all their services. The name of the song is "Al Rey de los Reyes" (To the King of Kings). We will provide a very literal translation of this and other examples:

To the King of Kings,
Jehovah the Glorious,
Let's start with joy
In holy communion.
With great reverence
To Him we'll get near,
His name we will exalt
Of all heart.

The King of Kings,
Jesus the loving one
Sublime and triumphal
To the world will return.
With all His saints,
With happy songs,
His anxious church
To Him will unite itself.

To the Holy Spirit,
Faithful and blessed,
Let us give credit (or acknowledge)

The celestial guest,
And with His presence,
Virtue and power,
Sin and violence
He ends, and all (other) evil.

From the only God
Let us hear His voice
And let's follow Him
To the celestial fatherland.
For your benefits
Receive propitiously
My humble services
Oh, celestial Father.

The following song has been traditionally sung by Apostolics for more than sixty years while they tarry for the baptism of the Holy Spirit. Once again we see how biblical the structuring of the song [is], which has never made the Apostolics feel shy about making an arrangement that to others might seem "Trinitarian." The name of the song is "Pon tu Espíritu en mi alma" (Put Your Spirit in My Soul) and in English it would read as follows:

Father, prostrate at your feet I fall.
Break my hard prisons (chains).
Oh, answer while I call,
Put your Spirit in me.

Chorus:
Put your Spirit in my soul,
Make me what I should be.
Make me pure in everything,
Free from sin.
Put your Spirit in me.

While Christ sustains me,
While Christ intercedes,
What I need, that give me.
Put your Spirit in me.

Deliver me from orphanhood,
Do not let me perish.
Keep me in your holy bosom.
Put your Spirit in me.

Apostolics in Mexico address their prayers both to the Father and the Son, and the same could be said of those in the USA, and in both groups occasional prayers are also addressed to the Holy Spirit. From this we could infer that a prayer structured in a Trinitarian form does not necessarily make one a Trinitarian, and a prayer addressed to the Son does not necessarily make the person a Oneness believer, but the hymns mentioned here would, at least, show us that Oneness people have never been afraid to use what could be construed as Trinitarian terminology. Those of us who strive for honesty and biblio-theological accuracy would feel that any meaningful effort to settl[e] the "unresolved issue" would have to begin by trying to adhere as much as possible to the Biblical language. In this we can affirm with confidence that the Oneness people in general have never tried to sidestep the question of the terms Father, Son, and Holy Spirit.[22]

For what little has been written on the subject, from what we find in the old hymnbooks, and from what some of the "old-timers" have told us, we gather that some of these Mexican believers were aware, albeit vaguely, of the New Birth controversies that seem to be a constant component of Oneness life in the USA. We can only speculate that the Mexican response, which was different from that of Anglo-Saxons and Blacks, was tempered by at least two factors. One was, as we have already mentioned, the constituency from which the Mexican church was destined to grow, made up mostly of nominal Roman Catholics, for whom the question of the New Birth, as expressed in the controversial terms of the other Oneness people, was not of immediate concern. The message that Mexicans preached was, and still is, simple but direct and consisted of three steps, after the order of Acts 2:38: (1) repent, (2) be baptized, and (3) receive the Holy Ghost. Even now there does not exist a theological formulation or an article of faith relative to the New Birth. Most Apostolics would seem to believe that there is such a thing and a time when such a thing takes place, but they would all rather refer to the "proofs" of a New Birth, to which we have referred before. We can only affirm that at no time has the New Birth been equated with the glossolalic experience. This may also be a good place to suggest, from personal observation, that in the average Apostolic sermon, Acts 2:38 is not quoted as often as it is in the average Anglo-Saxon service. The same observation is valid for some Black Oneness churches in England. This may be due to the fact that, in speaking to Mexican Catholics, they have to refer to other subjects and speak to people who know nothing about the existence of such texts, while the English-speaking people try to win their converts mostly from among other Protestants who have known the Bible for generations.

During the time, mentioned before, when some of the younger Mexican preachers began to attend Anglo-Saxon Bible colleges, some of them tried to have the Church adopt a more explicit and, consequently, radical position regarding the New Birth, but so far they have not succeeded. Some of them would argue that if the Church did not take a "tough stand," the people would not be interested in seeking the baptism of the Holy Ghost, but this is not borne out by the statistics. We know, for instance, that in Mexico more than seventy percent of baptized Apostolics have had the glossolalic experience. The statistics should be more or less the same for the Church in the USA and Central America. In all these churches, no man is accepted as deacon or minister if he has not previously spoken in tongues.

By way of contrast and comparison, we may mention that in Chile, Christian Lalive d'Epinay found that in autochthonous Pentecostal churches *fifty-one percent of the pastors had never spoken in tongues*, in contrast with ninety-two percent of pastors from the Church of God (Cleveland) who did have the glossolalic experience. At the time of the study (1965–66), d'Epinay found it a paradox that although "Pentecostalist pastors frequently speak about it (the baptism of the Spirit), nevertheless it does not seem to constitute a crucial activity in the Chilean congregations. . . . The things which seem to be most sought after are the gifts of the Spirit."[23]

Somewhere early along the line, the Mexican Oneness believers began to use the baptism[al] formula: "I baptize you in the name of Jesus Christ for the forgiveness *and remission* of your sins," but about thirty years ago the words *and remission* were dropped for no apparent reason. Our guess would be that the words were originally copied from an Anglo-Saxon or Black formula and were adopted without reference to the great discussion they caused in the other movements.[24] When the Mexicans dropped them, they did so simply because they do not appear in Acts 2:38.

The Apostolic churches in the USA, Mexico, Central and South America, and Europe all subscribe to eighteen "doctrinal principles," which make it a typical conservative premillennialist church. The second "principle" or statement about God begins: "We believe that there is only one God who has manifested himself to the world through the ages and who has especially revealed himself as Father in the creation of the universe, as Son in the redemption of humanity, and as Holy Spirit pouring himself in the hearts of the believers."

Notice that the statement speaks of a God "who has manifested himself through the ages" and "revealed himself" as Father, Son, and Holy Spirit. This has prompted some people to accuse the Apostolics of being Sabellians, but this is a false accusation, first, because they feel justified to use the word "manifestation," or its verb form, which is found in 1 Timothy 3:16, and, second, because they do not deny that God can be simultaneously Father, Son, and Holy Spirit, although no doctrine has been officially developed on the essence of God, and perhaps they could be better described as stressing the "Christo-dynamic" aspects of the godhead.

Equally important is what to us looks like a notably balanced statement on the Church as the body of Christ (First Doctrinal Principle): "We believe that the Church of our Lord Jesus Christ is one, universal and indivisible, formed by all men without distinction as to nationality, language, color, or customs, who have accepted our Lord Jesus Christ as their savior and who have been baptized into the body by the Holy Spirit."

These and other doctrinal statements represent an honest effort to face every subject within the bounds of the Bible, without making radical or extrabiblical statements. That is why, for instance, although there are some (including, especially, younger ministers in the USA) who honestly believe that to be born of the Spirit equals baptism in Jesus' name *plus* the experience of new tongues, and that consequently people are not saved if they have not experienced both things, we can view these as a miniscule group. The question has never been officially discussed in a general convention. In this and any other case, most likely the Church would refuse to put in writing something that it feels cannot be expressed in bibl[ical] language.

All the history and the doctrinal statements mentioned so far refer only to the Apostolic Oneness people who trace their origin directly to Azusa Street. No mention is made of the history or the official beliefs of other Latin American Oneness groups, which, as far as we can see, and with the exception of a few groups, would tend to be very similar. Although in no way do we pretend to speak of what all the Oneness groups might think of the idea, it might be that the conditions do exist now for the initiation of a dialogue that would eventually settle the "New Issue." Although we cannot at this stage predict what shape the settling would take, we can, at least, suggest a very broad outline.

ELEMENTS FOR THE PROBABLE SETTLING OF THE ONENESS ISSUE

As mentioned before, Pentecostalism, practically since its inception, embraced people who used different baptismal formulas.[25] It was only when the need for exclusively Pentecostal denominations arose that water baptism in Jesus' name and the Oneness of God became an issue, which eventually tore the American Pentecostal Movement in two. The issue, as we know it, was also related to an internecine leadership struggle in the nascent Pentecostal denominations.[26] The coexistence was broken; the fellowship was permanently injured, perhaps irremediably; the dialogue, if it ever existed between 1913 and 1916, was interrupted; and a state of animosity began to develop that all over the world has produced antagonists on both sides who had nothing to do with the New Issue controversy but are still fighting it on either side. And yet, one wonders if things could have been different, or one asks oneself what would have happened if there had not been other factors injected into the controversy.[27] Since we cannot possibly turn back the clock or change the history of the early Pentecostal Movement, we might as well try to move into the future . . . without forgetting the lessons of the past.

The past tells us, for instance, that the early church had a very serious controversy when Peter baptized the first Gentile believers (Acts 11). Peter defended his actions on the basis, first, that "the Spirit bade me go" and second, "that the Holy Ghost had fallen on Cornelius and his family "as on us at the beginning." Faced with such irrefutable evidence, Peter could not help but conclude, "then how could I possibly stand in God's way?" (Acts 11:17, New English Bible). All present-day Pentecostals of any persuasion must feel proud that none of them has questioned the power of the Spirit to fall "upon the flesh," and must feel very happy that they readily acknowledge as true the claim of any brother, Trinitarian or Oneness, to say nothing of present-day charismatics, to have received the Holy Spirit or spoken in new tongues. It would seem that, in this sense, all Pentecostals have kept, however unwillingly, an important degree of "the unity of the Spirit." This could open the way for a journey toward "the unity of the faith," with whatever expression this takes and whatever goals are to be followed.

The discrepancy between Matthew 28:19 and Acts 2:38 must be the object of a serious and profound historico-hermeneutical study and not be dismissed as a simple semantic expression. From our reading of commentaries on the subject we get the impression that, although the general feeling seems to be that baptism was first in the name of Jesus and then in that of the Trinity, this is simply accepted as an accomplished fact with no thought of its theological implications.

The doctrine of the Trinity may naturally turn out to be the most difficult to tackle, not only because of the deep wound it has left and a certain inability on both sides to describe their position in a less dogmatic, more historical, and more theologically disciplined way but also because of the nature of the doctrine of the Trinity itself.

Most Oneness people pride themselves on holding the original Apostolic doctrines, a position that, in the words of David Reed, makes them subscribe to "a sectarian form of Jewish Christian theology which manifests the characteristics of its theology of the Name of Jesus, a Christological model based on 'dwelling' and the 'Glory of God,' a zealous defense of the monarchy and transcendence of God, and the affirmation of the full humanity of Jesus in the Antiochene and particularly Nestorian traditions."[28]

Although Reed's conclusion is based on his study of the American Oneness Movement, his observations could well apply to other such groups in Latin America. One of the main inconveniences of this theology is the fact that the history of the Church does not end with the death of the last Apostle, a fact that has made some Oneness people claim that there was no church between the second and the nineteenth centuries or that the true name of God was hidden during that time, only to be revealed or discovered at the beginning of the Oneness Movement early in this century. Although many Oneness people have abandoned this theological position, they still face the problem of insisting that they represent the pristine Apostolic position on the godhead and, theoretically, do not accept as valid any doctrinal decision taken after the Apostles, although we know that many Oneness people do teach doctrines that came much later and that were not originally expounded by Oneness theologians.

For Trinitarian Pentecostals, particularly in Latin America, their problem takes a different form. Being Pentecostals, they claim to have gone back to the book of Acts, but when it comes to the question of water baptism and the godhead, they have to depend on extrabiblical arguments and defend their position by recurring to conciliar decisions that were taken long after the time of the Apostles. Except for the Trinity, they reject every decision or doctrine that was expounded or proclaimed between the second century and the Reformation, for, according to them, all of this was the work of the Roman Catholic Church. Some Oneness people, of course, tend to do the same in regard to other doctrines.

Oneness people cannot escape considering what Andrew Urshan calls "a divine three-ness of being."[29] The same author used terms like "Tri-Unity"[30] and "the Three-One God."[31] According to Reed, Urshan was of the opinion that "it was the Catholic and the Protestant Trinitarians, not the Oneness Christians, who had departed from the biblical position of the triune God."[32] It would seem that Oneness believers have some kind of conditioned aversion to the word "person," but since they cannot deny the terms Father, Son, and Holy Spirit, they want to use a different word or words to identify that "three-ness" they find in the New Testament, and which is also known as "economic" or "transitive Trinity," what Philip Schaff calls "the trinity of the revelation of God in the threefold work of creation, redemption, and sanctification; the trinity presented in the apostolic writings as a living fact."[33] By refusing to accept the word "person," Oneness people find themselves in need of a substitute word, swimming against a very strong historical current and bearing the epithet of heretics.

In evaluating the Oneness (mostly American Oneness) theology, Reed affirms that it is presently at a relatively unreflective or even prereflective stage. Therefore, it disregards certain substantial issues raised by its own teaching. It has not yet seriously engaged with the historical questions raised by its doctrine of a functional Trinity. It should abandon its preconceived definition of the word "person" in Trinitarian terminology in favor of one that is more historically and theologically accurate.[34]

While agreeing in essence with what Reed says in this respect, we should also ask ourselves the following questions: (1) Was early Pentecostalism, by embracing the doctrine of the Trinity as it did, acting only on the basis of expediency in order to solve a leadership struggle or to save the coherence of a new-born denomination? (2) By doing so (consciously or unconsciously), were early Pentecostals forfeiting, or at least retarding, the possibilities of making a positive and innovative theological contribution now that the Holy Spirit was being so exalted by the Pentecostals, who were also seeking His leading in a very serious way? Could we apply to the orthodox Pentecostal position what Hans Küng has said about the two natures, but which could undoubtedly be applied also to the doctrine of the Trinity? "Only too often behind the Christ image of the councils there can be perceived the unmoving, passionless countenance of Plato's God, who cannot suffer, embellished with some features of Stoic ethics. The names of the councils show that they are exclusively Greek. But Christ was not born in Greece. Both for these councils and the theology behind it the work of translation must be continued."[35]

Could the same author be speaking to the Oneness side when he reminds us that "The trinitarian confession of the early Church developed theologically through a long history into an increasingly expanded doctrine of the Trinity. The culminating points of this development came in the last century with Hagel's philosophy of religion and in the present century with Karl Barth's *Church Dogmatics. . . . Every attempt at a critical new interpretation will have to be justified in the light of this great tradition.*"[36]

Could Küng again be addressing all of us in these words:

> From the standpoint of the New Testament neither the *classical doctrine* of the Trinity nor the classical two-nature doctrine *are to be thoughtlessly repeated or thoughtlessly dismissed, but discriminately interpreted for the present time. . . . The attempts at interpretation based on* Hellenistic ideas *and the resultant dogmatic formulations of this co-ordination are however* time-conditioned *and not simply identical with this basic intention. Not that a doctrine of the Trinity can be rejected just because it makes use of Hellenistic categories. But neither can any future doctrine of the Trinity be tied to the use of such categories. The traditional formulas of the doctrine of the Trinity, defined in Hellenistic terms, however helpful they may have been, cannot be imposed as a timeless obligation of faith on all believers at all times.*[37]

Those among us who are interested in settling "the unresolved issue" must begin by reinitiating the dialogue that was so rudely interrupted more than seventy years ago.[38] In this respect we see encouraging signs. One would be the Harvard Symposium on Oneness Pentecostal Theology in 1984, in which papers were presented not only by people from traditional Oneness churches but also by a German Lutheran theologian, an Orthodox scholar, independent Oneness groups, and a scholar from Howard University, together with an Episcopalian priest. A future meeting of this kind will undoubtedly need the presence and participation of scholars from some of the traditional Trinitarian churches and theological institutions.[39]

Especially in the United States, it would seem that efforts have been made to deny the Oneness people the right to be part of organizations or assemblies where a Oneness presence could be deemed necessary or useful. The usual way to eliminate Oneness participation has been the imposition of a written statement of faith, which parties are required to sign before they can be accepted as participants in whatever enterprise is intended. Whether this is done intentionally or not, the important thing would be to find ways of bringing the Oneness people into greater contacts with other Pentecostals. It is true that doctrinal matters are of great importance and that people must be agreed on what they believe, but it is also true that according to the ideas of Paul (Ephesians), the goal of unity of the faith can be reached only if we begin with the unity of the Spirit, and, as can be gathered from what has been previously said, the unity of the Spirit exists in the whole Pentecostal Movement, for all Pentecostals have received, and are receiving, the same Spirit.

We can see practical examples of corrective measures that have been taken by certain bodies, which, unwittingly or on purpose, have opened the way for Oneness participation. Among these examples we find the Lausanne Covenant, which did away with the traditional mention of persons in the godhead and made it possible for it to be signed by some Oneness people. The Covenant includes the following: "We affirm our belief in one eternal God, Creator and Lord of the world, Father, Son and Holy Spirit, who governs all things according to the purpose of the will. He has been calling out from the world a people for himself, and sending his people back into the world to be his servants and witnesses, for the extension of his kingdom, the building up of Christ's body, and the glory of his name."[40]

Another good example would be the Society for Pentecostal Studies, which understood that in order to attract scholars of different persuasions it had to do away with the required acquiescence to a certain doctrinal statement prior to acceptance in the membership of the SPS. Although as of now there is only one Oneness member of the SPS, we can be sure that in the future others will join the society.[41]

CONCLUSION

The "New Issue" did not vanish by the simple expedient of having the Oneness people go away or forcing them to abandon the fellowship in which they had been so prominent. The "New Issue" was not simply a "new slant," or a "new revelation" rigged by preachers who did not want to be considered, in the words of the late H. A. Goss, "slow, stupid, unspiritual."[42] Nor was it "the work of Satan" who "adroitly maneuvered" the Oneness souls into heresy and fanaticism.[43] Both sides of the "New Issue" have grown over the years and undoubtedly have also matured. On their theological attitudes it would be good to ask ourselves if both sides have conformed to Martin Marty's model of Pentecostalism as "belief without theology," but who remain "'typically American' in their lack of theological constitutiveness and preoccupation."[44] In saying this, no disparagement of the American Pentecostal Movement is intended. Rather we take it as a starting point for what will now be said. We would rather accept Russell

Spittler's assertion that there is a theological opportunity before the Pentecostal Movement both on a popular level and at the level of "the reflective thinkers who also search for reality." Although Spittler admits that Pentecostals "have always been better at evangelism than at writing theology," he also offers some words of advice that all Pentecostals would do well to heed: "The time has come to pluck a ripened Pentecostal theology. The time has come to remind the intellectuals of the day that there are some folk around—not many mighty, not many noble among them—who've been saying long before Roszak, long before youthful protesters, that life is at its best, man has reached his highest and found God's best, when one not merely discovers truth beyond the material world, but when, more than that, one can by personal and individual experience so encounter that world as to be personally baptized into the Holy Spirit of God."[45] While saying a hearty "amen" to Spittler's words, we should add that in our opinion the seizing of the theological opportunity and the plucking of the "ripened Pentecostal theology" mentioned by Spittler has to include the Oneness people and should encourage all sides to settle the question of the "New Issue" and to try to answer the questions that for more than seventy years have been begging for an answer from all sides of the controversy. This paper is written with that intention in mind and to serve as a pointer in that direction.

Speaking of the development of ideas in various fields of learning, Maurice Wiles says that "the most important changes occur when somebody succeeds in seeing the object from a new perspective. It is a new frame of reference rather than new particular fact . . . which is most productive of advance," adding that "when you see something from a new perspective, everything is altered." Oneness Pentecostals at the beginning did alter everything and changed, perhaps forever, the character of Pentecostalism, but, still following Wiles's ideas, the image they were contemplating was the same. And that is exactly what has happened in Pentecostalism since the "New Issue" controversy: All Pentecostals have been looking at the same fact, that of Jesus, and have sought and received the same Spirit.

Since this is a Society for *Pentecostal* Studies, it means that its members are interested in studying all that relates to the experience of those who claim to have the baptism of the Spirit. For them and for everybody, an additional word from Wiles may be useful:

We have to go on with the hermeneutical task, trying to understand as fully as we can the scriptural witness to Jesus; we have to go on seeking to respond to God through him in prayer and worship. On the basis of all that, Christians have to try to say what seems to them to be true about God and his dealings with the world. We will certainly be limited, and we may well be wrong, even in what seems to us as individuals most clearly to be true. The Spirit is sovereign and does not guarantee to underwrite even our most faithful and devoted undertakings. But if we are working in the way I have outlined, and if we take seriously our own limitations and our own fallibility, we must then affirm what seems to us to be true. We have to take our stand there; we can do no other.[46]

NOTES

1. Editors' note: As noted in the introduction of this volume, this chapter is included as a tribute to Manuel Gaxiola (1927–2014). This paper was originally presented at the Annual Meeting of the Society for Pentecostal Studies held in Virginia Beach, Virginia, from November 12 to 14, 1987. Gaxiola was among the first Latin American Pentecostals to earn a doctoral degree (University of Birmingham with Walter J. Hollenweger, after master's-level studies at Fuller Theological Seminary with missiologists Donald McGavran and Ralph Winter). Gaxiola delivered a version of this essay three years earlier at the First Occasional Symposium on Aspects of the Oneness Pentecostal Movement held at Harvard Divinity School. The Society for Pentecostal Studies, founded in 1971, was the first academic society dedicated to the study of Pentecostal Movements. In 1990 Manuel Gaxiola served as the Society's first, and thus far only, Oneness Pentecostal and Latin American president. In 1991 he guest edited the Society's *Pneuma* journal's special issue on Latin American Pentecostalism, featuring scholars from the region; importantly, the typology proffered in his introductory essay, "Latin American Pentecostalism: A Mosaic Within a Mosaic," has been widely taken up by historians and social scientists. Gaxiola also left his imprint on the hemispheric study of Apostolicism; for example, coining and introducing the term "*unicitario*" (to distinguish from "unitario" [unitarian]) into the Latin American theological lexicon. In 1993 Gaxiola's denomination, the IAFCJ, hosted the SPS meeting in Guadalajara, Mexico. His work in this era opened doors for Oneness scholars in academia, and laid the basis for theological dialogue. As a result, SPS now counts dozens of Oneness Pentecostal adherents in its membership. Readers will need to bear in mind the timing of this essay as they read terms such as "now" or any references that employ a particular number of years or range of dates. Terms such as "Anglo-Saxons" when describing whites also reflect the academic conventions of his period and place as a leading Latin American Pentecostal scholar and church leader with deep ties to and affection for coreligionists in the United States and Canada. Minor editorial revisions such as slight changes in spelling are noted in brackets.

2. Brumback, *Suddenly*, 208. [Editors' note: During the historic 1916 Assemblies of God convention debate over the "New Issue," a Trinitarian advocate's denigration of the Oneness position as "hay, wood, and stubble," articulated by a "voice in the wilderness," was taken as a clear reference to (and possible racial slight against) one

of the main Oneness exponents (and sole African American speaker), Garfield T. Haywood, of Indianapolis, and his periodical, *Voice in the Wilderness*.]

3. Fauss, *Buy the Truth*, 34.

4. [Editors' note: By the time Gaxiola delivered this paper, the Oneness Pentecostal Movement was just over seventy years old.]

5. Piepkorn, "Profiles in Belief," 195–216.

6. Clark-Alfaro, "Grupos religiosos," 1–2; Greenway, "'Luz del Mundo'"; Ibarra and Lanczyner Reisel, "Hermosa Provincia," mimeo, 64.

7. [Editors' note: No full rigorous study of La Luz del Mundo had yet been conducted at the time of Gaxiola's presentation. Since then, Mexican scholars have published groundbreaking work on the movement. See Renée de la Torre, *Los hijos de la luz*.]

8. Reed, "Origins and Development." [Editors' note: Reed's revised dissertation was published in 2008; see Reed, *In Jesus' Name*.]

9. Gerloff's doctoral study culminated in her 1992 two-volume work; see Gerloff, *A Plea for British Black Theologies*.

10. [Editors' note: Gill's doctoral study culminated in his 1994 book: Gill, *Toward a Contextualized Theology*.]

11. The writer read at that symposium a paper on "The Spanish-Speaking Oneness Churches in Latin America: Search for Identity and Possibilities of Doctrinal Renewal."

12. [Editors' note: The term "New Issue" emerged during the controversies of the Jesus' name baptismal formula in the mid-1910s.]

13. Bartleman, *Another Wave*, 104.

14. Cantú et al., *Historia de la Asamblea*; *Apostolic Faith* 1, no. 3 (November 1906): 4. [Editors' note: The referenced issue of the *Apostolic Faith* periodical mentions a pioneering evangelist couple, Abundio and Rosa López; Cantú et al. record the baptism of lay pioneer Luís López in 1909.]

15. De León, *Silent Pentecostals*, 19–23. See also Holland, *Religious Dimensions*.

16. Holland, *Religious Dimensions*, 45–53.

17. Clanton, *United We Stand*, 85.

18. Foster, *Think It Not Strange*, 85.

19. Farrow, "New Birth," 3.

20. Clanton, *United We Stand*, 80.

21. See my "The Serpent and the Dove." [Editors' note: An earlier Spanish-language version was published in 1970 by William Carey Library in Spanish, under the title *La serpiente y la paloma: Análisis del crecimiento de la Iglesia Apostólica de la Fe en Cristo Jesús de México* ["The Serpent and the Dove: A History of the Apostolic Church of the Faith in Christ Jesus in Mexico"], with a preface by church-growth pioneer Donald McGavran, Gaxiola's adviser at Fuller.]

22. [Editors' note: See Gaxiola's fuller discussion, "Teología Uni-Pentecostal: Una aproximación," [Uni-Pentecostal Theology: An Approach], chapter 5 in Gaxiola's 1994 book revision, *La Serpiente y la Paloma*, 2nd ed., 51–65.]

23. D'Epinay, *Haven of the Masses*, 197.

24. Foster, *Think It Not Strange*, 56, 71.

25. Anderson, *Vision of the Disinherited*, 180–85.

26. Ibid., 179.

27. Foster, *Think It Not Strange*, 71.

28. Reed, "Origins and Development," 322.

29. Urshan, "Trinity," 2.

30. Ibid.

31. Urshan, *Almighty God*, 2.

32. Reed, "Origins and Development," 156.

33. Schaff, *History*, 567.

34. Reed, "Origins and Development," 375.

35. Küng, *On Being a Christian*, 131.

36. Ibid., 476; emphasis original.

37. Ibid., 476, 477; emphasis original.

38. [Editors' note: Gaxiola is again referencing the disputes beginning in the mid-1910s.]

39. This symposium was organized by Jeffrey Gill, formerly a Oneness minister who later joined the Episcopal Church. A book with the main papers presented at the symposium is expected to be printed by Peter Lang. In the meantime, those who are interested in copies of the papers read at that time could contact Kenneth D. Gill at the Billy Graham Center Library. [Editors' note: The book was never published.]

40. International Congress, *Let the Earth Hear*, 3.

41. [Editors' note: As of 2020 there are over a dozen Oneness Pentecostal members of the SPS. The SPS has also been a venue to examine Oneness scholarship such as theology, history, and ecumenical studies. From 2002 to 2007 the SPS sponsored a Trinitarian-Oneness dialogue with an interdisciplinary cohort of scholars and published their report and responses to the report in the society's peer-reviewed journal, *Pneuma* 30 (2008).]

42. Goss, *Winds of God*, 155.

43. Brumback, *Suddenly*, 191, 192.

44. Marty, "Pentecostalism," 205–6.

45. Spittler, "Theological Opportunity."

46. Wiles, *Remaking*, 7–8, 13–14.

BIBLIOGRAPHY

Primary Sources

Apostolic Faith 1, no. 3 (November 1906): 4.

Bartleman, Frank. *Another Wave Rolls In!* Monroeville, PA: Whitaker Books, 1962.

Farrow, George R. "The New Birth— What Is It; What It Does." *Apostolic Herald* (August 1930).

Urshan, Andrew D. *The Almighty God in the Lord Jesus Christ*. Los Angeles: By the author, 1919.

———. "The Trinity." *Witness of God* (September 1924): 2.

Secondary Sources

Anderson, Robert Mapes. *Vision of the Disinherited*. New York: Oxford University Press, 1979.

Brumback, Carl. *Suddenly . . . from Heaven: A History of the Assemblies of God*. Springfield, MO: Gospel Publishing House, 1961.

Cantú, Ernesto S., José A. Ortega, Isaac Cota, and Phillip Rangel. *Historia de La Asamblea Apostólica de La Fe En Cristo Jesús, 1916–1966* [History of the Apostolic Assembly of the Faith in Christ Jesus, 1916–1966]. Mentone, CA: Sal's Printing Service, 1966.

Clanton, Arthur L. *United We Stand: A History of Oneness Organizations*. St. Louis: Pentecostal Publishing House, 1965.

Clark Alfaro, Víctor. "Los grupos religiosos en Tijuana" [Religious Groups in Tijuana]. *Inventario*, no. 27 (April 27, 1986).

Epinay, Christian Lalive d'. *Haven of the Masses: A Study of the Pentecostal Movement in Chile*. London: Lutterworth Press, 1969.

Fauss, Oliver F. *Buy the Truth and Sell It Not*. St. Louis: Pentecostal Publishing House, 1965.

Foster, Fred J. *Think It Not Strange: A History of the Oneness Movement*. St. Louis: Pentecostal Publishing House, 1965.

Gaxiola-Gaxiola, Manuel J. "Latin American Pentecostalism: A Mosaic

Within a Mosaic." *Pneuma* 13, no. 2 (1991): 107–29.

———. "The Serpent and the Dove: A History of the Apostolic Church of the Faith in Christ Jesus in Mexico, 1914–1964." Master's thesis, Fuller Theological Seminary, 1975.

———. *La Serpiente y la Paloma: Análisis del crecimiento de la Iglesia Apostólica* [The Serpent and the Dove: Analysis of the Growth of the Apostolic Church]. 2nd ed. México, D.F.: By the author, 1994.

———. *La Serpiente y la Paloma: Análisis del crecimiento de la Iglesia Apostólica de la Fe en Cristo Jesús de México* [The Serpent and the Dove: Analysis of the Growth of the Apostolic Church of the Faith in Christ Jesus of Mexico]. South Pasadena, CA: William Carey Library, 1970.

Gerloff, Roswith I. H. *A Plea for British Black Theologies: The Black Church Movement in Britain in Its Transatlantic Cultural and Theological Interaction.* New York: Peter Lang, 1992.

Gill, Kenneth. *Toward a Contextualized Theology for the Third World: The Emergence and Development of Jesus' Name Pentecostalism in Mexico.* Bern, Switzerland: Peter Lang, 1994.

Goss, Ethel A. *The Winds of God: The Story of the Oneness Movement (1901–1914) in the Life of Howard A. Goss.* New York: Comet Press Books, 1958.

Greenway, Roger S. "The 'Luz del Mundo' Movement in Mexico." *Missiology* 1, no. 2 (1973): 113–24.

Holland, Clifford. *The Religious Dimensions in Spanish Los Angeles.* South Pasadena: William Carey Library, 1974.

Hollenweger, Walter J. *The Pentecostals.* London: SCM Press Ltd., 1972.

Ibarra Bellón, Araceli, and Alisa Lanczyner Reisel. "Hermosa

Provincia. Nacimiento y vida de una secta cristiana en Guadalajara" [Beautiful Province: Birth and Life of a Christian Sect in Guadalajara]. Master's thesis, Universidad de Guadalajara, 1972.

International Congress on World Evangelization, Lausanne. *Let the Earth Hear His Voice: Official Reference Volume.* Edited by J. D. Douglas. Minneapolis: World Wide Publications, 1975.

Küng, Hans. *On Being a Christian.* New York: Pocket Books, 1978.

León, Víctor de. *The Silent Pentecostals: A Biographical History of the Pentecostal Movement Among the Hispanics in the Twentieth Century.* La Habra, CA: By the author, 1979.

Marty, Martin E. "Pentecostalism in American Piety and Practice." In *Aspects of Pentecostal Charismatic Origins,* edited by Vinson Synan, 192–233. Plainfield, NJ: Logos, 1975.

Piepkorn, Arthur C. *Profiles in Belief: The Religious Bodies of the United States and Canada.* Vol. 3. New York: Harper & Row, 1979.

Reed, David A. *In Jesus' Name: The History and Beliefs of Oneness Pentecostals.* Blandford Forum, UK: Deo, 2008.

———. "Origins and Development of the Theology of Oneness Pentecostalism in the United Stated." PhD diss., Boston University, 1978.

Schaff, Philip. *History of the Christian Church.* Vol. 2. Grand Rapids, MI: Eerdmans, 1970.

Spittler, Russell P. "Theological Opportunity Before the Pentecostal Movement." In *Aspects of Pentecostal Charismatic Origins,* edited by Vinson Synan, 235–43. Plainfield, NJ: Logos, 1975.

Torre, Renée de la. *Los hijos de la luz. Discurso, identidad y poder en La Luz del Mundo* [The Children of the Light:

Discourse, Identity and Power in the Light of the World]. 2nd ed. Tlaquepaque, Jalisco, Mexico: Instituto Tecnológico de Estudios Superiores de Occidente, 2000.

Wiles, Maurice. *The Remaking of Christian Doctrine*. Philadelphia: Westminster, 1978.

CHAPTER 2

Evangelical Origins of Oneness Pentecostal Theology

David A. Reed

The formative years of the Pentecostal revival were tumultuous and full of surprises. Battles over doctrine, race, and leadership dogged, and even propelled, the spread of the new movement throughout North America. But none would produce the deep and lingering effects as did the Oneness Movement. Oneness Pentecostalism emerged as the third stream and second schism within the early Pentecostal Movement. Both schisms represented a Christocentric "correction." In the first, William Durham (1873–1912) called for a Christocentric soteriology, the Finished Work of Calvary. Evangelist Frank Ewart (1876–1947) led the second into a more radical Christocentrism—to preserve the "fulness" of deity in the revelation of Jesus, the one true God of the Bible must be without internal distinctions, and God's one revealed New Covenant name "Jesus" needs to be appropriated in water baptism. The distinctive teachings of both schisms bear Evangelical roots. But the scaffolding of the Oneness Pentecostals' exclusive claim to be the final restoration of Apostolic doctrine and practice before the return of Christ has left some to regard it as a heretical aberration. This chapter will explore the two fundamental doctrines of Oneness Pentecostals from within their historical context. First, it provides a narrative of the birth of the movement from 1913 to the movement's expulsion from the Assemblies of God in 1916. Second, it then turns to earlier Pietist, Evangelical, and Pentecostal origins to identify the leitmotifs that produced the fundamental contours of Oneness theology and spirituality. Third, it identifies early examples of cooperation and mutual recognition that may be a harbinger of a more inclusive future. The thesis of this chapter is that Oneness Pentecostalism is deeply rooted in its Evangelical heritage, that its restorationism led many early leaders to conclude their "revelation" was pure Apostolic truth, and that some early Oneness leaders recognized that this "precious truth" did not require complete separation from other Christian believers.

HOW IT ALL BEGAN

The first stirrings occurred in 1913 at what was advertised as a Worldwide Camp Meeting in Arroyo Seco on the outskirts of Los Angeles. Invitations were sent to the heirs of the first schism within the early movement called the Finished Work of Calvary, and originally spearheaded by Chicago-based William Durham (1873–1912). Two moments occurred within a twenty-four-hour period that would eventually become the catalyst for a new movement.

The first was a baptismal sermon delivered by Canadian evangelist Robert E. McAlister (1880–1953). Standing on a hastily built platform by a baptismal tank, McAlister launched into an exegetical exposition of the apparent inconsistency in the baptismal words spoken over the candidate between Jesus' triune invocation in Matthew 28:19 and the variants of "Lord Jesus Christ" as reported in the Acts of the Apostles. He proposed that the two were intended to be harmonized, since the name "Lord Jesus Christ" correlated with the triune name, "Father, Son, Holy Spirit." What occurred next was reported by Frank J. Ewart (1876–1947), first architect of the new doctrine. By his account, "an inaudible shudder" rippled through the preachers and the crowd. At that point, Frank Denny, a missionary from China, bounded onto the platform warning McAlister that this teaching was being promulgated by a local Dr. Sykes of questionable orthodoxy. Duly advised, McAlister returned to the podium to clarify that his observation was in no way intended to discard the triune name in baptism.[1]

Sykes (1860–1929) was never a significant figure in the narrative of Oneness origins. His name, however, was often repeated in secondary literature without elaboration, usually citing Ewart's account. Pentecostal historian Cecil M. Robeck identified him as Joshua Sykes, not a doctor but pastor of an "Apostolic Church" in east Los Angeles. He embraced the general teachings of the Azusa Street Mission, with one important exception: "He baptized his converts in the name of Jesus Christ and did not invoke the traditional Trinitarian formula."[2]

Sykes's reputation seemed to be of little consequence despite Denny's warning until a recent investigation was published by historian Andrea Johnson.[3]

To tie up this dangling thread of Pentecostal history, she follows Joshua Sykes from poor Virginian farmer to insurance salesman in Missouri, then to Baptist ministry in Detroit, where he reportedly had a vision to gather 144,000 followers in preparation for the Second Coming. In Los Angeles his controversial views on pacifism and extreme end-times prophecies became a warning signal to others. From there, Sykes would go on to split mixed-faith marriages and publicly oppose war support efforts, which earned him a prison sentence. He abandoned his wife for "a much younger, pretty, divorced, and wealthy woman."[4] For this indiscretion, he himself was promptly abandoned by many of his followers. When he died in 1929, only a handful of devotees remained to hold vigil for three days, waiting for him to resurrect.

As Johnson rightly concludes, nothing can be settled regarding Sykes's influence on the embryonic Jesus' name Movement, except possibly deterring some from baptizing in Jesus' name and depriving us of his writings and ideas. But history is never frozen in time. Without Denny's early warning signal, Sykes's potential for harm might have been considerable and the future revival been in for a rockier ride.

The second moment occurred after a less well-known listener, John B. Schaepe (1870–1939), was inspired by McAlister's sermon to study and pray through the night. In the early hours of the morning he ran through the camp shouting that God had shown him the truth on baptism in the name of Jesus Christ.[5] Schaepe left no account of his insights, but for some this night encounter became the coveted "revelation."[6] Although McAlister made no claim to a special revelation, Ewart credited him with the revelation that sparked a revolution. With characteristic hyperbole, he described the effect of the sermon: "the gun was fired from that platform which was destined to resound throughout all Christendom."[7]

The first echo from McAlister's homiletical gun blast was to be heard on April 15, 1914, precisely one year to the day from the opening of the Arroyo Seco Camp Meeting. McAlister had remained in Los Angeles for many months to assist Ewart in pioneer work, during which time Ewart reported that they discussed at length the baptismal issue. By the spring of 1914 Ewart was convinced of the truth of the new baptismal practice and, more importantly, its radical theological grounding:

> It was long after this preacher [McAlister] had left the city of Los Angeles, where I had a pastorate, before the revelation of the absolute Deity of our Lord Jesus Christ burst upon me. I saw that as all the fullness of the Godhead dwelt in Jesus, bodily; therefore, baptism, as the Apostles administered it,

in the Name of the Lord Jesus Christ, was the one and only fulfillment of Matt. 28:19. Instantly I conferred not with flesh and blood, but not wishing to trespass on the rights of those with whom I was associated in the ministry, I formed a band of helpers, rented and pitched a tent on the east side of the city of Los Angeles, and began to proclaim my new revelation.[8]

The Phrases "absolute Deity" and "all the fullness of the Godhead" are at least strong indicators of Ewart's new Modalistic view of the godhead in which there are no distinctions within God's being, and the "absolute" deity in Jesus is the one undifferentiated God and Father, not the *Logos* or Second Person of the Trinity. Ewart's account suggests that the basic contours of the Oneness view of the godhead were being formed by the time he launched his campaign.

Armed with the zeal of a convert with a revelation, Ewart and his assistant, former Azusa Street leader Glenn Cook, set up a revival tent outside Los Angeles in the area of Belvedere. On April 15 Ewart preached his first public sermon on Acts 2:38.[9] Since neither he nor Cook had been rebaptized, they acquired a baptismal tank and baptized each other, thus marking the beginning of a new and turbulent trajectory within the early Pentecostal revival. Within months, the New Issue, as it was initially called, spread like wildfire throughout the fellowship, which had that same month organized as the Assemblies of God.[10] It almost immediately made deep inroads along the West Coast, into the Midwest, and farther afield to Canada and Mexico.

Characteristically Pentecostal, the final vindication of the truth of the new teaching was not rational argument or confessional authority but the success of its spiritual effect. Ewart observed the power that attended the Belvedere meetings when people submitted to the new baptism: "One of the greatest, most startling characteristics of that great revival was that the vast majority of the new converts were filled with the Holy Ghost after coming up out of the water. They would leave the tank speaking in other tongues. Many were healed when they were baptized."[11] This appeal to "Pentecostal" power was undoubtedly a potent force in propelling the New Issue forward through the ranks of the Assemblies of God fellowship.

By the summer of 1915 it appeared that the new movement would engulf the entire leadership of the Assemblies of God. It had won over Indianapolis pastor Garfield T. Haywood (1880–1931), the only prominent African American leader in association with the fellowship. His influence resulted in large numbers of Blacks, including ministers and churches, entering the new movement.[12] E. N. Bell (1866–1923), a pivotal leader as editor of two Assemblies of God periodicals, was rebaptized. Throughout the summer, camp meetings witnessed a flurry of rebaptisms as New Issue preachers proclaimed their message. Prominent Canadians R. E. McAlister and Franklin Small (1873–1961) were rebaptized.

Clearly the new teaching had caught the Assemblies' fellowship by surprise. Those who were skeptical or confused found themselves on the horns of a dilemma. At the inaugural meeting of the Assemblies of God organization, the leadership had already established a minimalist standard for doctrinal beliefs, refusing to identify themselves as "a sect, that is a human organization that legislates or forms laws and articles of faith."[13] The year 1915 would test that resolve, and the Fourth General Council in 1916 would settle it.

By Council time in October, emotions were escalating and lines of division were hardening. The first item of business was the formation of a committee to draft a "Statement of Fundamental Truths." With all five members solidly Trinitarian, the result was predictable. There would be tolerance on the baptismal formula, but none on the New Issue's categorical rejection of the doctrine of the Trinity, its exclusive use of the name of the Lord Jesus Christ in baptism, or its insistence upon rebaptism. After debate and vote, the Trinitarians had triumphed. As 156 of the 585 ministers repaired outside the hall to contemplate their next move, a second schism in the early Pentecostal revival had just been realized and a new movement was born.

Now liberated from the restraint of contention, the new body marched forth confident that what they were preaching had been delivered directly from the Apostles. They were, however, unaware of the spiritual and theological forces that informed them on how to read the Bible, what themes to look for, who to read, and what to preach. To these forces we now turn.

BEFORE IT ALL BEGAN

By most accounts, the New Issue was a surprise—both unexpected and unfamiliar—or in Ewart's colorful words, "as startling and revolutionary as a thunder clap from a clear sky."[14] Not unlike the sweeping force of Durham's Finished Work teaching, which had captured the allegiance of a significant sector of Pentecostals within two years, the New Issue initially threatened to command the leadership of the newly formed Assemblies of God (AG). But its radical rejection of the doctrine of the Trinity and exclusionary practice of baptism in the name of Jesus Christ made the New Issue unfamiliar enough to raise suspicions regarding its source and spirit—unlike the more familiar Reformed themes of justification heralded in Durham's Finished Work theology.

As British sociologist Bryan Wilson points out, however, a sect is "a unique combination of variations, few of which in themselves are wholly distinctive of that sect alone."[15] Oneness Pentecostalism is no exception. Here we will briefly review spiritual and theological leitmotifs from Oneness's parentage in the revivalist evangelical and early Pentecostal Movements, rudiments of which contributed substantially to the scaffolding for construction of the New Issue.

Doxological Foundations of Oneness Doctrine

For all its singularities, the Oneness Movement was planted firmly in the long Pietist tradition of experiential faith, religion for which dry, intellectual confessionalism was insufficient without practical and affective purpose.[16] We can trace the lineage through the Great Awakenings and late nineteenth-century Holiness Movements. A common conviction throughout these movements is succinctly captured by H. Richard Niebuhr, "Gospel experience alone could convince of gospel truth."[17]

Two influences in particular, both focusing on Jesus, helped shape Oneness spirituality and doctrine. The first was its Pietist and Revivalist spirituality, best described as an orthodox expression of Jesus-piety. Hymns, poems, and devotion were often directed to Jesus. The doctrine of the Trinity was unquestioned, but its intellectual content was more formal than substantive, and interest was primarily directed to the *work* of the three Persons. Since the "New Birth," a centerpiece of Pietist faith, was cast as personal relationship rather than mere mental assent or sacramental seal, the personal name "Jesus" carried more spiritual weight in some circles than tepid titles like "Christ" and "Lord."

The second was an extension of the first name, the exaltation of the name, Jesus. Echoing the ancient Jewish belief that the personality resides in the name, praise to the name of God was an act of devotion to the Person of God. Sometimes the name was interchangeable with titles and metaphors for God. But they culminated with Jesus, and frequently with the name, Jesus. We can trace this stream of piety from the Pietists through the Wesleyan Revival and nineteenth-century Holiness Movements.[18]

More significant for Oneness theology was the *apologetic* use made of the name by early Evangelicals, especially representatives of the emerging Premillennial theology and Keswick Holiness Movement. The purpose was to defend the divine identity of Jesus and his atoning work. These fellow travelers were responding in part directly to the threat of liberalism. Unlike Fundamentalists of the next generation who attempted to secure the truth of Christ's deity through his virgin birth, the earlier generation directed its attention to a biblical study of the names and titles of God in the Old Testament to show that Jesus fulfilled all the qualifications as fully as Yahweh.[19] A classic example comes from Sam Green, an early Evangelical writer from the Boston area: "We have seen of Jesus, that His name is God, <u>Jehovah</u> of hosts, the Lord God, the Lord of glory, and the Lord of all. He is the true God, the mighty God, Lord of lords and God over all, the first and the last, and the self-existing I AM. We have seen that all the attributes and incommunicable perfections of Jehovah belong to Christ."[20] The unanimous conclusion of these Evangelical advocates, therefore, was that the Yahweh of the Old Covenant is the Jesus of the New.[21]

A variety of interesting descriptors began to appear among defenders of this magnified view of Christ. Jesus was being called "the supreme God,"[22] "supreme deity,"[23] "full deity,"[24] the "I AM,"[25] "all in all,"[26] and the "fulness of the God-head."[27] Clearly, the urgency was to assert in the strongest terms possible that in his deity Jesus was none other than the God of the Old Covenant. In contrast to the fourth-century debates over the ontological distinctions between the eternal Father and the *Logos* or Son, the mandate in the Evangelical culture of late nineteenth-century Anglo-Protestantism was to champion the *oneness* of the Father and Son. This effort, I suggest, is the first theological plank that would prepare the way for Oneness thought.

More immediately, this shift helped shape what might be best described as a form of Christocentric Trinitarianism among some Evangelicals. J. Monro Gibson, noted Presbyterian theologian, one-time coworker with D. L. Moody, and in later years moderator of the Presbyterian Church in England, decried a modernist sentiment of his time, the attempt to find God only in his "absolute essence of Deity." He countered that the Father can be found only in the Son: "The whole knowledge of the Father is provided in Christ. We are 'complete in him.'"[28] Taking Paul's statement that in Christ "dwelleth all the fulness of the Godhead bodily" (Colossians 2:9), Gibson concluded that we will see the Trinity only by "sitting at the feet of Jesus and looking into his face." All that God as Father, Son, and Holy Spirit has revealed of himself for us "is manifest in Christ."[29]

The Name and William Phillips Hall's "Remarkable Discovery"

Two pre-Oneness events contributed more directly to the theological construction of the New Issue. First was the 1913 publication of a study on the name of God by an Evangelical leader, William Phillips Hall. Hall was a wealthy inventor, businessman, and lay evangelist from Brooklyn, New York.[30] Encouraged by

Arno C. Gaebelein, his friend and early Dispensational Fundamentalist, Hall undertook the project.[31]

Hall's goal was to demonstrate that the mystery of the true identity of Jesus, lost in the rubble of church history, was to be found in the biblical name of God, especially through a Semitic understanding of the name in the Old Testament.[32] The critical practice that had been lost to the church was the invocation of the true name in water baptism. Hall's premise for presuming that the "discovery" would be revolutionary was that the modern church was spiritually powerless. A recovery of the *name* of God would bring people into life-changing contact with the *Person* of God: "'the Name' of God is . . . in a very true sense, the very Essence, or Essential Personality, of God Himself."[33]

The exegetical dilemma for Hall was the discrepancy between Jesus' commission to baptize in "the name of the Father, and of the Son and of the Holy Spirit" (Matthew 28:19) and the Apostolic practice of baptizing in some variation of "Lord Jesus Christ" as recorded in the Acts of the Apostles—and paradigmatically stated in Acts 2:38. There must be an internal explanation since the reigning hermeneutical principle in Hall's time was the complete harmonization of scripture—no contradictions.

The key for Hall was the parable: Jesus was speaking in parabolic form to his inner circle of disciples, as he had often done. His words were not intended to be repeated but were a parabolic reference to himself as the full revelation and embodiment of the Trinitarian God. Hall was aware that challenging the common practice of Trinitarian baptism was a radical affront to most of Christendom. While only the Christocentric name had been employed in New Testament practice, the Trinitarian formula became the normal, and required, usage throughout most of the church's history.[34]

With the enthusiasm of a detective, Hall set out to solve the mystery. First, he concluded that the Trinitarian names in Matthew are "relationship" names, not personal names, and therefore do not qualify to be the New Covenant name of God. On the Day of Pentecost the veil of the parabolic words of Jesus was lifted when the Apostles declared that the full name of "Lord Jesus Christ" was the designated name of the Triune God, the One through whom we have access to the Father and the Spirit, and the name that encompasses the whole enterprise of salvation.[35] Since Jesus was made both "Lord and Christ" (Acts 2:36), the baptismal name must be the same, or in Hall's words, "The true baptismal 'Name' is the saving 'Name of the Lord Jesus Christ.'"[36]

For Hall, the name "Lord Jesus Christ" perfectly embodies the name of the Trinity. As Yahweh is called Lord (Jeremiah 16:21), now Jesus claims to come in his *Father's* name (John 5:43, 10:25).[37] Jesus is the personal name of the incarnate *Son* of God, not merely the human name of a man from Nazareth.[38] The name of the *Holy Spirit* is the name of "Christ," since the Spirit "is of, incarnate in, and proceeds from" the incarnate Son of God. The Holy Spirit is one with the Spirit of the Father and the Son. More importantly here, the Pauline language of "Christ in you" is another way that scripture expresses the indwelling Holy Spirit.[39]

This brings us full circle to the 1913 Worldwide Camp Meeting and R. E. McAlister's sermon on the name to be invoked in baptism. The clue that connects his sermon with Hall's 1913 edition of *What Is the Name?* is McAlister's explanation given to Ewart some months later: "Lord, Jesus, Christ, being the counterpart of Father, Son, and Holy Ghost, . . . made Jesus' words in Matt. 28:19, one of those *parabolic statements* [emphasis mine] of truth, which was interpreted in Acts 2:38 and other scriptures."[40] The question lingers: Did McAlister acquire his novel interpretation from reading Hall's book, which had been published that same year? That Hall is the source is virtually conclusive, given that both Hall and McAlister believed Jesus was speaking parabolically. Many years later, McAlister credited George Studd, a Pentecostal pioneer working in the Los Angeles area, with the insight. It so happens that Studd was one of the organizers of the Worldwide Camp Meeting at Arroyo Seco and eventually converted to the Oneness Movement.[41] Ewart himself reported later that he had read Hall's book, following which they engaged in correspondence with each other.[42]

Hall's alternative to the traditional Trinitarian baptismal formula did not diminish his belief in the doctrine of the Trinity. But it did shift the emphasis theologically and spiritually toward a Christocentrism in which the name "Lord Jesus Christ" was both revelation and power in the age of the New Covenant.

Salvation and William Durham's Finished Work of Calvary

The second contribution critical for earliest Oneness theology came from the first schism, led by Chicago evangelist William Durham.[43] The initial enthusiasm of the Azusa Street Revival was waning, and fissures of race, doctrine, and organization were threatening the unity of the movement. For some years Durham had preached the Holiness doctrine of sanctification as a second work of grace. But following his dramatic Pentecostal experience at Azusa Street in 1907, his theology was so rearranged that, as he later acknowledged, "From the day the Holy Spirit fell on me and filled me I could never preach the second work theory again."[44] The day of public declaration was May 10, 1910, at a large annual convention of Pentecostal leaders from the Midwest in Chicago's prominent Stone Church. The title of his address was, "The Finished Work of Calvary"— and with it a movement and new stream of Pentecostalism was born, netting a significant sector of Pentecostals at the time.

Durham's bold move was a seismic Christocentric shift, a move away from what he perceived to be a two-stage salvation process in the Holiness teaching, in which justification leaves one minimally saved until sanctified. The new theological center of Durham's teaching was one act of grace through total identification with Christ in his atoning work on Calvary.[45] This is achieved by identifying with Christ in his death, burial, and resurrection. The paradigmatic text, Romans 6:4, states that by faith and baptism a person dies to sin and receives new life through Jesus' resurrection. It is noteworthy—and astonishing—that water baptism would become for Durham a central and even essential act of identifying with Christ, inseparable from the inward act of faith. While he rejected baptismal regeneration, he elevated baptism to the point where he could state that it is "the dividing line between the old life and the new."[46]

Durham's next move was to shift his paradigmatic text from Romans 6:4 to Acts 2:38, the defining text for the Oneness Movement and central to Hall. While Durham did not abandon the Romans text, the Acts passage incorporated, along with water baptism, the two great experiences of the Christian—conversion and Spirit baptism. Acts 2:38 articulated both Durham's Finished Work of Calvary teaching and the divine *ordo salutis*.[47]

Durham and his Finished Work teaching reconfigured the future of the Pentecostal revival. The Assemblies of God was organized by newly committed Finished Work adherents, most notably E. N. Bell and Howard Goss. From his vantage point in Chicago, Durham captured the major Canadian centers from Winnipeg to Ontario, drawing into his circle leaders like R. E. McAlister, A. H. Argue, and Franklin Small. But by 1912 his health began to fail. In late June he returned to Los Angeles, where he had moved to be with his family. He died on July 7 at age thirty-nine of pulmonary tuberculosis. Frank Ewart, his associate and successor in the city, preached his funeral sermon.[48]

Durham's theology and work were prematurely cut off. He left a large following in the wake of his death, many of whom had been deeply affected by the monumental Christocentric shift he had orchestrated. For a few, the effect was radical as they contemplated the implications of the all-encompassing Christ for their faith. They would soon emerge to write their own chapter of an unfinished story. These include the familiar names of Frank Ewart, R. E. McAlister,

Garfield T. Haywood, Franklin Small, and later, Andrew D. Urshan. By 1930, three out of five Pentecostals would become followers of Durham's Finished Work teaching.[49]

Interracial Vision and the Azusa Street Revival

Oneness Pentecostalism is interracial at its core. This is the claim argued by Oneness historian Talmadge L. French. Not only was the first Oneness organization, the Pentecostal Assemblies of the World (PAW), fully interracial from 1918 to 1924, its earliest incarnation was as a child of the Azusa Street Revival with an unwavering commitment to the interracial ideal. Corroborating evidence supports French's conclusion that the PAW was formed in 1906 by the Azusa Mission as a loose association, "for the purpose of evangelism and keeping pace with its expanding, increasingly visible ministry."[50]

Pentecostal meetings were first held in Indianapolis in 1907 with the visit of William Seymour, Azusa's recognized leader. The ensuing two-year revival became popularly known as the "Indianapolis Azusa." In 1907 Haywood, already living and working in Indianapolis, was converted to the movement. In 1911 he registered as a minister with the PAW and in 1915 embraced the New Issue, eventually to become one of its most influential leaders and theologians.[51] Haywood was a remarkable communicator. As theologian Roswith Gerloff observes, he was capable of thinking and preaching in the language of another culture, but also of introducing a bridge-building process by which elements of one culture became incorporated into another.[52]

The interracial ideal ran deep within Haywood. He had been formed by the racism of his time, especially through his work as political cartoonist and satirist for two Black newspapers in Indianapolis, *The Freeman* and the *Recorder*.[53] He had also been spiritually and theologically influenced by the interracial vision of Azusa and Seymour. He was unwavering in his commitment to racial equality and interracial marriage, even as the interracial ideal was collapsing during the waning years of the Azusa Street Revival. Haywood's vision of a fully interracial body persisted, though briefly, through the earliest years of the PAW. French captures this achievement: "The interracial unity that had failed in Parham's ministry . . . and the later unraveling of racial unity at Azusa itself, was accomplished to a great extent, though temporarily, in the visionary dream of Oneness integration and unification."[54]

A close reading of the roots of the Oneness doctrine of God suggests that, within Haywood, who had struggled and labored so hard over the interracial

unity of the human race, there would have been a subterranean echo of a revelation that only the "one" true God—not the racist and partitioned god of the
Trinitarians—could create all humans as one and equal, with offer of salvation
to all.[55]

Convergence

Historical movements ferry leitmotifs that eventually capture the imaginations
of those caught up in the flow "around the bend," even if unaware of the source.
The Oneness pioneers appropriated such themes from a Jesus-centric Evangelicalism, which applied the names and titles of God in the Old Testament
to Jesus, from a book that applied those themes to water baptism, and from
the primal Azusa Street Revival, which preached the "oneness" of all races.
The Oneness gospel spread rapidly from state to state and within months was
crossing borders, both south and north.

AFTER IT ALL BEGAN
First Border Crossing—A Mexican Immigrant Story

The Oneness connection with Azusa Street does not stop with Haywood.
For Hispanics it began with Azusa Street participant Juan Navarro who was
baptized by Apostolic Assembly of the Faith in Christ Jesus (AAFCJ) founder
Francisco Llorente in 1913. The AAFCJ also celebrates Luís López's 1909 Jesus'
name baptism in San Diego.[56] The first account of Oneness Pentecostalism
moving beyond the southern American border occurred in late 1914, within
months of Ewart's inaugural tent meeting. The message was carried by Romana
Carbajal de Valenzuela, an immigrant woman from Chihuahua, Mexico, who
had arrived with her husband in Los Angeles in 1912 to escape the Mexican
Revolution.

Formerly Catholic and later Congregationalist, they began attending a
Latino Pentecostal house church that had already embraced the Oneness teaching in the aftermath of the Azusa Street Revival. Desiring to share this new
faith with her family, Valenzuela returned home and at a house gathering on
November 1, 1914, twelve of those present received Spirit baptism. She immediately persuaded a nearby Methodist minister, Rubén Ortega, to perform the
baptismal ritual, but only after he had received Spirit baptism and was himself
baptized in Jesus' name. To perform the latter, Valenzuela sought out the assistance of a Black minister in El Paso, who was likely affiliated with the PAW.[57]

A striking feature emerging from this story is that Oneness Pentecostalism is not a distant cousin of the Azusa Street Revival but a close relative—a near-seamless extension. Not only is it interracially integrated through Haywood and the earliest PAW, many within the Mexican Apostolic community, in both Mexico and United States, were initially participants in the Azusa Street Revival and its aftermath. As Mexican Oneness leader Manuel J. Gaxiola-Gaxiola points out, "Later, most of these Mexicans became part of the Oneness movement."[58]

Northern Border Crossing—A Unique Canadian Story

Border crossing between Canada and the United States has always been brisk. Early Pentecostal leaders traversed the continent as leaders, preachers, and organizers of a nascent but spirited movement. Some were born in one country and settled in the other; some served in one and returned home; many remained home but wielded influence in the other. A classic Oneness example is Howard Goss (1883–1964): convert to Pentecostalism through the ministry of its first pioneer, Charles Parham (1873–1929); signatory to the formation of the Assemblies of God; pastor in Ontario from 1919 to 1945 (eighteen of those years with the confessionally Trinitarian Pentecostal Assemblies of Canada while holding credentials with the Pentecostal Church Inc., a Oneness organization); and eventually first general superintendent of the United Pentecostal Church.[59]

The Canadian Oneness Movement was also shaped by its own geographical, personal, theological, and institutional forces, which contributed to its unique character. *First, the Canadian Pentecostal Movement did not suffer the painful schism over the New Issue as did the Assemblies of God.* This was largely due to the leadership of R. E. McAlister, early leader and general secretary of the Pentecostal Assemblies of Canada (PAOC) from 1919 to 1932. He, along with Franklin Small (1873–1961), a Canadian leader in Winnipeg who embraced the Oneness teaching, had already embraced Durham's Christocentric "Finished Work" teaching.[60] Although McAlister never accepted the Oneness doctrine of God, he approved of the baptismal formula and was baptized in Jesus' name in 1915.[61]

Equally important was McAlister's ability to lead with a light touch. Since many pastors were baptized in Jesus' name and invoked it in their baptismal ministry, there was no requirement to add the Trinitarian name in the baptismal invocation. When the fellowship received its charter as PAOC in 1919, McAlister supported a Trinitarian statement in the face of pressure from Goss and Small. Yet, as general secretary, he never pressured Goss to conform or yield his ministerial credentials during eighteen years as pastor of Danforth Gospel Temple in Toronto. McAlister had been deeply distressed over the division occurring in the Assemblies of God from the beginning of the Oneness controversy. Although he was Trinitarian, he appeared to honor as best he could his own final admonition to fellow ministers in Los Angeles before returning to Canada. As Ewart reported, "Before he went he deplored anyone causing a split in the movement over this issue."[62]

Second, the Canadian Oneness Movement made a unique theological contribution to Oneness Pentecostalism. This was chiefly the work of Franklin Small, his theology and ministry. When it was clear that the emerging PAOC would officially embrace the doctrine of the Trinity, Small withdrew in 1921 to form the Apostolic Church of Pentecost (ACOP), based on Oneness principles. His contribution was threefold. First, he was the only Pentecostal leader of that era who thoroughly grasped Durham's "Finished Work of Calvary" teaching and fervently promoted it throughout his ministry.

Small's second contribution is a corollary of the first. He recognized that Durham's theology was fragmentary and needed development, which he was determined to carry out. It was likely this trajectory that led him finally to embrace the popular Reformed doctrine of "eternal security."[63] This teaching was unique and exceedingly rare among Pentecostals anywhere. In 1945, Small revealed that he had embraced the doctrine of "eternal life" as early as 1919 and noted that his credibility with leaders in the east may have been damaged more by this doctrine than with the "New Issue."[64] Unsurprisingly, it became a stumbling block in efforts to cooperate with fellow Oneness leaders in Atlantic Canada with whom there had been early organizational cooperation.[65]

Small's third contribution is institutional and woven into the others. His founding of ACOP distinguished it as the first chartered Oneness organization in Canada, and the only one in North America to embrace the teaching of eternal security.[66] In 1953, over Small's protestations, ACOP received a small Trinitarian group, Evangelical Churches of Pentecost (ECP), including the adoption of their preferred term, "Tri-unity."

Finally, the earliest Oneness Movement in Canada sowed the seeds of tolerance. As noted above, this tolerance was first exemplified in the ministry of R. E. McAlister. It came a few years later in Atlantic Canada, particularly New Brunswick's Saint John River Valley near the Maine border. The pioneer was John H. Dearing (1880–1940), a Oneness evangelist from Idaho. He arrived in northern Maine shortly after revival meetings with Aimee Semple McPherson and in 1921 was invited to preach at a convention in the town of Woodstock, New Brunswick. Unfortunately, within days the pastor, Edgar Grant, fell ill and died, but not before he prevailed upon Dearing to continue the ministry there, which he did until 1926.

Throughout his ministry, Dearing was clear and consistent that as deeply as he believed in the Oneness message, he was insistent that it must not be cause for division within the fellowship. In his 247-page "Bible Lessons," he challenged those promoting division: "We are not putting out these lessons to separate a little bunch of followers off to themselves, who all believe the same thing; but we put them out believing we are putting forth the truth. If any man differ with us, it will be nice to see how much real love we have to one another. The test is, can we agree to disagree in their views and still hold a sweet spirit of fellowship?"[67] To carry through with his conviction, in 1932 Dearing was instrumental in forming the Full Gospel Ministerial Fellowship, comprised of both Trinitarian and Oneness leaders. He wrote, "We might as well settle it now that any person or assembly that is not out to promote unity among all the Spirit filled people of God regardless of doctrinal views, is not in the way of an overcomer's life."[68]

In 1946, a significant number of Oneness leaders joined the United Pentecostal Church.[69] But as historian Shane Flanagan concludes, the Full Gospel Pentecostal Movement in the Atlantic Northeast eventually indigenized in ways that produced several innovations: "Trinitarians baptized in Jesus' Name; foundation of a Latter Rain Jesus' Name ministerial network; and lastly the ability of Trinitarian and Oneness ministers to work together in a spirit of collegiality."[70] Dearing's vision may not have transpired as he had hoped. But it was discernible for years to come.

These two border crossings firmly established the third stream of the early Pentecostal revival on North American soil. Like other Pentecostals, its leaders evangelized and established local missions and churches. They soon became launching platforms for global missions.

CONCLUSION

A constellation of religious and cultural forces had been shifting and shaping North American Evangelical Christianity throughout the late nineteenth and early twentieth centuries. It was a time of Revivalist experiential faith and

Biblicist warfare. These forces eventually converged to create new religious movements. At a moment in time, one of them was Oneness Pentecostalism. Initially, this divisive New Issue appeared to lack familiar markers except for an apparent similarity with Sabellianism, a third-century Modalist teaching rejected a century later by the Nicene Council.[71] But it is clear that a timely set of circumstances, spiritualities, ideas, and polemics within the wider Evangelical and Pentecostal cultures had coalesced with resources for the new trajectory. The New Issue was simply the radicalization of movements already set in motion. Finally, there is no reason to doubt Ewart's account that he was responsible for these initial theological building blocks.[72] He and Glenn Cook had already been propagating their message for a year before other key leaders would be recruited to the cause in 1915.

Throughout their history, Oneness Pentecostals in North America have been, with some exceptions, both exclusive and excluded. The roots of exclusion lay deep within the restorationist impulse whose goal it is to deliver an unadulterated Apostolic Christianity. As historian Grant Wacker writes, "the only problem was knowing where to draw the boundaries, knowing who was in and who was out."[73] The Oneness rejection of a core Christian doctrine and its relative isolation from the wider Christian community have left it tenacious in its beliefs for more than a century.

One effect of this isolation has been its slow theological development. But this is changing as demonstrated in the founding of the first accredited Oneness seminary—Urshan Graduate School of Theology (UGST)—in 2001 by the United Pentecostal Church International (UPCI). This portends increased opportunity for ecumenical dialogue, mutual understanding, and an enrichment of the deep themes of faith that are inhabited by Oneness and Trinitarian adherents alike. Three foundational doctrines that will surely be mined are these: the doctrine of the threefold God, the covenantal name of God in baptism, and diverse soteriologies that coexist even within the Oneness tradition.[74] As important as are these doctrinal foundations, increased cooperation between Oneness and Trinitarian bodies may well be the agency for building a lasting bond of fellowship.[75]

As we move into the second century, there has been progress to be acknowledged and more to be accomplished. The history and experience of Oneness Pentecostals and Trinitarians alike suggest that the future holds potential for mutual enrichment, recognition, even resemblance. Oneness Pentecostal's Evangelical forebears will not be a disinterested party to future Oneness identity.

NOTES

1. Ewart, *Phenomenon*, 76–77.

2. Robeck, *Azusa Street Mission*, 189.

3. Johnson, "Shudder Swept," 312–29. The following is a brief summary of Johnson's findings.

4. Ibid., 16.

5. Brumback, *Suddenly*, 191; Clanton, *United We Stand*, 15; Foster, *Think It Not Strange*, 52.

6. Harry Morse, an early convert to the Oneness Movement, was present and listened intently to Schaepe's ideas, which he recounted in 1943 as "new ideas on water baptism in Jesus' name, and the oneness of the Godhead"; quoted in Clanton, *United We Stand*, 16. His claim that the "oneness of God" was part of Schaepe's revelation is dubious at best, since the Oneness doctrine of God was formulated later by Frank Ewart, the initial leader of the new movement.

7. Ewart, *Phenomenon*, 77. Ewart was a Baptist evangelist who initially migrated from Australia to Canada for health reasons. While pastoring in Winnipeg he received the Pentecostal experience of Spirit baptism in 1908 in Portland, Oregon. He moved to the Los Angeles area where he became a leading Pentecostal evangelist, pastor, and contributor to the later formation of the New Issue doctrine; see Ewart, *Phenomenon*, 4–5.

8. Ewart, *Name,* 40.

9. Ewart, *Phenomenon*, 51.

10. The leadership of the Assemblies of God represented those who had followed William Durham's "Finished Work of Calvary" theology.

11. Ewart, *Phenomenon*, 52.

12. A 1964 report estimated that over half of Oneness Pentecostals were Black. See Synan, *Holiness-Pentecostal Tradition*, 163. Haywood never officially held credentials with the Assemblies of God but was the only prominent African American leader in Durham's Finished Work ranks.

13. Minutes of the General Council of the Assemblies of God, 4.

14. Ewart, *Name*, 40. Ewart apparently regarded himself as the leading spokesperson for the movement, describing himself as "the ring-leader of the Oneness crowd," in *Phenomenon*, 34. While it is accurate that Ewart was responsible for the initial theological framework for the Oneness view of the godhead, baptism in Jesus' name had already been practiced by Seymour, Andrew Urshan, and others.

15. Wilson, *Sects and Society*, 7.

16. For a detailed account of German Pietism, especially its influence on subsequent revivalism, see Stoeffler, *Rise of Evangelical Pietism*; Brown, *Understanding Pietism*; David Bundy, "European Pietist Roots," 279–81.

17. Niebuhr, *Kingdom*, 108.

18. See O'Malley, "Pietistic Influence," 69. Examples from this period can be found in A. B. Simpson's hymns, such as "The Power of His Name" and "Glory to the Name of Jesus," in *Songs of the Spirit*, 100, 101; see also Essek W. Kenyon's popular book *The Wonderful Name of Jesus*; Arno C. Gaebelein's "That Worthy Name," excerpt from his book, *The Lord of Glory*; and early Pentecostal hymn writer, L. C. Hall, *Songs of Power*.

19. For the most thorough apologetic treatment of the virgin birth of Christ, see Machen, *Virgin Birth*.

20. Green, *More Than One Hundred*. The pamphlet was written as a refutation of Unitarianism. It is worth noting that in mid-nineteenth-century Unitarianism there was a movement that historian Timothy Smith justly calls "Evangelical Unitarianism." See Reed, "Aspects of the Origins," 163.

21. Numerous examples from early Evangelical writers include Arno C. Gaebelein's study of the name "Jesus" to show that "the Greek *Jesus* is the same as the Hebrew

Joshua—Jehovah saves. . . . Jehovah Himself is the great Hope," in *Hope of the Ages*, 34; Presbyterian J. Monro Gibson who likewise traced the meaning of the name of Jesus to Joshua and Jehovah-our-salvation in *Gospel of Matthew*, 10; and A. B. Simpson's similar point in *Names of Jesus*, 18. Keswick writers in particular highlighted the theological importance of the threefold name, Lord Jesus Christ. See Pierson, "Jesus-Christ-Lord"; Webb-Peploe, "Jesus Christ, Lord"; Hopkins, "Our Lord's Names and Their Message."

22. The central point of the sermon preached by Elijah Hedding was, "Jesus Christ Is the Supreme God," 4.

23. Hall, *"What Is the Name?,"* 76.

24. The phrase used by J. D. Davis and Clarence MacKinnon in referring to the deity of Christ, "Bible Scholarship and the Deity of Christ."

25. Gaebelein, *Lord of Glory*, 8.

26. Gibson, *Christianity According to Christ*, 102.

27. A phrase taken from Col. 2:8–9, by Gibson, ibid., 80.

28. Ibid., 73–74, 102.

29. Gibson, "Mystery," 5. It is ironic that a movement that so vigorously opposed the traditional doctrine of the Trinity admiringly and without qualification quoted Gibson. The *Pentecostal Herald* is the official periodical of the largest American Oneness organization, United Pentecostal Church International. At least two early Oneness writers published quotations from Gibson in their periodicals: Urshan, *Almighty God*, 79–80; Small, *Living Waters*, 85. This suggests that the primal impulse of the Oneness Movement was less a rejection of the Trinity than an effort to secure the highest regard for the deity and centrality of Christ as possible, even when expressed within the categories of the traditional doctrine of the Trinity.

30. See "Plainfield Revival Meetings."

31. Hall acknowledged the initial encouragement to undertake a study of the Divine Name in scripture by Gaebelein in his final edition of *Remarkable Biblical Discovery*, 13.

32. Gaebelein and Hall were both strong advocates of the Jewish people as the people of the Covenant. This explains Hall's statement in the beginning of his book, that it is being addressed first to "God's ancient and beloved people the Jews; who, according to the flesh, are the children of Abraham," in *What Is the Name?*.

33. Ibid., 15.

34. Hall opens the preface of his book with these words: "In publishing this book the writer is fully aware of the fact that he is presenting an interpretation of 'the Name' and 'Personality' of the Triune God that cannot be considered otherwise than as revolutionary in itself and in its prospective influence upon the teachings and practice of the Christian Church in all lands." Ibid., 21.

35. One of Hall's favorite and paradigmatic texts is Col. 2:9, "For in him dwelleth all the fulness of the Godhead bodily."

36. Hall, *What Is the Name?*, 70.

37. See John 5:43, 10:25, and others; ibid., 87–98.

38. See Luke 1:31–32, Matt. 3:16–17, 16:13–17, 1 John 5:5, and others. Hall, *What Is the Name?*, 99–103.

39. See John 14:26, Gal. 2:20, Col. 1:27, Rom. 8:9–11, and others. Hall, *What Is the Name?*, 105–15.

40. Quoted in Ewart, *Phenomenon*, 77. It was not until December 1915 that McAlister claims to have understood the theological significance of the new baptismal formula; see Larden, *Our Apostolic Heritage*, 87, and Ewart, *Phenomenon*, 99.

41. McAlister, "Is the 'New Thing' New?" *Truth Advocate* 1, no. 2 (1949): 16; quoted in Thomas Fudge, *Christianity*, 46n16.

42. Ewart, *Phenomenon*, 83–84. Although Ewart cited only Hall's later edition and claimed that his own view was a "revelation," he would have been

already introduced to and influenced by Hall's views during 1913–14. He writes that, during the months following the 1913 Camp meeting, he and McAlister had long discussions over the matter of the baptismal formula. Ewart, *Phenomenon*, 77.

43. For a brief introduction to Durham, see Blumhofer, "William H. Durham." For a broader treatment of his life and ministry, see Farkas, "William H. Durham."

44. Durham, "Sanctification," 16.

45. For a detailed analysis of Durham's Finished Work teaching, see chapter 4 in Reed, *In Jesus' Name*.

46. Durham, "Sanctification," 17.

47. Durham finally replaced Rom. 6:4 with Acts 2:38 on the masthead of his magazine, *Pentecostal Testimony*.

48. Ewart, *Phenomenon*, 75.

49. Reed, *In Jesus' Name*, 97.

50. French, *Early Interracial*, 64.

51. Ibid., 68.

52. Gerloff, "Theology en Route," cited in French, *Early Interracial*, 156.

53. French, *Early Interracial*, 47.

54. Ibid., 196.

55. See also the theological argument for the unity and dignity of all races in the monograph by Haywood's early protégé, Robert C. Lawson, *Anthropology of Jesus Christ*. Lawson deftly shifts attention from the biblical Jew-Gentile Covenantal division to the Creation account in which all humanity is promised salvation (Gen. 3:15).

56. Ramírez, *Migrating Faith*, 35.

57. For a detailed account of the beginnings of Apostolic (Oneness) Pentecostalism in Mexico (1909–14), see Ramírez, *Migrating Faith*, 62–72. See also Gill, *Toward a Contextualized Theology*, 43–46.

58. Gaxiola-Gaxiola, "Latin American Pentecostalism," 115.

59. See Johnston, *Howard A. Goss*; Reed, "Oneness Seed."

60. See Faupel, *Everlasting Gospel*.

61. Reported in Ewart, *Phenomenon*, 98.

62. Ibid., 77.

63. Small, "Theories and Traditions of Men Exploded"; Small, "Finished Work of Calvary."

64. Small, "Historical and Valedictory Account."

65. Flanagan, "From Tent to Tabernacle," 87–88.

66. See Larden, *Our Apostolic Heritage*; more recently, Wegner, *Streams of Grace*. In a review of *Streams of Grace*, Darrin H. Rodgers reports that ACOP is the only Pentecostal organization to embrace eternal security teaching: https://ifphc .wordpress.com/tag/eternal-security. See also Wegner, *Streams of Grace*, 50. Small's reference to his personal convictions refers to the freedom of conscience clause in the PAOC charter, "allowing liberty of conscience in matters of personal conviction"; printed in Small, "Historical and Valedictory Account," 2. Small's analysis was that his "disfellowship" was due to both his Oneness stand and his belief in eternal security; see Larden, *Our Apostolic Heritage*, 90.

67. Dearing, "Pentecostal Home Study Course," 243.

68. Ibid., 79.

69. See Flanagan, "Wynn T. Stairs," 215–37.

70. Flanagan, "From Tent to Tabernacle," 93.

71. "Sabellianism" was finally the label permanently stamped on the New Issue at the Assemblies of God's Fourth General Council in 1916. It remains so today, without review.

72. In 1916, Ewart reported that it was after he began to preach on baptism according to Acts 2:38, and pressed by listeners to explain Matt. 28:19, "we saw that if the name of the Father, Son and Holy Spirit was Jesus Christ, then in some mysterious way the Father, Son and Holy Ghost were made one in the person of Jesus Christ. We saw from this premise that the old trinity theory was unscriptural." Ewart, "Unity of God."

73. Wacker, "Playing for Keeps," 199.

74. Reed, *In Jesus' Name*, 310–13.

75. The Society for Pentecostal Studies sponsored a six-year official dialogue between Oneness and Trinitarian Pentecostals; see "Oneness-Trinitarian Pentecostal Final Report."

BIBLIOGRAPHY

Primary Sources

Davis, J. D., and Clarence MacKinnon. "Bible Scholarship and the Deity of Christ." *Sunday School Times* 52, no. 50 (December 25, 1910): 635.

Dearing, John. "Pentecostal Home Study Course." Lesson 34/1. Self-published, ca. 1938.

Durham, W. H. "Sanctification—The Bible Does Not Teach That It Is a Second Definite Work of Grace." In *Articles Written by Pastor W. H. Durham, Taken from Pentecostal Testimony*, 16. Springfield, MO: Assemblies of God Archives, n.d.

Ewart, Frank J. *The Name and the Book.* Chicago: Daniel Ryerson, 1936.

———. *The Phenomenon of Pentecost: A History of the Latter Rain.* Houston, TX: Herald Publishing House, 1947.

———. "The Unity of God." *Meat in Due Season* 1, no. 13 (June 1916): 1.

Gaebelein, Arno C. *The Hope of the Ages— The Messianic Hope in Revelation, in History and in Realization.* New York: "Our Hope," 1938.

———. *The Lord of Glory—Meditations on the Person, the Work and Glory of Our Lord Jesus Christ.* New York: "Our Hope," 1910.

Gibson, John Monro. *Christianity According to Christ.* 2nd ed. Nisbet's Theological Library. London: James Nisbet, 1889.

———. *The Gospel of Matthew.* The Expositor's Bible 15. New York: A. C. Armstrong, 1902–8.

———. "The Mystery of the Father, Son, and Holy Spirit." *Pentecostal Herald* 28 (December 1953): 5.

Green, Sam. *More Than One Hundred Scriptural and Incontrovertible Arguments for Believing in the Supreme Divinity of Our Lord and Saviour Jesus Christ.* New York: American Tract Society, 1828. http://www.wholesomewords.org/resources/deityofchrist.html.

Hall, L. C. *Songs of Power.* Rev. and enl. Zion City, IL: Privately published, 1914.

Hall, William Phillips. *A Remarkable Biblical Discovery or "The Name" of God According to the Scriptures.* New York: The American Tract Society, 1929.

———. "What Is the Name?" Or "The Mystery of God Revealed." Greenwich, CT: Published by the author, 1913.

Hedding, Elijah "Jesus Christ Is the Supreme God." In *The Substance of a Sermon Delivered in Bath (Maine), July 4, 1822*, 4. Boston: Lincoln & Edmands, n.d.

Hopkins, Evan H. "Our Lord's Names and Their Message." In *The Keswick Week, 1911*, edited by Evan H. Hopkins, 157–61. London: Marshall Brothers, 1911.

Kenyon, Essek W. *The Wonderful Name of Jesus.* Los Angeles: West Coast, 1927.

Lawson, Robert C. *The Anthropology of Jesus Christ Our Kinsman.* Piqua, OH: Ohio Ministries, 1925. Reprint, 2000.

Machen, J. Gresham. *The Virgin Birth of Christ*. Grand Rapids, MI: Baker Book House, 1930.

Minutes of the General Council of the Assemblies of God, April 2–12, November 15–19, 1914. St. Louis: Gospel Publishing House, 1914.

Pierson, A. T. "Jesus-Christ-Lord." In *The Keswick Week, 1909*, edited by Evan H. Hopkins, 16–21. London: Marshall, 1909.

"Plainfield Revival Meetings." *New York Times*, March 4, 1901, 1.

Simpson, A. B. *The Names of Jesus*. New York: Christian Alliance, 1892.

———. *Songs of the Spirit*. New York: Christian Alliance, 1920.

Small, Franklin. "The Finished Work of Calvary—Original Sin and Sins of Omission Contrasted." *Living Waters* 1, no. 10 (September 1946): 1–3.

———. "Historical and Valedictory Account of the Origin of Water Baptism in Jesus' Name Only, and the Doctrine of the Fulness of God in Christ, in Pentecostal Circles in Canada." *Living Waters* 1, no. 4 (April 1941): 2.

———. *Living Waters—A Sure Guide for Your Faith*. Winnipeg: Columbia, n.d.

———. "Theories and Traditions of Men Exploded, Work of the Holy Spirit—The Finished Work of Calvary." *Living Waters* 1, no. 1 (January 1930): 21–24.

Urshan, Andrew. *The Almighty God in the Lord Jesus Christ*. Los Angeles: Published by the author, 1919.

Webb-Peploe, Prebendary. "Jesus Christ, Lord." In *The Keswick Week, 1910*, edited by Evan H. Hopkins, 125–31. London: Marshall Brothers, 1910.

Secondary Sources

Blumhofer, Edith. "William H. Durham: Years of Creativity, Years of Dissent." In *Portraits of a Generation: Early Pentecostal Leaders*, edited by James R. Goff Jr. and Grant Wacker, 123–42. Fayetteville: University of Arkansas Press, 2002.

Brown, Dale. *Understanding Pietism*. Grand Rapids, MI: Eerdmans, 1978.

Brumback, Carl. *Suddenly . . . from Heaven: A History of the Assemblies of God*. Springfield, MO: Gospel Publishing House, 1961.

Bundy, David. "European Pietist Roots of Pentecostalism." In *Dictionary of Pentecostal and Charismatic Movements*, edited by Stanley M. Burgess and Gary McGee, 279–81. Grand Rapids, MI: Zondervan, 1988.

Clanton, Arthur L. *United We Stand: A History of Oneness Organizations*. Hazelwood, MO: Pentecostal Publishing House, 1970.

Farkas, Thomas G. "William H. Durham and the Sanctification Controversy in Early American Pentecostalism, 1906–1916." PhD diss., The Southern Baptist Theological Seminary, 1993.

Faupel, D. William. *The Everlasting Gospel: The Significance of Eschatology in the Development of Pentecostal Thought*. Sheffield, UK: Sheffield Academic Press, 1996. Reprint, Blandford Forum, UK: Deo, 2007.

Flanagan, Shane. "From Tent to Tabernacle: A History of the Origins and Development of the Atlantic Northeast Pentecostal Tradition." Master's thesis, Acadia University, 2005.

———. "Wynn T. Stairs: Atlantic Canadian Full Gospel Pentecostal Leader." In *Winds from the North: Canadian Contributions to the Pentecostal Movement*, edited by Michael Wilkinson and Peter Althouse, 215–37. Boston: Brill, 2010.

Foster, Fred J. *Think It Not Strange: A History of the Oneness Movement*. St. Louis: Pentecostal Publishing House, 1965.

French, Talmadge. *Early Interracial Oneness Pentecostalism: G. T. Haywood and the Pentecostal Assemblies of the World, 1901–1931*. Eugene, OR: Pickwick, 2014.

Fudge, Thomas. *Christianity Without a Cross: A History of Salvation in Oneness Pentecostalism*. Parkland, FL: Universal Publishers, 2003.

Gaxiola-Gaxiola, Manuel J. "Latin American Pentecostalism: A Mosaic Within a Mosaic." *Pneuma* 13, no. 1 (Fall 1991): 107–29.

Gerloff, Roswith. "Theology en Route of Migration: The Inner Dynamics of the Pentecostal Oneness (Apostolic) Movement from North America to the Caribbean to British and Beyond." Society for Pentecostal Studies, Fresno, CA, November 1989.

Gill, Kenneth. *Toward a Contextualized Theology for the Third World: The Emergence and Development of Jesus' Name Pentecostalism in Mexico*. Bern, Switzerland: Peter Lang International, 1994.

Johnson, Andrea Shan. "A Shudder Swept Through Them: An Identification of the Controversial Joshua Sykes." *Pneuma* 38, no. 3 (2016): 312–29.

Johnston, Robin. *Howard A. Goss: A Pentecostal Life*. Hazelwood, MO: Word Aflame Press Academic, 2010.

Larden, Robert A. *Our Apostolic Heritage—An Official History of the Apostolic Church of Pentecost, Inc.* Calgary, AB: Kyle Printing & Stationery Ltd., 1971.

Niebuhr, H. Richard. *The Kingdom of God in America*. New York: Harper & Row, 1959.

O'Malley, Steven. "Pietistic Influence on John Wesley: Wesley and Gerhard Tersteegen." *Wesleyan Theological Journal* 31, no. 2 (Fall 1996): 40–70.

"Oneness-Trinitarian Pentecostal Final Report, 2002–2007." *Pneuma* 30, no. 2 (January 2008): 203–24.

Ramírez, Daniel. *Migrating Faith, Pentecostalism in the United States and Mexico*. Chapel Hill: University of North Carolina Press, 2015.

Reed, David A. "Aspects of the Origins of Oneness Pentecostalism." In *Aspects of Pentecostal-Charismatic Origins*, edited by Vinson Synan, 143–68. Plainfield, NJ: Logos International, 1975.

———. *In Jesus' Name: The History and Beliefs of Oneness Pentecostals*. Blandford Forum, UK: Deo, 2008.

———. "Oneness Seed on Canadian Soil: Early Developments of Oneness Pentecostalism." In *Winds from the North: Canadian Contributions to the Pentecostal Movement*, edited by Michael Wilkinson and Peter Althouse, 191–213. Boston: Brill, 2010.

Robeck, Cecil M., Jr. *The Azusa Street Mission and Revival: The Birth of the Global Pentecostal Movement*. Nashville: Thomas Nelson, 2006.

Rodgers, Darrin H. "Review: Apostolic Pentecost Church of Canada." https://ifphc.wordpress.com/tag /eternal-security.

Stoeffler, F. Ernest. *The Rise of Evangelical Pietism*. Studies in the History of Religions 9. Leiden: E. J. Brill, 1965.

Synan, Vinson. *The Holiness-Pentecostal Tradition: Charismatic Movements in the Twentieth Century*. Grand Rapids, MI: William B. Eerdmans, 1997.

Wacker, Grant. "Playing for Keeps: The Primitivist Impulse in Early Pentecostalism." In *The American Quest for the Primitive Church*, edited by Richard Hughes, 196–219. Chicago: University of Illinois Press, 1988.

Wegner, Linda. *Streams of Grace: A History of the Apostolic Church of Pentecost of Canada*. Edmonton, AB: New Leaf Works, 2006.

Wilson, Bryan R. *Sects and Society: A Sociological Study of the Elim Tabernacle, Christian Science, and Christadelphianism*. Berkeley: University of California Press, 1961.

CHAPTER 3

Sounding Out Diversity in Pentecostal History

Early Oneness Hymnody

Daniel Ramírez

Holy, Holy, Holy, Lord God Almighty
Early in the morning my song will rise to thee
Holy, Holy, Holy, merciful and mighty
God in three persons, Blessed Trinity

This anthem still rings with power today, much as it did when John Bacchus Dykes set it to the new tune of "Nicea" in 1861. Dykes cast the by then four-decades-old text—composed for Trinity Sunday by Reginald Heber, Anglican Lord Bishop of Calcutta, India—in resonant musical form and provided Anglo Protestantism a doxological hymn to wield the length and breadth of the British empire and the expanding American one. As a major supporter of the Anglican Church Missionary Society and a cofounder of the British and Foreign Bible Society, the well-born and bred Heber (he was installed in his bishopric by the Crown's governor-general) exemplified the leadership that helmed the Anglo-led missionary enterprise of the nineteenth and early twentieth centuries. (Another of Heber's compositions, "From Greenland's Icy Mountains," fired the missionary imagination of that era.) In June 1910, American and European missionary leaders gathered at the World Missionary Conference in Edinburgh,

Scotland, to take note of a century of success and chart the next century of missions. Heber's doxology, of course, was included in the conference hymnal. Little did Heber or Dykes imagine that their liturgical poem would also serve to demarcate contested doctrinal and ideological turf in St. Louis, Missouri, six years after Edinburgh, when the nascent US Pentecostal Movement (Anglicanism's great-granddaughter) divided over theological and soteriological questions. According to several sources, when Assemblies of God ministers definitively approved an ultra-Trinitarian "Statement of Fundamental Truths" at the AG's Fourth General Council, the exit out of the assembly hall by the losing advocates of the Oneness "New Issue" was heralded with the spontaneous singing of Heber and Dykes's hymn. Doubtless, for those within the auditorium, this half-century-old song acquired a triumphalistic valence tied to the ancient namesake council of Dykes's "Nicea" tune. That valence was not lost on the losing side. "New Issue" champion (and Azusa Street Revival participant) Frank Ewart described the anxious sensation felt by the clustered dissidents gathered in the lobby, as the auditorium doors that now excluded them swung with the strain: "Holy, Holy, Holy, Merciful and Mighty, God in Three Persons, Blessed Trinity." Months later, African American pioneer G. T. Haywood, who had been verbally tarred and bullied in the heated floor "debate" (the "New Issue" proponents were excluded from key committees and meaningful input), reported on the General Council to readers of his *Voice in the Wilderness* magazine, and borrowed from the Epistle to the Hebrews (13:13–14) to assure them that they would "now press on with the Lord 'without the camp, bearing his reproach, for here we have no continuing city, but we seek one to come.'" Of such glorious episodes is church and religious history made: exclusions, demarcations, and contestations. The auditorium-lobby frame provides an apt metaphor for church history: insiders versus outsiders, center versus periphery, hegemon versus subaltern, etc.

Ironically, the winning side's choice of anthem demonstrates precisely the problem in historical orthodoxy that the primitivist Oneness folks were seeking to point out, namely its extrascriptural dimensions. Had Heber hewed faithfully to the words of the "Sanctus" of the Roman Catholic mass, from which he derived his lyrics, his doxology would be acceptable to Apostolics today. The "Sanctus," as preserved in the English Book of Common Prayer (1549), conjoins Isaiah 6:3, Revelation 4:8, and Matthew 21:9 to render: "Holy, Holy, Holy, Lorde God of Hostes / Heaven and earth are full of thy glory / Hosanna in the highest / Blessed is he that commeth in the name of the Lorde / Glory to thee, o Lorde, in the highest." The extrascriptural tag, "God in three persons, blessed Trinity," is, of course, the Greco-Roman bone that cannot go down

Hebraic-Christian throats. These throats erupted instead in alternative versions of Zion's songs. This chapter explores that heterodox repertoire.

Of course, sectarian exclusion is a two-way street. The ninety-four songs compiled in the first Oneness Pentecostal hymnal, G. T. Haywood's *The Bridegroom Songs*, ran the gamut from gentle to not-so-gentle persuasion, directed toward recalcitrant coreligionists to accept the restorationist "light in the evening time." Several stanzas and the chorus of Hattie E. Pryor's 1919 "Water Way" (see fig. 3.1) pointedly upped the soteriological stakes:

The Water Way
(Hattie E. Pryor)

2. So God's servants come to tell you
Of a Bridegroom in the sky,
Looking for a holy people
To be His bride soon, by and by;
He sends to us refreshing water
In this wondrous latter day;
They who really will be raptur'd
Must go through the water way.

Chorus
It shall be light in the evening time;
The path to glory you will surely find
Thru the water way; It is the light today.
Buried in His precious name.
Young and old, repent of all your sin,
Then the Holy Ghost will enter in.
The evening time has come;
'Tis a fact that God and Christ are one.

3. Are you on your way to ruin,
Cumber'd with a load of care?
See the quick work God is doing
That so His glory you may share.

Fig. 3.1. Hattie Pryor, "The Water Way," 1919. In G. T. Haywood, *The Bridegroom Songs* (Indianapolis: Voice in the Wilderness, 1926).

> *At last the faith he once deliver'd*
> *To the saints, is ours today;*
> *To get in the Church triumphant*
> *You must go the water way.*

> *4. Have you looked and often wondered*
> *Why the power is slack today?*
> *Will you stay in that back number*
> *And go on in the man-made way?*
> *O saints who never have been buried*
> *In the blessed name of God,*
> *Let the truth now sanctify you:*
> *'Tis the way the apostles trod.*

A growing arsenal of short choruses also provided weapons for sectarian pugilism. These did not need hymnals to travel. And they could be inserted into any part of a Pentecostal service, or tagged onto a longer medley of choruses, masking their pointed message in a praise-filled environment. For example:

One Way to God
One, one, one, one way to God,
One, one, one, one way to God,
One, one, one, one way to God,
Baptized in Jesus' Name!

Any number of alternative words could be poured into the chorus's simple lyrical musical frame, in order to bring the message clearly and directly home, such as

///Acts 2:38, one way to God///
Baptized in Jesus' Name!

or

///Holy Ghost and Fire, one way to God///
Baptized in Jesus' Name!

RECKONING WITH ONENESS PENTECOSTAL HISTORY

The story of the 1916 Assemblies of God schism looms large in the history of American Pentecostalism. Nearly a century after that rupture, in 2014 the Society for Pentecostal Studies (SPS) held its forty-third annual meeting at Evangel University, the AG's flagship school in Springfield, Missouri. In a remarkable gesture, the host institution shared welcoming duties with the United Pentecostal Church International's (UPCI) Urshan Graduate School of Theology and Urshan College; the College's chorale graced the opening plenary with a musical performance. The irony of the conference site (at the AG headquarters) was lost on no one. The event marked a reunion of sorts between the AG and a flagship Oneness rival based in the St. Louis suburb of Hazelwood. (In 2015 the UPCI celebrated the seventieth anniversary of its creation as a merger of two major Oneness denominations.) For three days, at least, old shibboleths were laid aside as scholars, many of them church-tied, explored and respected common ground, including devotional and liturgical ground. The shared hymnody helped to guide the exploration. And it will help to frame our exploration of early Pentecostal identity and culture.

The careful scholarship of David Reed and Doug Jacobsen has begun to render a more systematized understanding of early Oneness thought.[1] Still, the material available remains limited. It could be gathered on a few sets of shelves in the AG Flower Heritage Center's archives. And that has always been heterodoxy's burden and orthodoxy's advantage: scant written material by the heterodox and its custodianship in the hands of the orthodox. Like the Nag Hammadi Library, which seemed destined to remain dust in the wind, the historical documentation of Oneness Pentecostalism awaits deeper retrieval and analysis, especially in its diverse, multipolar, multiracial, multilinguistic, and multinational dimensions. These dimensions matter for a movement that has taken deeper root and acquired wider breadth among Black and Mexican populations in the United States, in Mexico, and elsewhere in the global South (e.g., Colombia and Ethiopia).

In a provocative 1998 address to the American Theological Library Association, historian David Bundy called for a careful ethical approach to the "newly minted traditions of the poor." Historical charity, according to Bundy, should go beyond mere archiving and "text"-centricity, in order to more faithfully capture the important social, oral, and aural dimensions of global Oneness Pentecostalism. The stakes, as Bundy saw them, were high indeed:

And what are the ethical implications of not documenting these traditions? Think, if you will, of how different life in the Christian church might have been for women if the early Christian Association for Theological Library Acquisitions (CATLA) had documented the Montanist traditions, or the Messalians and provided accurate information about the roles of women and praying people? Think how the tiny library found at Nag Hammadi and Medinet Madi transformed our understanding of the early Church and of Manichaeism. Most of the information about all these groups that circulated in the dominant cultures of the day was skewed, misleading, or downright incorrect. The same is generally true today. We have a moral obligation to try to find ways to document the "other" so that we can avoid being party to an intellectual pogrom against the "other." . . . The provision of accurate information will not only assist the decision-making of the dominant culture. If it is ethically and cooperatively produced, it will assist the "other" to respect their own traditions more and to be more ready to bring these traditions into the halls of their "cultured despisers" for a meaningful conversation.[2]

To its credit, the Society for Pentecostal Studies earnestly pursued such a conversation in its Trinitarian-Oneness Dialogue, 2002–7. The Dialogue's Final Report, delivered in 2008, contributed, in part, to the generous gesture of hospitality at the 2014 SPS meeting.[3] In truth, the generosity began decades earlier when Manuel Gaxiola was welcomed into membership as the SPS's first Oneness member and later elected (1990) as the Society's first and only Oneness president. Its 1993 meeting in Guadalajara, the Society's first and only conference held outside of the United States, was hosted by Gaxiola's denomination, Mexico's Iglesia Apostólica de la Fe en Cristo Jesús. The Dialogue, thus, represented the culmination of a process of earnest engagement. The Final Report and Frank Macchia's subsequent assessment cleared through the detritus of misunderstanding and caricature and pointed toward future possibilities of doctrinal synthesis, at least among theologians. The situation on the ground may look different, however. While the shouting matches of yesteryear—"Patripassianism," "Jesus Only," "Three God-ism," etc.—have attenuated somewhat in an era of evangelical homogenization and convergence over common political and cultural agendas (and anxieties) in the United States, the distinctives remain and the epithets retain their currency, especially behind closed doors and pulpits.

MAPPING ONENESS PENTECOSTAL DIVERSITY

To its discredit, though, the Dialogue entered in and exited out only one ear, that of the global North. The narrow process and outcome did not capture the breadth and diversity of Oneness (or *"unicitario"*) belief and experience in other places; it also did not capture the ecumenical experience of Oneness and Trinitarian believers caught in the desperate existential trenches of the global South. Thus, in this sonic excursion, I suggest that we pay attention not only to the resonant, musical response of the Oneness Pentecostal heterodox— including, especially, African Americans—to the 1916 exclusion in St. Louis, but also to the creative riffs on a Oneness theme heard in places far removed from Middle America. The nuances are important. By grounding the story of Pentecostal origins and schisms along the two-thousand-mile border swath that unites/divides the United States and Mexico, for example, we can relativize the prominence of Hot Springs (1914) and St. Louis (1916) in the dominant origins narrative. Put simply, there weren't any Mexicans in the South's Aguascalientes

(Hot Springs) and the Midwest's San Luis (St. Louis). Yet, they were there in Los Angeles in 1906, cleaning out the dung and flies from the old African American Episcopal church-turned-livery stable on Azusa Street. Arthur Osterberg characterized the O'Neil company construction workers upon whom the Bonnie Brae prayer warriors laid hands for their Spirit baptism as "Catholic."[4] In turn-of-the-twentieth-century Los Angeles, that usually meant "Mexican." In other words, Mexicans not only cleaned out the muck from the barn, but they may have been among the very first to have their spiritual thirst slaked at Azusa.

Months later, the Mission's *Apostolic Faith* magazine reported on the "Spanish [a polite moniker for Mexicans] Receiv[ing] Their Pentecost," and even included matching testimonials concerning a "poor," "rough" Indian from central Mexico who happily converted upon hearing a German woman speak his indigenous tongue and then laid healing hands on a woman suffering from consumption.[5] The anonymous pilgrim apparently testified at some length in his own language. Thankfully, someone who had traveled in Mesoamerica provided the translation of the pilgrim's testimonial discourse; the only intelligible words (to the gathering), however, were "Jesus Christ" and "Hallelujah." Unfortunately and ironically, given the Revival's claims about xenolalia, the linguistic captivity of the *Apostolic Faith* editors redacted this fascinating datum, this subaltern discourse, out of the historical record. Pentecostalism's subsequent preferential shift to glossolalia over xenolalia glossed over the theological, historical, and sociological significance of the diasporic migration story of Acts 2:5–12—linguistic hospitality, diasporic migration, etc.—and the borderlands complexity of Azusa. Nevertheless, we can assume that Mexicans contributed to the linguistic cacophony of Azusa, and that Spanish was one of the constitutive languages of the borderlands revival (so too was our phantom's indigenous language), much like the languages of the Jewish diaspora were of the Day of Pentecost. In any case, the participation of Mexicans at Azusa allowed Latino/a Apostolicism to root its modern identity squarely in the Revival.

This return to Los Angeles allows us to examine the rise of Pentecostal heterodoxy through a borderlands prism. Indeed the much-discussed catalytic events leading up to the 1916 Assemblies of God rupture in St. Louis unfolded in the Los Angeles area in 1913 at the Worldwide Pentecostal Camp Meeting held in Arroyo Seco (near Pasadena). However, the attendance of Mexicans at Arroyo Seco awaits documentation, and hence so does the conclusion that they may have carried away any impressions from there. That gap presses us to focus, rather, on long-neglected protagonists, sources, and expressions of the controversy.[6] Historical sequence matters here. In addition to the pre-1914

Jesus' name water baptisms of pioneers Juan Navarro, Luís López (1909), and Francisco Llorente (1912), the robust Oneness doctrine carried by Romana Valenzuela to her native Chihuahua in 1914 (and preserved by the derivative *Apostólico* Movements in Mexico) argue for a ratcheting down of Arroyo Seco and the subsequent musings of Ewart et al. as the sole watershed of Oneness Pentecostal history. This entails, of course, a deprivileging of the dominant narrative of Assemblies of God rupture.[7]

The SPS conference year (2014) also marked the centenary celebration of Mexico's flagship Oneness denomination, the Iglesia Apostólica de la Fe en Cristo Jesús. In 1914, the most violent year of the Mexican Revolution, the IAFCJ's founding matriarch, Romana Valenzuela, carried Azusa's revival embers to her native Villa Aldama, Chihuahua, in Mexico's northern interior. Also in 1914 in southern California, pioneer preacher Francisco Llorente, an immigrant from Acapulco, baptized an immigrant from Torreón, Marcial de la Cruz, early Latino Pentecostalism's most prolific songwriter. Llorente, in turn, had been baptized in 1912 in Jesus' name by Azusa participant Juan Navarro. As we note at a century's distance the points of modern Pentecostal origins and organizing, a new, careful hearing of the sonic and multipolar dimensions of Pentecostal history is in order. This is especially important for the heterodox side.

If the records of more privileged orthodox antagonists are any indication (keeping in mind Bundy's caveat), it is safe to surmise that by 1920, most of the Latino Pentecostal movement in Arizona and southern California had embraced the heterodox belief in radical monotheism and Jesus' name baptism. Or so it seemed to Alice Luce, whose dispatches on the AG's "Mexican work" (carried in that denomination's *Pentecostal Evangel* organ) lamented the wholesale defection being fomented by "many false teachers."[8] An earlier appeal by Luce underscored the high stakes as she saw them: "Dear helpers-together-by-prayer, if ever we needed your help in prevailing intercession it is now. False teachers have been among the flock in these parts, and they have been tossed and torn by many winds of doctrine, so that it is hard to find any who are standing together in unity."[9] A gifted educator and former Anglican missionary in India (we can place her in the long imperial ecclesial pedigree that stretches back to Lord Bishop Reginald Heber), Luce deemed the best defense against heresy to be sound biblical pedagogy and Bible institutes.[10]

One such "false teacher" surely was Antonio Nava, whose work eclipsed that of AG pioneer M. M. Pinson in the border town of Calexico, radiated out from there across the border to Baja California, and overlapped that of other ministers throughout California, Arizona, and New Mexico.[11] Along with Francisco Llorente, Nava convened the first organizing conventions of the Iglesia de la Fe Apostólica Pentecostés (San Bernardino, 1925; Indio, 1926; and Colonia Zaragoza / Mexicali, 1927). Nava, Llorente, and Marcial de la Cruz held licenses issued by the Pentecostal Assemblies of the World to its distant "Mexican representatives." By 1927, the IFAP counted thirty works, mostly in agricultural and mining towns in California, Baja California, Arizona, and New Mexico. (In 1930, the IFAP incorporated in California as the Apostolic Assembly of the Faith in Christ Jesus. The connected but more loosely organized movement in Mexico—the future Iglesia Apostólica de la Fe en Cristo Jesús—stretched from the northcentral states of Coahuila and Chihuahua to the northeastern ones of Nuevo León, Tamaulipas, as well as to Texas's Rio Grande Valley.) The minutes of the first two IFAP conclaves (1925, 1926) reveal a search for harmony and doctrinal consensus among the ministers. They also dutifully record the hymns sung by the conventioneers, all readily identifiable standards of the received missionary repertoire of Mexican *evangelicalismo*, save for several new compositions by Marcial de la Cruz.[12] The flock, though, clamored for more.

APOSTOLIC CATECHISM

Away from the ministerial gatherings, music began to assume an important catechetical function, namely to teach Oneness doctrine, including Christological, soteriological, and holiness themes. One of the earliest resources arrived in the form of G. T. Haywood's hymnal, *The Bridegroom's Songs*. The compilation was musically scored. This allowed young, bilingual pianist Luis Herrera to share Haywood's "Baptized into the Body" with the monolingual Nava, who immediately transformed the melody into a *freely* translated hymn, "El Nombre del Mesías" (The name of the Messiah), for his flock's eager consumption. (Importantly, Haywood's 1914 composition predated his own rebaptism in Jesus' name in 1915 and the 1916 Assemblies of God schism; clearly by the time of the St. Louis conference, the Oneness party had at the ready apologetic ripostes to the exclusionary doxology.) Elsewhere I have discussed the deep resonance and broad diffusion of Nava's song throughout the Americas. At nine decades it can rightfully be accorded pride of place as the Apostolic Movement's doctrinal anthem par excellence.[13]

    To be sure, Antonio Nava could have picked from any of twenty-seven of Haywood's songbook's ninety-four songs that deployed a Oneness theme (29 percent). Jesus' name folk were busy in those days! This is understandable.

Lacking the theological acumen and infrastructure of mainline Protestantism, Oneness Pentecostals reached for one of the few means available to them to give witness to the doctrinal restoration. The approach also allowed for a broad, popular catechesis, one that facilitated the memorization of key scriptural passages. Take, for example, George Farrow's bouncy proof-texting song, "It's All in Him." Here too, as with Nava's appropriation, we can match this pioneering Oneness song with its later borderlands version, authored by one of Apostolicism's expert translators, the bilingual *tejano* Methodist-turned-Apostolic Benjamín Cantú (who served as the Apostolic Assembly's second presiding bishop, 1959–63):

It's All in Him George Farrow	Es Todo en Él Benjamín Cantú	(Translation of Cantú lyrics mine)
1. The mighty God is Jesus, the Prince of Peace is He, The Everlasting Father, the King eternally, The wonderful in wisdom, by whom all things were made, The fullness of the Godhead in Jesus is displayed.	En Isaías veintiocho, En el verso dieciséis, Y primera de San Pedro, Capítulo dos seis; La Roca puesta en Sión, Honor a los creyentes. Para tropezadero De los desobedientes.	In Isaiah twenty-eight, In verse sixteen, And I Peter, Chapter two [verse] six; The Stone laid in Zion, Honor to the believers. A stumbling stone To the disobedient.
Chorus: It's all in Him, it's all in Him, the fullness of the Godhead is all in Him; It's all in Him, it's all in Him, the mighty God is Jesus, and it's all in Him.	Es todo en Él, es todo en Él, La plenitud de Dios habita en Él; Es todo en Él, es todo en Él, Dios fuerte es Jesucristo, Es todo, todo en Él.	It's all in Him, it's all in Him, the fullness of the Godhead is all in Him; It's all in Him, it's all in Him, the mighty God is Jesus, and it's all in Him.
2. Emmanuel God with us, Jehovah, Lord of hosts! The omnipresent Spirit, who fills the universe, The Advocate, the High Priest, the Lamb for sinners slain, The Author of redemption; O glory to His name!	Admirable, Consejero, Dios fuerte y Padre es Él, Emanuel, Dios con nosotros, El Santo de Israel; Es el Dios verdadero; Cristo el maná del cielo, El lirio perfumado, El primero y el postrero.	Admirable, Counselor, Mighty God and Father is He, Emmanuel, God with us, The Holy One of Israel; He is the true God; Christ the manna from heaven, The fragrant lily, The first and the last.
3. The Alpha and Omega, Beginning and the End, The Living Word incarnate, the helpless sinner's Friend, Our wisdom and perfection, our righteousness and power, Yes, all we need in Jesus, we find this very hour.	Es Alfa y Omega, Es Principio y es fin; Es Todopoderoso Que al mundo ha de venir; Renuevo de David Es por generación, También es la raíz; Eso es por revelación.	He is Alpha and Omega, He is beginning and end; He is the All-Powerful one Who is to come to the world; The seed of David By generation, He is also the root; This is by revelation.

4. "Our God for whom we've waited"	¿De quien es hijo el Cristo?	Of whom is Christ the son?
will be the glad refrain	Dijeron: de David.	Of David, they said.
Of Israel recreated,	¿Cómo lo llama el Padre	What does the Father call him
when Jesus comes again;	Vosotros, pues, decís?	Can you tell us?
Lo! He will come and save us,	Fué manifestado en carne	He was manifested in flesh
our King and Priest to be,	Por ángeles fué visto,	Seen of angels,
For in Him dwells all fullness,	Siendo el velo del Padre,	Being the veil of the Father
the Lord of all is He.	El cuerpo de Jesucristo.	The body of Jesus Christ.

While Nava and Cantú kept the melodies of both songs intact and communicated the gist or heart of the original message, what is striking in both cases is the divergence in lyrics. Clearly, these were not faithful translations. Given the different contexts of composition and reception, the songs' new content served as much a catechetical as an apologetic function. Cantú's lyrics, for example, coincide with Farrow's *only* in the chorus (and even then not completely). While Haywood and Farrow could count on a biblically literate audience as they evoked familiar passages for their intra-Pentecostal apologetics, Nava and Cantú's broader audience included popular Catholics (with a lower biblical literacy) along with fellow *evangélicos* (not just Pentecostals). Accordingly, Cantú proffered chapter and verse for new and potential converts. This drew attention to the relevant Bible passages and equipped laypeople—still in a honeymoon with the recently available *Reina y Valera* Bible—with easily apprehended apologetic tools via musical recitation. Put simply, there were too few Trinitarian Pentecostals to win over in Mexico and the US Southwest. In many places, Apostolics were the first and only Pentecostals on the ground. Indeed, they often arrived at places where historic Protestant missions had been weakened considerably by macro forces and events like the Mexican Revolution (which prompted temporary missionary exodus), migration, and deportation; Apostolics buttressed Protestantism in Mexico as much as they fragmented it. As they successfully evangelized proletarian and peasant niches long neglected by Mainline Protestantism, they could not count on a high rate of general, let alone biblical literacy in a population long denied ready access to public education and to the Bible. Thus, Apostolics joined Bible distribution efforts with alacrity as soon as organization allowed. Similar to earlier *evangélicos*, Apostolics consumed the *Reina y Valera* text with gusto; the new reading and musical framing impelled literacy. Pioneer José Ortega's original "Divinidad Plena de Jesús" (Full divinity of Jesus) (see fig. 3.2), composed on a hilltop in Zacatecas in 1937 for a group beset by Catholic and cristero partisans,[14] exemplifies hymnody's catechetical function:

Fig. 3.2. José Ortega, "Divinidad Plena de Jesús" / "Full Divinity of Jesus," 1937. Musical scoring by Ramón Rentería, ed., *Himnos de Suprema Alabanza* (Guadalajara: Iglesia Apostólica de la Fe en Cristo Jesús, 2022).

Divinidad Plena de Jesús
(José Ortega)

Full Divinity of Jesus
(Translation mine)

1. Si alguien tiene entendimiento,
hallará el fundamento,
del Padre, del Hijo
y del Espíritu que es Dios;
si tiene revelación
halla la combinación
que estos tres, en Uno son.
Mientras unos edifican
en arenas movedizas,
otros en la roca firma y eternal;
unos creen a la mentira,
otros creen a la verdad.
la verdad en Cristo está.

If one has understanding,
the foundation will be found,
of the Father, the Son
and the Spirit, who is God;
if one has revelation
the combination will be found
that these three, are in One.
While some build
on shifting sand,
others build on the firm and eternal rock;
some believe the lie,
others believe the truth.
The truth is in Christ

Coro
Es Jesús la verdad,
el camino y la luz.
Él es Dios, la plenitud
de la gran divinidad.

Jesus is the truth,
the way and the light.
He is God, the fullness
of the great Godhead.

2. Unos aceptan el bautismo
que la Biblia nos enseña,
el bautismo de inmersión;
otros por no obrar justicia,
creen al bautismo de hombres,
basado en la tradición.
En Mateo 28:9,
Cristo da el mandamiento
del bautismo
que se debe obedecer,
por eso el apóstol Pedro
en Hechos 2:38,
nos lo da a conocer.

Some accept the baptism
that the Bible teaches us,
the baptism by immersion;
others, not practicing righteousness,
believe in men's baptism,
based on tradition.
In Matthew 28:19,
Christ gives the commandment
of baptism
that should be obeyed,
that is why the apostle Peter
in Acts 2:38,
makes it known to us.

3. Tres testigos en la Biblia,
nos confirman el bautismo
en el nombre de Jesús;
tres apóstoles de Cristo:
Pedro, Juan y también Pablo
nos confirman esta luz.
Tres testigos en el cielo,
dan un mismo testimonio,
el Padre, el Verbo
y el Espíritu que es Dios;
y este glorioso misterio,
Juan muy bien nos lo declara,
que estos tres, en Uno son.

Three witnesses in the Bible,
confirm baptism to us
in the name of Jesus;
three apostles of Christ:
Peter, John and also Paul
confirm this light to us.
Three witnesses in heaven,
give a like testimony,
the Father, the Word
and the Spirit who is God;
and this glorious mystery,
John very clearly declares,
is that these three, are in One.

4. Este Uno es Jesucristo,	This One is Jesus Christ,
Emanuel,	Emmanuel,
Dios con nosotros,	God with us,
Padre eterno	eternal Father
y también Príncipe de Paz;	and also Prince of Peace;
en el principio era el Verbo	in the beginning was the Word
y el Verbo era con Dios.	and the Word was with God
y este Verbo era Dios	and this Word was God.
Si alguien tiene entendimiento	If one has understanding,
hallará el fundamento	the foundation will be found,
del Padre, del Hijo	of the Father, the Son
y del Espíritu que es Dios.	and the Spirit, who is God.
Si tiene revelación,	If one has revelation
halla la combinación	the combination will be found
que estos tres, en Uno son.	that these three, are in One

The recent (and long overdue) musical scoring of Ortega's song demonstrates the difficulty of tightly aligning the uneven syllabic patterns with the musical notation. The elongated syllables in the chorus allow for a slowed bridge to contrast with the percussive momentum of the verses. These arresting features were not common in either received *evangélico* hymnody or newer Pentecostal compositions. This novelty enhanced the song's popularity. In order to circulate effectively and faithfully, however, and lacking a musical score, the song—and its irregular syllabic percussion—needed to be taught orally. This process of transmission doubled as a theological workshop, reinforcing the catechetical function of the music. Once committed to memory, any part of the hymn could be deployed either as spoken verse or as musicalized proof-text for bearing witness and giving account of Apostolic convictions. The song is still celebrated eight decades after its composition.[15]

Other early compositions addressed frontally the term "Trinity." The first stanza of Marcial de la Cruz's "El Mensaje" (The message) offered a protoeconomic Trinitarian scheme (a single God working in complementary modalities and not necessarily comprised of ontologically separate persons) to counter tritheistic and ditheistic tendencies:

El Mensaje	The Message
(Marcial de la Cruz)	(Translation mine)
Este es el Mensaje,	This is the Message,
dado a a la humanidad:	given to humanity:
Es que en Jesucristo,	That in Jesus Christ,
se encierra la Trinidad.	the Trinity is contained.
Hijo según la carne,	Son according to the flesh,
en espíritu Él es Dios.	in spirit He is God.
Él es uno con el Padre.	He is one with the Father.
No hay tres dioses, no son dos.	There are not three gods, they are not two.

Other songs were more explicit and less nuanced. One combined an anti-Trinitarian message with the idea of dispensational revelation and shift:

Jesus es Dios	Jesus Is God
(Anonymous)	(Translation mine)
1. Sólo Jesucristo es Dios,	Jesus Christ alone is God,
y ninguno otro hay;	there is none other;
ni en el cielo, ni en la tierra,	neither in heaven, nor on earth,
ni en lo profundo del mar.	nor in the deepest sea.
Es Autor del Universo,	He is the Author of the Universe,
que al hombre vino a salvar;	who came to save mankind;
el que se está preparando,	the one who is preparing
para venir a juzgar.	to come and judge.
Coro	
Y la Iglesia de su nombre,	And the Church of his name,
la que Cristo estableció,	the one Christ established,
es la puerta que está abierta,	is the door that is open,
al que busca salvación.	to whomever seeks salvation.
Aunque hay otras muchas puertas,	Although there are many other doors,
que no prevalecerán;	these will not prevail;
y si han estado abiertas,	and if they have been open,
Cristo las viene a cerrar.	Christ is coming to close them.
2. Muchos niegan hoy a Cristo	Many deny Christ today
y anuncian la Trinidad	and declare the Trinity
con palabras arrogantes,	with arrogant words,
que son pura vanidad.	that are pure vanity.
Estos son falsos doctores,	These are false doctors,
que engañan la humanidad,	who deceive humanity,
que no quieren adorar,	who do not wish to worship,
en Espíritu y verdad.	in Spirit and truth.

NEW WINE IN CULTURAL WINESKINS

The processes of transmission and memorization were also facilitated by recourse to familiar secular tunes, as seen in the case of Elvira Herrera's "El Nombre de Dios" (The name of God). Herrera, musically trained, like her brother Luis, by Methodists in Calexico, fastened upon a country tune familiar to borderlanders: "Red River Valley."[16] The popular melody allowed her to insert a Oneness message in the chorus for the ready memorization and transmission.

El Nombre de Dios	**The Name of God**
(Elvira Herrera)	(Translation mine)
1. He escuchado la voz del Maestro,	I have heard the voice of the Master,
le he seguido sin más dilatar;	I have followed him without delay;

Él me ha dado del agua de vida.	He has given me living water.
Me ha lavado de toda maldad.	He has washed me from all sin.
Coro	
Yo he creído en el nombre de Dios	I have believed on the name of God
y admiro su divinidad.	and I admire his divinity.
¡Qué misterio saber que su nombre	What a mystery to know that his name
es Jesús, el gran Rey celestial!	is Jesus, the great celestial King!

The recognizable melody (it included three more verses) facilitated the song's easy circulation along congregational and migration circuits; these included farmworker families and congregations traversing the length of California's agricultural valleys, as well as Tejano circuits to the Midwest. That proletarian diffusion layered on even more meaning to the new hymnody. The shared music knitted pilgrims and converts together in the midst of harsh anomic circumstances.

Two original songs, in particular, were accorded a privileged status in baptismal practice. Baptisms, in turn, were accorded a sacred centrality, usually as the denouement of a service. The first, "Seguiré a Mi Jesús" (I will follow my Jesus) (see fig. 3.3) noted the convert's faithful adherence to the baptismal command (in Jesus' name, of course), celebrated the turning away from the old life, and committed the believer resolutely to the new pathway of faith. Customarily, the congregation would launch into the invigorating first stanza (of three) at the sound of splashing water.

Seguiré a Mi Jesús	I Will Follow My Jesus
(L. Vega)	(Translation mine)
1. ¡Soy bautizado como manda el Salvador!	I am baptized as the Savior commands!
¡Qué grande gozo siento yo en mi corazón!	What a great joy I feel in my heart!
Ya mis pecados los borró mi Salvador.	My sins have now been erased by my Savior.
Quiero llegar puro y limpio a su mansión.	I want to arrive pure and clean to his mansion.
Coro	
Seguiré a mi Jesús,	I will follow my Jesus,
pues para mí lo del mundo se acabó;	now that for me the world is no more;
y ayudado de su luz,	and aided by his light,
proseguir en su camino quiero yo.	I wish to continue in his way.

At the conclusion of the service, converts would be received into fellowship with a hymn about new fraternal bonds: "Sepultados Juntamente" (Buried together) (see fig. 3.4). In one account (drawn from a memoir replete with instances of musical enchantment), the Francisco and Secundino Avalos families, repatriated Apostolic converts from southern and Baja California,

Fig. 3.3. L. Vega, "Seguiré a Mi Jesús" / "I Will Follow My Jesus," n.d. Musical scoring by Ramón Rentería, ed., *Himnos de Suprema Alabanza* (Guadalajara: Iglesia Apostólica de la Fe en Cristo Jesús, 2022).

introduced the movement's new baptismal songs into their native Nayarit on
Palm Sunday, 1932. The region's first Apostolic baptisms occurred in the face of
heated intolerance and drew a large crowd of the curious and critics, including
Coamiles village officials, to the San Pedro River. The breakthrough moment
occurred when the most dogged opponent, upon seeing an angelic epiphany
during her friend's baptism, flung her rosary into the water, and begged her husband for permission to join the ritual. The moment transformed the repatriated
family's lament and joyfully confirmed Francisco Avalos's prior prayer request
for a Gideon-like confirmation of his ministerial calling: that his first convert
would emerge from water baptism speaking in tongues. The event marked the
beginning of an impressive ministry and the building of Nayarit state into a
future bulwark of Oneness Pentecostalism in Mexico.[17] The service that night
at the Avalos home included the welcoming anthem, sung as became customary,
while the congregation filed up to warmly embrace the initiates.

Sepultados Juntamente

Buried Together
(Translation mine)

Todos fuimos sepultados
como aquel siervo Naamán;
sepultada nuestra lepra
en las aguas del Jordán.

We all have been buried
like the servant Naaman;
our leprosy buried
in the waters of the Jordan.

Coro
Y sepultados juntamente
en el bautismo de Cristo Jesús,
en esperanza de su muerte,
porque Él es nuestra guía y nuestra luz.

And buried together
in the baptism of Jesus Christ,
in the hope of his death,
for He is our guide and our light.

2. "En la mar y en la nube,"
vemos en Corintios diez,
"todos fueron bautizados"
juntamente en Moisés.

"In the sea and in the cloud,"
We see in Corinthians 10,
"they were all baptized"
unto Moses.

3. También Pedro nos recuerda,
de la familia de Noé,
de la salvación en agua,
sepultados por la fe.

Peter also reminds us,
of the family of Noah,
of salvation in water,
buried through faith.

4. Te recibimos, hermano,
con cariño y con amor,
por haberte sumergido
como mandó el Salvador.

We welcome you, brother,
with affection and love,
for having submerged yourself
as the Savior commands.

Fig. 3.4. D. Parra Huerta, "Sepultados Juntamente" / "Buried Together," n.d. Musical scoring by Ramón Rentería, ed., *Himnos de Suprema Alabanza* (Guadalajara: Iglesia Apostólica de la Fe en Cristo Jesús, 2022).

As evident from the lyrics, the concern for scriptural recitation (and biblical metaphors) remained a primary one for a community still in its honeymoon with the *Reina y Valera* Bible. In fact, the Coamiles episode was preceded by one in Yago (also in Nayarit) three years earlier (Francisco Avalos was repatriated twice) in which a startled woman reacted to Avalos's invitation to read the Bible aloud. Unaccustomed to the practice, and mistaking Avalos's demeanor for that of a clandestine priest (the Cristero War was subsiding in 1929), she requested a clean cloth so that her hands would not stain the forbidden Holy Writ. Her cry, "Blessed be God, He has allowed me to read the genuine words spoken by Jesus Christ," was echoed three years later in the Coamiles episode by the first baptismal candidate whose grandparents' account of a clandestine Bible intrigued her. The trope was not uncommon. Repatriated Pentecostals' successful harvest in the mountain town of Quebrada Honda (Deep Ravine), Coahuila, was made possible by the seed spread by prior Bible colporteurs.[18]

HETERODOX REDACTION

One of the drivers of early composition among Latino Apostolics was the doxological content of hymns in the translated missionary corpus. Pioneer Emeterio Reta of Monterrey, Nuevo León, recalled how Trinitarian lyrics caused believers to choke as they hewed to the lyrics' rhymes; hence, the need for musical alternatives.[19] Besides fecund composition, another option was simply to excise the problematic lines. In one example, Apostolic hymnals removed J. P. Cragin's Trinitarian interpolation in his translation of William P. Mackay's original 1863 hymn, "We Praise Thee, O God" ("Revive Us Again").

We Praise Thee, O God (William P. Mackay)	Te Loamos, Oh Dios (J. P. Cragin)	Te Loamos, o Dios (Translation of Cragin's lyrics mine)
We praise thee, O God, For the Son of thy love, For Jesus who died, And is now gone above.	Te loamos, oh Dios, Nuestro Padre de amor, Pues en Cristo, tu Hijo, Nos diste perdón.	We praise you, oh God, Our father of love, For in Christ, your Son, You gave us pardon
Chorus Hallelujah! Thine the glory, Hallelujah! Amen! Hallelujah! Thine the glory, Revive us again.	Aleluya, te alabamos, Oh, cuán grande es tu amor. Aleluya, te adoramos, Bendito Señor.	Hallelujah, we praise you, Oh, how great is your love. Hallelujah, we praise you, Blessed Lord.

2. We praise thee, O God,	Te loamos, Jesús,	We praise you, Jesus
For thy Spirit of light	Pues tu trono de luz	Since you left your throne
Who has shown us our savior	Tú dejaste por darnos	Of light to give us
And scattered our night.	Salud en la cruz.	Salvation on the cross.

3. We praise thee, O God,	Te damos loor,	We give you praise,
For the joy thou hast giv'n	Santo Consolador,	Holy Comforter,
To the saints in communion,	Que nos llenas de gozo	Who fills us with joy
These foretastes of heav'n.	Y santo valor.	And holy valor.

4. Revive us again,	Unidos load	United we praise
Fill each heart with thy love.	A la gran Trinidad,	The great Trinity,
May each soul be rekindled	Que es la fuente de gracia,	Who is the fount of grace,
With fire from above	Poder y verdad	Power and truth

The Apostolic version retained the Holiness missionary's third verse, with its Pentecostal inflection. As Latin American Pentecostals, they would not have found a plea for renewed revival as resonant as in Mackay's Scotland of the early nineteenth century; thus Cragin's elimination of the "Revive us again" phrase would have been agreeable. But not so with Cragin's fourth stanza, which the Apostolic versions left off altogether. Whereas the defeated dissidents in St. Louis in 1916 could only seethe at the extrascriptural lines in "Holy, Holy, Holy," Latino Apostolic hymnal compilers freely redacted when necessary.

DIVERSE SETTINGS, DIVERSE ANTAGONISTS

The above examples suggest that a shared doctrinal principle, when viewed in different settings of popular reception and practice, can acquire different meanings and resonances. Whereas for white and Black Apostolics, Oneness hymnody reflected a sectarian apologetical posture vis-à-vis exclusionary orthodox Pentecostals and Evangelicals, for Mexican Apostolics, doctrinal hymns planted a flag in more hostile (Catholic-dominated) terrain, a banner around which sinners and even fellow *evangélicos* could gather. No banner glowed brighter and more provocatively than "Carga sobre Roma" (A charge against Rome), a litany that stridently decried, like Martin Luther's Theses four centuries earlier, Catholic practices and teachings. The endearing melody (to the tune of "Jesus Loves the Little Children") was not meant to soften the blow of the bellicose lyrics; rather, it facilitated the song's memorization. The musical iconoclasm strengthened the symbolic arsenal with which Apostolics and other evangélicos withstood perennial and often violent intolerance instigated by priests, prelates, and lay organizations like the Caballeros de Colón (Knights of Columbus). To be sure, cristero partisans wielded their own war hymns, like "Tropas de María" ("Troops of Mary / Follow the banner / None shall faint / We go to war / We go to war"), to protect symbolic and religious turf. The hymnodic wars would be unthinkable, of course, in the United States, with its long-standing and widening pluralism. There, Oneness believers aimed their apologetic arsenal against fellow Pentecostals and Protestants. In Mexico, Apostolics could let their guard down only in the post–Vatican II era. In 1966, the IAFCJ removed the pugilistic hymn from its revised *Suprema Alabanza* (Supreme Praise) hymnal.[20]

Carga sobre Roma | **Charge Against Rome**
(Anonymous) | (Translation mine)

1. Predicamos la verdad, protestamos contra el mal.
Rechazamos las doctrinas de error.
Desechamos la invención, lo que es mera tradición,
Que invalida la palabra del Señor

We preach the truth, we protest against wrong.
We reject the doctrines of error.
We cast off invention, which is mere tradition,
That invalidates the Word of the Lord

Coro:
Sólo Jesucristo salva.
Cristo salva al pecador.
No hay otro Salvador, ni hay otro mediador.
Sólo Cristo salva y guarda al pecador

Chorus:
Only Jesus Christ saves.
Christ saves the sinner.
There is no other Savior, nor other mediator.
Only Christ saves and keeps the sinner

2. No podemos encontrar que debemos confesar
Los pecados a un hombre pecador.
Él que acude a su Dios con sincera contrición
Hallará que Él perdona con amor

We cannot find that we should confess
Sins to a sinful man.
He who comes to his God with sincere contrition
Will find that He forgives with love

3. Preguntamos el por qué han quitado de la ley
El segundo mandamiento que Dios dió:
"Un imagen no te harás: a ella no te inclinarás.
Servirás y adorarás sólo a tu Dios."

We ask why they have removed from the law
The second commandment given by God:
"A graven image you shall not make: you shall
    not bow down to it."
"You shall serve and worship only your God."

4. No queremos el latín, mas al Evangelio sí,
Las promesas del bendito Salvador.
Cristo dijo: "Escrudiñad la Palabra de verdad
Y hallaréis la vida eterna y salvación."

We do not want Latin, but just the Gospel,
The promises of the blessed Savior.
Christ said: "Search the Word of Truth
And you shall find eternal life and salvation."

5. Sirve para explotar a la pobre humanidad
El hablar de un purgatorio de terror.
Mas sabemos que Jesús dió su sangre en la cruz
Por lavar de toda mancha al pecador.

Poor humanity is exploited
By talk of a purgatory of terror.
But we know that Jesus gave his blood on the cross
To cleanse the sinner from all stain.

6. ¿Cuando y donde dijo Dios que se rinda
    adoración
A una imagen de madera o de metal?
De las bulas ¿cuando habló?
De indulgencias, ¿qué mandó?
En la Biblia no se pueden encontrar.

When and where did God say to adore
An image made of wood and metal?
When did He speak of [papal] bulls?
Decreed indulgences?
These cannot be found in the Bible.

Many of the above songs were consecrated throughout the ensuing decades as identity markers and today serve as nostalgic reminders of that identity. *Apostólico* identity, unlike white Oneness Pentecostal identity, was shaped and grounded by *evangélico* memory and solidarity vis-à-vis a hostile and hegemonic Catholicism. Thus, the pointed Oneness choruses of Black and white Apostolicism—directed against fellow Pentecostals—were entirely absent from the Spanish-language Apostolic repertoire. This is probably owing to something other than the challenge of clumsy translation. Choruses like "I've Got Joy Like a River" and "Send Down the Rain, Lord" crossed smoothly into the Spanish-language repertoire. Clearly, the stakes differed, according to the setting and ostensible antagonists.

ONENESS PENTECOSTAL DIVERSITY

Oneness Pentecostalism's exit from the hall controlled by the orthodox was a noisy affair. Apostolics did not go quietly into a dark night; neither did they walk in lockstep. The lobby, the periphery, the rim of Christendom brims and vibrates with sound and song, with diverse sounds and songs. Historians and other students of Pentecostalism—theologians, sociologists, anthropologists, and others—must keep our ears attuned to this even as our eyes search out the textual data (the fugitive sources), and as we continue to revisit and reopen the question of Pentecostal and Oneness Pentecostal origins. The religious and cultural soils in which Oneness imbedded itself in Mexico and Nicaragua and Colombia were very different from, say, Indianapolis and Louisiana. The *pentecostalismos unicitarios* that grew in these other places reflect the historical ecology of proto-*evangelicalismo* and a more tenuous existential reality in regions of Catholic hegemony; hence a more peaceable approach to fellow *evangélicos*. The question of Oneness Pentecostal origins and history, then, remains an open-ended project, an "unsettled issue," as Manuel Gaxiola put it in 1987.[21] And as David Bundy reminds us, its retrieval and understanding will require ethical and charitable commitment.

POSTSCRIPT: SINGING A SHARED CHRISTOLOGY

Ethnomusicology—the study of music and its role in society—teaches us that much creativity revolves around the popular sphere, where songs are composed, received, performed, transformed, and consumed. Here, music travels from heart to heart, changing hearts, and is changed in the process. In truth, the vast

majority of Oneness songs could be heartily embraced by Trinitarian Pentecostals and vice versa. This may have something to do with the attenuation of
sectarian songs in hymnal compilations. Whereas 29 percent of the hymns in
G. T. Haywood's *Bridegroom's Songs* articulated a clear Oneness content, two
decades later, only 2 percent (six out of 337) of the newly merged (1945) United
Pentecostal Church's first *Pentecostal Praises* hymnal (1947) did so (including
George Farrow's "It's All in Him"). By contrast, Mexico's Iglesia Apostólica and
her sister US denomination, the Apostolic Assembly, maintained a 9 percent
Oneness content in their respective hymnals, *Himnos de Suprema Alabanza*
and *Himnos de Consolación* (Hymns of Consolation), through the end of the
twentieth century. In total, their shared thirty-three songs and separately published ones amounted to fifty-seven total songs with a clear Oneness message
or imprint (godhead, Jesus' name baptism, etc.). The twin Apostolic hymnals
freely crossed the border (the Apostolic Assembly's *Consolación* hymnal was
even published for a season in Mexico City by the Iglesia Apostólica) and represented a joint resource for the churches' faithful and their daughter churches
in Central America and the Southern Cone.

Of course, as with Evangelicalism in general, hymnals have been eclipsed as
a ready resource. Contemporary global systems of Christian music production
have contributed to the attenuation of sectarian musical difference. David Reed's
insight about the ubiquity of popular Jesus-centric hymnody among nineteenth-
century Evangelicals facilitating the emergence of Oneness Pentecostalism in
the early twentieth century may still obtain in the early twenty-first century.
This shared Jesus-centrism and Oneness Pentecostalism's high Christology may
make for a felicitous meeting place. In fact, folks across the doctrinal divide have
been meeting here all along, around Oneness pioneer William Booth-Clibborn's
celebrated hymn about God in Christ redeeming the world to God's self, "Down
from His Glory." Like Elvira Herrera's appropriation of the "Red River Valley,"
Booth-Clibborn's masterful appropriation of the Italian aria "O Sole Mio"
ensured the popularity and longevity of his song. If YouTube recordings are
an indication, it remains popular (especially among Baptists!) and continues
to open up an inviting space for Christian fellowship, in English and Spanish
(with the inevitable and interesting divergence in lyrics).

"Down from His Glory" (William E. Booth-Clibborn)	Que Bella Historia (Anonymous)	Que Bella Historia (Translation mine)
1. Down from His glory ever living story, my God and Savior came	Qué bella historia, de su excelsa gloria bajó el Salvador,	What a beauteous story, from his lofty glory the Savior came down,

and Jesus was His name.	Jesús mi Redentor.	Jesus my Redeemer.
Born in a manger,	nació en pesebre,	born in a manger,
To His own a stranger,	despreciado y pobre,	despised and lowly,
a Man of sorrows,	varón de lágrimas	man of tears
tears and agony.	y de dolor.	and sorrow.

Chorus:

O how I love Him!	Oh cuánto le amo	Oh how I love him
How I adore Him!	y fiel le adoro.	and faithfully adore him.
My breath, my sunshine,	Cuida me vida	My Redeemer
my all in all.	mi Redentor.	guards my life.
The great Creator	El Rey de Gloria	The King of Glory
became my Savior,	vino a salvarme,	came to save me,
and all God's fullness	y a revelarme	and to reveal to me
dwelleth in Him.	al Dios de amor.	the God of love.

2. What condescension	Qué gran misterio	Oh great mystery
bringing us redemption,	tan incomprensible,	so incomprehensible,
that in the dead of night	que el Verbo se encarnó	the Word was made flesh
Not one faint hope in sight;	y al mundo descendió;	and descended to the world;
God, gracious, tender	el plan oculto	the hidden plan
laid aside His splendor	revelose al hombre,	was revealed to man,
stooping to woo, to win,	y por su tierno amor	and by his tender love
to save my soul	se levantó.	He arose.

3. Without reluctance,	Don admirable,	Admirable gift,
flesh and blood His substance,	tan incomparable,	so incomparable,
He took the form of man,	de plena salvación	of full salvation
revealed the hidden plan;	e eterna redención;	and eternal redemption;
O glorious myst'ry	el sol divino	the divine sun
Sacrifice of Calv'ry,	brilla en mi camino,	lightens my path,
and now I know	su luz alumbrará	his light shall shine
Thou art the great "I Am."	mi corazón.	in my heart.

NOTES

1. Reed, *In Jesus' Name*; Jacobsen, *Thinking in the Spirit*.

2. Bundy, "Documenting 'Oneness' Pentecostalism," 155–75.

3. See the final Report and Responses in the special issue of the Society's journal, *Pneuma* 30, no. 2 (2008): 197–269.

4. Osterberg, "I Was There," 342–45.

5. *Apostolic Faith* (Los Angeles), November 1906, 1; September 1906, 3.

6. See Ewart, *Phenomenon*, 94–144; Foster, *Their Story*, 88–122. See also Reed, "Oneness Pentecostalism," 644; Reed, *In Jesus' Name*.

7. See my discussion of this in Ramírez, "Historian's Response," 245–54. Douglas Jacobsen has systematized the theological ideas of Oneness pioneers Garfield T. Haywood (African American), Andrew Urshan (Persian American), and Robert C. Lawson (African American). Jacobsen, *Thinking in the Spirit*.

8. Luce, "Mexican Work Along the Border."

9. Luce, "Mexican Work in California," 11. Luce's 1920 application for license renewal—sent from Los Angeles—lamented heterodox incursions: "All our

converts have been immersed according to Matt. 28:19. The 'new issue' error is the greatest difficulty here. They are trying to steal away our flock all the time." Luce, "License Application."

10. McGee, "Pioneers of Pentecost," 5–6, 12–16.

11. "Missionary Department."

12. Ramírez, *Migrating Faith*, 179.

13. Ibid., 56–60. Nava's reworking of the original lyrics forced Haywood's interrogatory into a more declarative and catechetical form for ready repetition and memorization. It also hewed more closely to scriptural text. In doing so, it softened the sectarian edge to Haywood's pointed "New Light" soteriological challenge (to Trinitarian Pentecostals) and rendered a song that, save for the chorus's final line, "En el debeís ser bautizado" ([The name] into which you should be baptized), could be sung in any *evangélico* setting in Latin America. The redaction of that line allowed for the increasingly popular hymn's inclusion in one of the hemisphere's most widely distributed hymnals: J. Paul Cragin's *Melodías Evangélicas* [Evangelical Melodies].The missionary simply replaced the baptismal imperative with the more obtuse "[his name] for all eternity," thereby blurring the Apostolic distinctive concerning water baptism in Jesus' name.

14. Ortega, *Mis memorias*, 125, 228–29.

15. See the Apostolic Assembly's (US) musical recovery project, Nuestro Canto (1995) and Nuestro Canto II (2011). The Iglesia Apostólica (Mexico) has sponsored similar projects and the musical scoring of its *Suprema Alabanza* hymnal.

16. The hit "cowboy" song of the mid-1920s had roots in the late nineteenth-century Métis-French-Scottish borderlands of the Canadian plains. Elvira Herrera also proved adept at metaphorical subversion, as seen in her free adaptation of Holiness composer F. Lehman's 1909 "Telephone to Glory." Her "Es la Oración" [Prayer Is] excised completely Lehman's clever metaphor (for prayer), probably owing to the novel appliance's absence in most borderlands farmworker households. Instead, she substituted clearly understood Christocentric prayer metaphors of popular Mexican piety and thereby freed the song to circulate widely throughout the century, including to the Caribbean and Andes. By contrast, over time, Lehman's original lost its novelty—due to ever-changing communication technologies—and nestled into nostalgic folkloric repertoires. Ramírez, *Migrating Faith*, 175–78.

17. Avalos Orozco, "Historia de la Iglesia," 57–62.

18. Ibid., 48–49; Ramírez, *Migrating Faith*, 95.

19. Ramírez, *Migrating Faith*, 180.

20. Ibid., 147–53.

21. See chapter 1 in this volume.

BIBLIOGRAPHY

Primary Sources

Apostolic Faith (Los Angeles), November 1906, 1; September 1906, 3.
Luce, Alice. "License Application." 1920. Assemblies of God Archives, Springfield, MO.

———. "Mexican Work Along the Border." *Evangel*, June 15, 1918, n.p.
———. "Mexican Work in California." *Evangel*, April 20, 1918, 11.
"The Missionary Department." *Evangel*, November 1, 1919, 23.

"Nuestro Canto" (1995). https://www
.youtube.com/watch?v=rJC9jrjE1j4.

"Nuestro Canto II" (2011). https://
www.youtube.com/watch?v=
zlJQVvVnubE.

Ortega, José A. *Mis memorias en la Iglesia
y la Asamblea Apostólica de la Fe
en Cristo Jesús* [My Memoirs in the
Apostolic Church and Apostolic
Assembly of the Faith in Christ
Jesus]. Indio, CA: By the author,
1998.

Secondary Sources

Ávalos Orozco, José. "Historia de la Iglesia
Apostólica de la Fe en Cristo Jesús
en el Estado de Nayarit, República
Mexicana" [History of the Apostolic
Church of the Faith in Christ Jesus
in the State of Nayarit, Republic
of Mexico]. In *Laboriegos al jornal.*
[Laborers for Hire], Absalón Ávalos
Gómez, 37–118. Monee, IL: Absalón
Ávalos, 2020.

Bundy, David. "Documenting 'Oneness'
Pentecostalism: A Case Study in
the Ethical Dilemmas Posed by
the Creation of Documentation."
In *Summary of Proceedings—Fifty-
Third Annual Conference of the
American Theological Library
Association, June 9–12, 1999*, edited
by Margaret Tacke Collins, 155–75.
Evanston, IL: American Theological
Library Association, 1999.

Ewart, Frank J. *Phenomenon of Pentecost:
A History of the Latter Rain.* Houston, TX: Herald Publishing House,
1947.

Foster, Fred. *Their Story: 20th Century
Pentecostals.* Hazelwood, MO: Word
Aflame Press, 1983. Revision of *Think*

It Not Strange. St. Louis: Pentecostal
Publishing House, 1965.

"Historia de los primeros años de las
Asambleas de Dios latinas: El prin-
cipio" [History of the First Years
of the Latino Assemblies of God:
The Beginning]. Cap. 1, *La Luz
Apostólica* (March 1966): 2.

Jacobsen, Douglas. *Thinking in the Spirit:
Theologies of the Early Pentecostal
Movement.* Bloomington: Indiana
University Press, 2003.

McGee, Gary B. "Pioneers of Pentecost:
Alice E. Luce and Henry C. Ball."
Assemblies of God Heritage (Summer
1985): 5–6, 12–15.

Osterberg, Arthur. "I Was There." In *Wil-
liam J. Seymour and the Origins of
Global Pentecostalism: A Biography
and Documentary History*, edited by
Gaston Espinosa, 342–45. Durham:
Duke University Press, 2014.

*Pneuma: The Journal of the Society for
Pentecostal Studies* 30, no. 2 (2008):
197–269.

Ramírez, Daniel. "A Historian's Response
to the Trinitarian-Oneness Pentecostal Dialogue." *Pneuma* 30, no. 2
(2008): 245–54.

———. *Migrating Faith, Pentecostalism in
the United States and Mexico.* Chapel
Hill: University of North Carolina
Press, 2015.

Reed, David. *In Jesus' Name: The History
and Beliefs of Oneness Pentecostals.*
Blandford Forum, UK: Deo, 2008.

———. "Oneness Pentecostalism."
In *Dictionary of Pentecostal and
Charismatic Movements*, edited by
Stanley Burgess and Gary B. McGee.
Grand Rapids, MI: Zondervan, 1988.

CHAPTER 4

Andrew D. Urshan

An Eastern Voice in Early Oneness Pentecostalism

Daniel L. Segraves

Andrew Bar David Urshan (1884–1967) was one of the four pioneers of early twentieth-century Oneness Pentecostal[1] theology.[2] Like the other three—Frank Ewart, Garfield T. Haywood, and Franklin Small—Urshan was prepared by his social context and theological background to make a unique contribution to this segment of Pentecostalism.

Urshan testified to baptism with the Holy Spirit on July 4, 1908. Beginning as early as 1911, he wrote and published his understanding of scripture in a variety of formats. This included tracts, magazines, periodicals, sound recordings on 78 rpm discs, and books. Beginning in 1919, Urshan published the monthly journal *The Witness of God*. He continued this publication until his death in 1967. In addition, he wrote articles that appeared in a variety of publications produced by others.

FRANK J. EWART

Frank J. Ewart, a Baptist minister from Australia who immigrated to Canada in 1903 and who was baptized with the Holy Spirit in 1908, made his way to Los Angeles, California, after being dismissed from his pastorate in Canada by the Baptist organization with which he was affiliated. In 1911 Ewart became assistant pastor to William Durham in Los Angeles. Upon Durham's death in

1912, Ewart became pastor of the church.[3] While attending the 1913 World-wide Camp Meeting in Arroyo Seco Park in Los Angeles, he heard Canadian evangelist R. E. McAlister point out that "the apostles invariably baptized their converts once in the name of Jesus Christ" and "that the words Father, Son, and Holy Ghost were never used in Christian baptism."[4] After studying the matter for one year, Ewart began baptizing in Jesus' name on April 15, 1914. Through the periodical *Meat in Due Season* and at least eight books, he contributed to the development and spread of Oneness Pentecostal theology.[5]

G. T. HAYWOOD

G. T. Haywood was an African American born in Greencastle, Indiana, who obtained ministerial credentials in 1911 with the Pentecostal Assemblies of the World (PAW) before the rise of Oneness Pentecostalism.[6] Haywood was baptized with the Holy Spirit in 1908 and founded what is now known as Christ Temple Apostolic Faith Assembly in Indianapolis, Indiana.[7] In 1915, after hearing the "Jesus name message" from Glenn Cook—who was the first person to be baptized in Jesus' name by Frank Ewart and who had, in turn, baptized Ewart—Haywood accepted Cook's message, was rebaptized in the name of Jesus, and likewise rebaptized 465 members of Christ Temple. A prolific author and songwriter, Haywood also contributed to the development of Oneness Pentecostal theology by means of his charts and paintings.[8]

FRANKLIN SMALL

Franklin Small, a Canadian who was ordained by the American Assemblies of God in 1914 and who became a charter member of the Pentecostal Assemblies of Canada (PAOC) in 1917, withdrew from the PAOC in 1921 to found the Apostolic Church of Pentecost of Canada. Like Ewart and Haywood, Small contributed to the development of Oneness Pentecostal theology as a writer and publisher. In addition to writing a history of the Winnipeg Revival of 1916–26, Small wrote *Living Waters: A Sure Guide for Your Faith* and edited *Living Waters, The Apostolic Church Advocate,* and *The Beacon.*[9]

URSHAN'S THEOLOGICAL ASSUMPTIONS

Andrew D. Urshan was born in Persia. His theology and Christology valued what he understood to be that of the Church of the East, sometimes also described as Nestorianism.[10] Since his understanding of a critical term in the church's doctrinal statements is not that of the church itself, it is essential not only to understand what the church means by this term but what Urshan understood it to mean. This approach alone produces a reliable perspective on Urshan's theology and Christology.

In the final version of his autobiography, published the year of his death, Urshan devoted the entire first chapter to his perspective on the Assyrian-Chaldean people, the Aramaic (Syriac) language, the history of Assyria, and the Nestorians, whom he described as "Apostolic Faith Christians."[11] He saw the theology and Christology of the Church of the East as the New Testament antecedent of his view.

> They believed in the God-head being a triunity of three Kenoomas and never a trinity of three separate distinct persons. "Ke-noo-ma" to them was an image, attribute, or a manifestation of God. For instance, they taught that Jesus, one Being, or His one person, contained two "Ke-noo-mas." That is: two distinct natures; one absolutely divine, the other perfectly human, though conceived by the Holy Spirit and born in the Virgin Mary.
>
> Tri-unity of God to them was like mind, wisdom, and power. As mind produces wisdom, and wisdom and mind together produce power and action, so Father (the Supreme Mind) produces the Son (the Heavenly wisdom), and the Father in the Son produced the power (the Holy Spirit). All these three attributes of the one Divine Being were in Jesus of Nazareth; that is why He was not man-God, but the perfect God, and the perfect man; hence "Aman-El," the Lord over all, or the God-man with us.[12]

The solidarity Urshan felt with the Church of the East is seen in what he perceived to be a rejection of Western Trinitarianism. Until he discovered the textual variant in 1 John 5:7–8,[13] he was willing to describe God as a triunity and even as the "three-one" God.[14] But he understood Western Trinitarianism to teach that God is "three separate and distinct persons," with the word "person" describing a self-conscious individual just as it refers to individual human beings. He could not believe this.

Urshan viewed the Pentecostal Movement as a restoration of the faith once held by these early Eastern Christians. His restorationism went beyond that typically seen among early twentieth-century Pentecostals in the Western world. From the perspective of the West, the Pentecostal experience was restored progressively as the result of Martin Luther's discovery of justification by faith,

John Wesley's preaching of sanctification as a second work of grace, and the late nineteenth-century's holiness emphasis on the baptism of the Holy Spirit as a distinct third work of grace.[15] By connecting restorationism with Eastern Christianity, Urshan's view was a world apart from Western Pentecostalism.[16] His idea of Pentecostalism as a restoration of the faith once held by Eastern Christianity goes further than the typical Western view; he also saw Oneness Pentecostalism as standing in solidarity with the view of the godhead held by the Church of the East.

THE THEOLOGICAL LANGUAGE

The language used to describe this view is a challenge to those unaccustomed to wrestling with the subtleties of the Greek and Latin vocabularies typically used to describe the doctrine of the Trinity, but the Syriac vocabulary has its own challenging subtleties as well. As Sebastian Paul Brock points out, "there were different understandings, not only of the term *qnoma*, but also of the term 'nature' (Greek *physis*, Syriac *kyana*)."[17]

The words that created theological and Christological conflict between Western Christianity and the Church of the East are the Greek *hypostasis*, *physis*, and *theotokos*[18] and the Syriac *kyana* and *qnoma*. Of these words, we will focus on *qnoma* and its derivatives since this was Urshan's primary concern.

Urshan did not distinguish between *qnoma* in relation to the doctrine of the Trinity and in the context of Christology. This lacuna complicates an accurate understanding of Urshan's comprehension of the theology and Christology of the Church of the East. To grasp the subtle distinctions between the Greek and Syriac words pertinent to this point, we should first consider the use of the Greek *hypostasis* at the Council of Chalcedon of 451. The Council employed *hypostasis* in the context of the Son's two "natures," deity and humanity, which formed one person and *hypostasis*.[19]

The Church of the East rejected the Chalcedonian Definition due to conflict between the Greek *hypostasis* and the Syriac *qnoma*, the word used to represent *hypostasis*. The Chalcedonian Definition declared Christ had two natures that formed one person and *hypostasis*. For the Church of the East, this was impossible. The Syriac *qnoma* has a broader range of meaning than *hypostasis*, and it was the word used to represent both *hypostasis* and nature (*physis*). To say that Christ had two natures implied that he had two *qnome*, but the Syriac use of *qnoma* to translate *hypostasis* interpreted the Chalcedonian Definition to mean that Christ had only one *qnoma*. How could he simultaneously have one and two?

Table 4.1. Distinctions Between Terms Used in Alexandrine (e.g., Cyril) and Antiochene (e.g., Nestorius) Christologies

Alexandrine Christology	Antiochene Christology
Hypostasis: Concrete realization of *ousia* (e.g., concrete person)	*Prosopon* (Syriac *parsopa*): Concrete person Nestorius: *Usia*[a] [Greek, *ousia*] *qnoma*[b] [Greek, *hypostasis*] *parsopa*[c]

a. *Ousia* refers to general species.

b. *Qnoma* refers to a material reality bound up with its species; an individual, representative realization of its nature, not yet the *prosopon*; real, existing realization; inner reality.

c. *Parsopa* refers to the sum of accidental qualities that make the appearances of two *hypostases* different; appearance of an actual person; external appearance.

As Brock points out, this puzzle is due to the fact that "when the Church of the East uses *qnoma* in connection with 'nature' it usually speaks of 'the two natures and their *qnomas*,'" where *qnoma* means something like 'individual manifestation.'"[20] In addition, the Syriac word *kyana* and its relationship to *qnoma* further contribute to the rejection of the Chalcedonian Definition: "a *qnoma* is an individual instance or example of a *kyana* (which is understood as always abstract), but this individual manifestation is not necessarily a self-existent instance of a *kyana*."[21] Thus, *kyana*, corresponding to the Greek *ousia*, refers to "a general and immutable type in the sense of a species. So there is the usia [*ousia*] of God or the general species of human being."[22] Christoph Baumer's explanation of the philosophical terms "nature," "hypostasis," and "person" is helpful. Tables 4.1 and 4.2 provide a summary of the language used in Alexandrine and Antiochene Christology. Cyril, an opponent of Nestorius, held to the Alexandrine perspective, whereas Antiochene Christology reflects Nestorius's view.

In a theological disputation between the Syrian Orthodox Church and the Church of the East, which took place in 612, the official teaching of the Church of the East was, for the first time, declared to be "the two natures and two *qnome*" in Christ.[23] The formula that God is a single being or nature consisting in three *qnome* [persons] appeared for the first time in the early fifth century.[24]

George David Malech served as professor of Oriental languages and literature at the Presbyterian Mission College, where Urshan was a student. After leaving Urmia, Persia, on May 27, 1901, Malech published the Syrian nation's history. It included a quotation from the Synod of Mar Akakios, the Nestorian

Table 4.2. Key Terms Applied to Human Species in Antiochene Christology

Greek	Syriac	
Ousia	Kyana	General species of human
Hypostasis	Qnoma	A real, existing realization
Prosopon	Parsopa	Appearance of the actual person

Church's patriarch in AD 486 when the synod convened: "In God [there] is one nature and three perfect personalities (*kenume*)[25] who are one true eternal Trinity, Who is Father, Son and Holy Spirit, which cleanses out paganism and judges Judaism."[26]

Malech offered an extended treatment of his understanding of Christology by focusing on the Syrian words *parsufa* (person)[27] (Greek: *Prosopon*), *kejane* (natures),[28] and *kenuma* (person). For our purposes, the last of these is the most critical. The Syrians and Nestorius confessed that Jesus Christ has one person (i.e., *parsufa*) and two natures (i.e., *kejane* or *kyana*). But they also said Christ had two *kenume*. This was expressed by the phrase "One person double in natures and their kenume."

Malech asserted there had been development in the vocabulary used to explain the theology and Christology of the Syrians: "In the early days the Syrians used [*kenuma*] when they spoke of the three persons of the holy Trinity, saying that there are three *kenume* in God, and *one divine 'essence.'* . . . Now, the Syrians use more the word '*Parsufa,*' to signify *person*, when speaking of the three persons in God; and *kenume* when they speak of the two natures in Christ."[29]

Regarding the Nicene Creed, the Syrians said there is one person (i.e., *parsufa*) in Christ. But by affirming two *kenume* (i.e., *qnome*) in Christ, they did not mean two persons in Christ. Instead, *kenume* referred to Christ's two natures, deity and humanity. From a Western perspective, *kenume*, in this case, was close in meaning to personality. In Malech's words, this would be "the attributes, taken collectively, that make up the character of an individual, that which distinguishes and characterizes a person."[30]

On February 22–27, 1996, the Second nonofficial Syriac Consultation organized by the foundation Pro Oriente met in Vienna. Participants from the Oriental Catholic Churches (Chaldean, Syrian, Maronite, Malabar, and Malankara), the Oriental Orthodox Churches (Syrian Orthodox from Antioch, Malankara Orthodox from India), and both jurisdictions of the

Assyrian Church of the East mutually agreed that "in the context of Christology (as opposed to the situation in Trinitarian theology), there is a clear and important difference between the understanding in the Church of the East of the term *qnoma* (i.e., individuated, but not personalized nature) and that of other Syriac Churches where *qnoma* is regularly understood as the equivalent of *hypostasis* in the sense of person."[31]

This agreement led to the following explanation of *qnoma*: "In Christology, as expressed in the synodical and liturgical sources of the Church of the East, the term *qnoma* does not mean *hypostasis* as understood in Alexandrine Tradition, but instead, individuated nature. Accordingly, the human nature which the Holy Spirit fashioned and the Logos assumed and united to Himself without any separation, was personalized in the Person of the Son of God. When we speak of the two natures and their *qnome*, we understand this very much in the same sense as two natures and their particular properties (*dilayatha*)."[32] The consultation participants emphasized the importance of noting that the term *qnoma* is used differently in the Trinitarian theology of the Church of the East.[33]

Although the Church of the East employs a different vocabulary than is used in the theology of the Roman Catholic Church and the Syrian Orthodox Church, there may be no real difference in meaning. The fourteenth-century Mar Odisho, "the last outstanding theologian of the Church . . . was convinced that the differences and disputes among the three great Christian communities of his time were founded only on words and terms, not in the religious ideas they expressed."[34] In 1994 Pope John Paul II and Patriarch Mar Dinkha IV reiterated this understanding when they signed the Common Christological Declaration, which acknowledged, "The Lord's Spirit permits us to understand better today that the divisions brought about . . . were due in large part to misunderstandings."[35]

According to *A Compendious Syriac Dictionary*, published two years after Urshan's 1901 arrival in the United States, when *qnomas* is used in the context of Trinitarian theology by the Church of the East, the word represents "the persons of the Godhead." When used in the context of Christology, "Christ is two natures and two qnumi united in the person of the Son."[36] Since the Church of the East used *qnoma* to represent "person" in its Trinitarian theology and said that Christ had two *qnomas*, others misunderstood the church to believe that in Christ there were two persons. This misunderstanding was an error from the beginning.

As it relates to the Christology of the Church of the East, *qnoma* means individuated or individualized nature, but nature in this context doesn't mean person. Just as human nature is distinct from a specific human person, so an individuated nature is not yet an *hypostasis*. So in the Incarnation, there were two *qnomas* (individualized natures), each with its own set of properties (divine nature [deity] for one; human nature [humanity] for the other). These two *qnome* are instantiated in the personal identity of Jesus Christ, the Son of God. In the Trinitarianism of the Church of the East, *qnoma* means personal identity but not individuated nature because Father, Son, and Holy Spirit are not individuated natures in the way the divine nature and human nature are in Christ. Rather, *qnoma* underscores the personal identity in the sense that Father, Son, and Holy Spirit each have personal properties analogous to how an individuated nature has its own set of properties. Whether *qnoma* is used in Christology or theology, the connection seems to be a *unique set of properties* with the difference being the application of this unique set to an individuated nature or a personal identity.

In a lecture titled "Christology in the Patristic Period," Andrew Younan explains the use of *qnome* as it relates both to the Trinity and to Christology:

> God—as in Father, Son, and Holy Spirit—did not become man. Only the Son became man. The Father did not become flesh. The Holy Spirit did not become man. Only the Son. One *qnoma* of the three became man. . . . [N]or was it human nature that was united perfectly to God the Son, but Christ the man. So this is a new kind of category. It's not the kind of thing you're going to find in the West. . . . Particular nature versus abstract nature—this is the contribution of the term *qnoma*. . . . *Qnoma* does not mean hypostasis, but individuality. . . . *Qnoma* does not mean individual, but individuality. Christ is not two individuals. . . . Distinct doesn't mean separate.[37]

To further explain the difference between "distinct" and "separate," Younan referred to the black color of his coat and to the softness of the fabric of his coat. The blackness and the softness are distinct from each other, but not separated from one another.

URSHAN'S THEOLOGICAL JOURNEY

In Urshan's understanding of the godhead as he perceived the formulation of the Church of the East, it is essential to note that while the Church of the East makes a distinction between the meaning of *qnome* in the context of the doc-trines of the Trinity and Christology, Urshan made no such distinction. Thus, he defined *qnoma* as "an image attribute [*sic*] or a manifestation of God"[38] and applied this definition both to the three *qnome* in the godhead and the two *qnome* in Christ.

Urshan's commendation of the view of the godhead held in the Church of the East and his conviction that this view harks back to the first-century Apostles and Christians leaves open a question. Even if Urshan's grasp of the Eastern view of the godhead was not precise, how does his understanding shape his personal theology and Christology differently than the Oneness theologies and Christologies developed within the Western perspective?

It may seem presumptuous to question the accuracy of Urshan's under-standing of the doctrine of the godhead and Christology of the Church of the East. It was, after all, the cultural and religious milieu in which he grew up. But we must remember that his father was a Presbyterian minister, and we don't know the extent of his father's grasp on the subtle nuances of the Greek and Syriac languages on these subjects. Further, we know that many who claim to hold to the Trinitarian doctrine in the Western world have views that bear little resemblance to the historic creedal formulations.

URSHAN'S AUTOBIOGRAPHY

A comparison of the five editions of Urshan's autobiography reveals an ongoing and theologically significant reshaping of his story. The story does not change, but Urshan understands parts of it differently as his theological journey devel-ops. Because of the significance of these changes, it is essential to examine each edition of his autobiography.

The first edition of Urshan's autobiography, *The Story of My Life*, was pub-lished in 1917 by the Gospel Publishing House, the official publishing house of the Assemblies of God. This version, which chronicles events in Urshan's life from his birth (May 17, 1884) to his marriage to Mildred Harriet Hammergren (August 9, 1917), includes no notice of his practice of baptizing in the name of the Lord Jesus Christ or of his view of the Oneness of God. Although Urshan attended the Arroyo Seco Camp Meeting in 1913, where he heard God's call to return to Persia to preach the gospel, he included nothing about the controversy that arose at that camp meeting concerning baptizing in the name of the Lord Jesus Christ. He described his conversion experience as being "born again" and distinguished it from his later experience of baptism in the Holy Spirit with the sign of speaking with tongues. This first version of Urshan's autobiography was released with a press run of five thousand.

The second edition, a revision of the first, was printed as chapters in *The Witness of God* from the October 1922 issue through the combined June-July 1925 issue. To save the cost of printing the second edition in book form, Urshan had four hundred extra copies of each issue of *The Witness of God* printed so that when the project was finished, all thirty chapters could be collected and sent to those who wanted the complete autobiography. This second edition contains two concluding chapters that are omitted from the third edition.

The most immediate difference between the second edition and the previous edition is the addition of a first chapter concerning the Assyrian-Chaldean race and religion. It becomes quickly apparent that Urshan added this chapter for theological purposes. He discussed the Syriac language, which he claims to have heard spoken on occasion by those who were speaking in tongues. He identified the Assyrians as Nestorians who rejected a "trinity of three separate distinct persons" in favor of "a tri-unity of three Kenoomas," a "Ke-noo-ma" being "an attribute, and not a person." Further, these Nestorian Assyrians saw the "tri-unity of God" as being "like mind wisdom [*sic*] and power."[39]

This chapter indicates the influence of Eastern Christianity—and specifically Syrian Christianity—on Urshan. He approved of Nestorianism and embraced the concept of incomprehensible mystery in the threeness of the one God.[40]

Urshan made additional revisions in the third edition that are apparently for theological purposes. In parallel accounts where the first edition uses the word "saved," the third edition consistently replaces "saved" with "blessed." On at least one occasion, the word "saved" was replaced by "convicted." In some cases, the changes are even more remarkable. For example, in the account of Urshan's conversion while attending an American Presbyterian school in Persia, the first edition reads, "I had been born again and had been made a new creature in Christ Jesus."[41] In the account of the same event in the third edition, those words are replaced with these: "I had truly been blessed and the branch of the Divine tree in the bitter water of my life was planted afresh."[42] This reference to "the Divine tree" may be intentionally connected to the theology of the Church of the East that identifies the Cross of Christ with the "Tree of Life."[43]

Another significant and apparently theologically motivated change is also seen in Urshan's recollection of his conversion. In the first edition, he reports that the memory "is burning even now as a clear blaze of glory of God the Father, God the Son, and God the Holy Ghost."[44] The second edition revises this to read, "is burning even now as a clear blaze of glory of God, my Father, my elder Brother and my Comforter."[45] Regardless of these kinds of changes, Urshan continued in the second edition to use terms like "the Trinity in Christ" and "the One Name of the triune God."[46] Again, as in the previous edition, there is no mention of the idea of baptism in Jesus' name in connection with Urshan's visit at the 1913 Arroyo Seco Camp Meeting, even though Urshan now revealed that his profile at the camp meeting was quite high, which included sitting on the platform with about seventy ministers and speaking in some of the simultaneous sessions.[47]

Throughout the second edition, Urshan discussed his practice of baptizing in the name of the Lord Jesus Christ, which he saw as the revealed name of the Father, Son, and Holy Ghost for this dispensation. It is clear that Urshan saw the fulfillment of Christ's command in Matthew 28:19 to require the use of the words "Lord Jesus Christ," although he sometimes reordered the words as "Jesus Christ, the Lord." The word "Lord" represented "Father," "Jesus" represented "Son," and "Christ" represented "Holy Ghost."[48] Urshan wrote, "Since the Father has given His Name and Title to His Son to bear, therefore it is right and scriptural for us to do all things, which includes the Baptism in Water, in the Name of Jesus Christ, the LORD; why? because JESUS is the name of God the Son, CHRIST stands for the fullness and name of the Holy Ghost ... and the Name of the Father ... is JEHOVAH, the LORD."[49]

The third revised and enlarged edition of Urshan's autobiography is still titled *The Story of My Life*. It is self-published. Although it is undated, internal evidence indicates that it was printed in 1933.[50]

Beginning with the January 1962 issue of *The Witness of God* and continuing through the May 1963 edition, Urshan again serialized his life story. In *The Life and Experiences of Andrew David Urshan*, the fourth edition of his life story, Urshan referred to this serialization as the third edition.[51] This serialized third edition includes, apparently for theological purposes, material not found in the second edition or third edition as it appeared in book form. For example, in his discussion of the reasons for his baptism in Jesus' name in the third edition as it appeared in book form, Urshan wrote, "The question is then what that one name of the Deity (Trinity) is into which we are commissioned to baptize."[52] In the serialized third edition, this line is revised to read, "The question is then: 'What was that one name of the Diety [*sic*] used in practice by all of His faithful Apostles, or Christian Pioneers, or Trail-blazers?'"[53]

Although no publication date is found, the front cover puts Urshan's age as eighty-two. This means the fourth edition was published sometime after May 17,

1966, and before March 1967, since the fifth and final edition was published in March 1967. This fourth edition is taken from the serialized third edition as it appeared in *The Witness of God*, with some rearrangement. It was published at the request of the Mississippi District Pentecostal Conquerors.[54] Urshan mistakenly says that the third edition appeared in eighteen issues of *The Witness of God*. It actually appeared in seventeen.[55]

The fifth edition and final version of Urshan's autobiography was printed in 1967.[56] This version is identified on the inside title page as originally printed in *The Witness of God*. The most significant difference between this fifth edition and the third edition as it was serialized from January 1962 through May 1963 is that the fifth edition concludes with a selection of pictures that do not appear in previous editions and with a chapter that reprints some material not seen since the second edition.[57]

The successive editions of Urshan's life story reveal more than simply the events of his life. They reveal a man who was on a theological journey, but one who wished to continue to honor all his spiritual experiences even as he redefined them. What he once understood to be salvation became a blessing. The baptismal formula he consistently used ceased to be an option and became a necessity, even for himself. His understanding of the godhead at first continued to be expressed in selected Trinitarian terms, but those terms eventually fell away. The developments in his theological perspectives did not, however, lead him to reject any of his experiences that were once understood differently. Nor did they lead him to reject the experiences of others who continued to understand them as once he did.

There is tension in the idea that Urshan was on a theological journey even as he honored his redefined spiritual experiences. But this is a tension that must be accepted in view of the value he placed on his ancient Syrian heritage. In a sense, Urshan was a man going in two directions. He went forward as he experienced new dimensions of spiritual life, but as he went forward, he found himself looking back to a perceived recovery of the theological vision of his forebears.

This tension is seen in the final version of Urshan's autobiography. In a discussion of the relationship between Nestorius and the Apostolic Church of the East, Urshan described those who came to be known as "Nestorians" as Christians who lived and died "for the true and unadulterated Apostolic teachings of the founders of the Church of Jesus Christ."[58] Nestorius was welcomed by these Christians "as their brother in the original Apostolic Faith."[59] Church history, according to Urshan, indicates "that most of the Eastern Christians of Mesopotamia and Persia were Apostolic in their doctrine."[60] The "Bible fundamentals" for which the Eastern Christians were passionate included the atonement, the deity of Christ, the depravity of human nature, the mysteriousness of God's being, the Incarnation, the rejection of the use of pictures and images in worship, and the belief "in the God-head being a triunity of three Kenoomas and never a trinity of three separate distinct persons."[61]

Urshan's description of Eastern Christianity was not intended to be a mere retracing of history. Instead, he believed that the blood of the martyrs—Eastern Christians whose lives had been taken by Islamic oppressors—was still crying out with the result that God had "graciously left us a remnant to raise His glorious Apostolic Standard now before this present generation."[62] As he viewed his own spiritual progress, it was a journey that led him back to recapture the authentic voice from the past and to bring along with him the "remnant" that remained of those who still clung to the vestiges of that voice. In this sense, Urshan was a renewal theologian. In redefining his spiritual experiences, he saw himself as one rebuilding a crumbling edifice. It was his task to "raise [the] glorious Apostolic Standard" anew.

An examination of Urshan's theology and Christology compared with what these doctrines have become, at least in North America, suggests that they would not be the most enduring influences. Urshan's understanding of theology and Christology reflected his Eastern cultural and theological heritage as influenced by the Church of the East. Even though he did not fully grasp the subtleties of *qnoma*, a key term in the theological and Christological vocabulary of the Church of the East, his views nevertheless represented a largely Syriac trajectory of thought with its implicit suspicion of Western forms of Trinitarianism. For Urshan, these suspicions focused on the term "person" and its implications of tritheism.

Urshan's willingness to embrace mysteriousness as inherent in God's being was not acceptable to those whose Oneness views were shaped in the Western world. The concept of mystery, especially as it relates to any notion of "threeness" within the godhead, was eventually eliminated or at least minimized in mainstream Oneness theology,[63] but Urshan maintained his views until his death.[64]

CONCLUSION

The life story of Andrew Bar David Urshan is a remarkable saga of a man who acknowledged his frailties, embraced his weakness and suffering, attempted to be at peace with those who disagreed with him, but who would not compromise his convictions. This led to the loss of his fellowship with Trinitarian Pentecostals, a fellowship he treasured and enjoyed, and which he would have continued had he not been required to surrender his credentials in response to the rejection of his "Confession of Faith" by the Assemblies of God.

Not only did Urshan grieve over his forced departure from the Assemblies of God and the doors of fellowship that were thereby closed to him; he also saw Satan at work in attempts to thwart the unification of Oneness groups.[65] In his opinion, those who shared a common experience should be able to find a level of fellowship despite doctrinal, social, and cultural differences.[66]

Urshan died as he lived, active in the work of the Lord, proclaiming a simple gospel message while embracing divine mysteries, and loving his Pentecostal friends everywhere. In his words, written at the age of seventy-nine, Urshan declared: "We were forced to stop our ministry to all the Pentecostal faiths, blessing them, encouraging them to love one another, to have fellowship and worship together in such soul-saving campaigns, overlooking their difference on some Bible subjects." If that had not happened we would have been still preaching to thousands of different groups of the Pentecostals together to this very day.[67]

There was never a time when Urshan decided to be a Oneness pioneer. He knew what he believed, but he respected those with whom he did not agree. His destiny was shaped by those who did not share his willingness to seek unity in diversity. The distance to which he was willing to go in an effort to find unity gained little traction in his day, and the subsequent history of the relationship—or lack of it—between Trinitarian and Oneness Pentecostals indicates that Urshan's experience was prescient.

Although Urshan failed to heal the division between Trinitarian and Oneness Pentecostals and was not the defining voice of Oneness Pentecostal theology and Christology, his remarkable, vibrant faith and devout life left a lasting and positive imprint on the spiritual shape of Oneness Pentecostalism.

NOTES

1. I will use the term "Oneness Pentecostal," "Oneness Pentecostalism," or simply "Oneness" throughout this chapter unless quoting from sources that use other terms to describe the non-Trinitarian branch of Pentecostalism.

Although the term "Jesus' name" is used widely to describe Oneness Pentecostalism both by those within this branch of Pentecostalism and by observers, it is my opinion that the term is too narrow to define all aspects of the movement. The term "apostolic" is also widely used, but it is not specific enough. Many denominations and traditions that have no connections with Oneness Pentecostalism use the word "apostolic."

2. Reed, *In Jesus' Name*, 168.

3. Hall, "Frank J. Ewart," 623–24.

4. Ewart, *Phenomenon*, 93–94.

5. Ibid., 97. See also Ewart, *Name*; Ewart, *Revelation*; Reed, "Aspects of the Origins," 145–47; Warner, "1913 Worldwide Camp Meeting."

6. Robeck, "Garfield Thomas Haywood," 693–94.

7. Christ Temple, "Church History."

8. Dugas, *Life and Writings*; Haywood, *Divine Names and Titles of Jehovah*; Haywood, *Birth of the Spirit*.

9. Gohr, "Franklin Small," 1075.

10. The identification of this Eastern branch of Christianity as the Church of the East or Nestorianism is not supported by all adherents and scholars. See Brock, "'Nestorian' Church," 23–35; Baumer, *Church of the East*. Baumer says the official name is the "Holy Apostolic and Catholic Assyrian Church of the East," although "East Syrian Church" is appropriate. "Nevertheless, for the sake of simplicity, 'Nestorians' and "Nestorian' are used along with 'East Syrian' and "Assyrian'" (8). For the same reason, and since it is the term used by Urshan, we will in this chapter use the term "Church of the East." See also Cross and Livingstone, *Oxford Dictionary*, 354.

11. Urshan, *Life Story*, 15.

12. Ibid., 16.

13. In 1921 Urshan wrote, "It is an evident fact that the Scriptures no where indicate the word 'Three' in connection with the Godhead, except in one place (1 John 5:7) which is no Scripture but was simply inserted into the Scriptures by Constantine during the third century, and you will not find it in any original writings at all"; see Urshan, "Scriptural Facts,"

5. The text to which Urshan referred is commonly known as the *Johannine Comma*, and it includes these words: "in heaven: Father, Word, and Holy Spirit; and these three are one; and there are three who testify on earth"; see Brown, *Epistles of John*, 775. No evidence supports the claim that Constantine was involved with inserting the *Comma* into the text of scripture. The earliest Greek manuscript, including the *Comma* in the biblical text, dates from about AD 1400.

14. Urshan, *Almighty God*, 6, 10, 14, 42, 43, 44, 45, 47, 66, 74, 75, 77, 78, 82, 84, 87, 88, 93.

15. See Dayton, *Theological Roots*.

16. Urshan, *Almighty God*, 46.

17. Brock, "'Nestorian' Church,"

25. Urshan transliterated *qnoma* as "Ke-noo-ma."

18. *Theotokos* ("God-bearer," used in the Christianity of the West to describe Mary as the "Mother of God") is the term rejected by Nestorius in favor of *Christotokos* (Christ-bearer). Nestorious is linked with the Church of the East to the extent that this expression of Christianity is sometimes referred to as the Nestorian Church.

19. Bettenson, *Documents*; emphases in original.

20. Brock, "'Nestorian' Church," 28.

21. Ibid., 28.

22. Baumer, *Church of the East*, 46.

23. Taylor, "Syriac Tradition," 214.

24. Lange, *Portrayal of Christ*, 161n26. For additional references to the one God in three *qnome* in the official documents of the Church of the East, see Brock, "Christology of the Church," 292–96.

25. Variations in transliteration in Malech's book from current standards is probably due to the fact that Malech wrote the original work in Syriac, his son translated it from Syriac into Norwegian, and it was finally translated from Norwegian into English by Ingeborg

Rasmussen, MD, with stenography done by Cherrie M. Sly.

26. Malech, *History of the Syrian Nation*, 343. Malech says the same confession can be found in Mar Sabrishu's Synod, AD 596.

27. Usually transliterated *parsopa*.

28. Usually transliterated *kyane*.

29. Malech, *History of the Syrian Nation*, 348–49.

30. Ibid., 348–49.

31. "Joint Communiqué."

32. Ibid.

33. Ibid.

34. Baumer, *Church of the East*, 280.

35. Ibid., 280.

36. Smith, *Compendious Syriac Dictionary*, 510.

37. Younan, "Christology in the Patristic Period."

38. Urshan, *Life Story*, 16. I assume Urshan means "image, attribute, or a manifestation."

39. In the fourth edition of his life story, Urshan corrected the phrase "mind wisdom and power" to "mind, wisdom and power" (Urshan, *Life*, 3).

40. Urshan, "First Chapter."

41. Urshan, *Story of My Life*, 30.

42. Urshan, "Third Chapter—Story of My Life," 4. He continued, however, to use the language of regeneration: "It was here in this school that God met me one night in March 1900, convicted me of sin and regenerated my soul which transformed my character." See Urshan, "Second Chapter—Story of My Life." These revisions continue into the third edition of Urshan's life story. In the fourth edition of his life story, Urshan corrected the phrase "mind wisdom and power" to "mind, wisdom and power." Urshan, *The Life and Experiences of Andrew David Urshan*, 3.

43. Baumer, *Church of the East*, 118.

44. Urshan, *Story of My Life*, 31.

45. Urshan, "Third Chapter—Story of My Life," 4. See also Urshan, *Story of My Life*, 22.

46. Urshan, "Story of My Life—10th Chapter," 4. See also Urshan, *Story of My Life*, 94, 179.

47. See Urshan, "Story of My Life—13th Chapter," 3–4.

48. See, e.g., Urshan, "Republication of Our First 1918 Open Letter," 2–5; Urshan, *Apostolic Faith Doctrine of the New Birth*, 12.

49. Urshan, "Republication of Our First 1918 Open Letter," 4; emphases original.

50. See Urshan, *Story of My Life*, 108.

51. Urshan, *Life and Experiences*, 1.

52. Urshan, *Story of My Life*, 179.

53. Urshan, "Andrew in Russia," 5.

54. At that time, the General Youth Department of the United Pentecostal Church, Inc. used the phrase "Pentecostal Conquerors" to describe an aspect of their work.

55. Urshan, *Life and Experiences*, 1.

56. Urshan, *Life Story*.

57. Compare Urshan, "My Arrival in the United States," with Urshan, *Life Story*, 262. Both identify Urshan as being seventy-nine years old at the time of writing. Thus, oddly, Urshan was older (eighty-two) when the fourth edition of his life story was published than he was when he wrote the bulk of the content of the fifth edition (seventy-nine). This oddity is due to the fact that both the fourth and fifth editions are drawn from the third edition as it appeared in the *Witness of God*. Urshan was actually eighty-three when the fifth edition was published in 1967, the year of his death.

58. Urshan, *Life Story*, 15.

59. Ibid.

60. Ibid.

61. Ibid., 16.

62. Ibid., 15–16. The original wording of this phrase indicates forcibly Urshan's conviction that the Church of the East had a substantial role in the restoration of first-century Christianity: "He has graciously left us a remnant to raise His

glorious standard through them before this present generation" (Urshan, "First Chapter—Story of My Life," 3).

63. See Bernard, *Oneness*, 65, 289, 296; Norris, *I Am*, 57–59.

64. Urshan, *Life Story*, 14–16.

65. Urshan, "Grand and Good New Merger," 6.

66. Urshan, "Story of My Life—28th Chapter," 3.

67. Urshan, "The Final and the Conclusion," 7. Urshan's reference to "soul-saving campaigns" alluded to his seven-month campaign in Los Angeles in 1918.

BIBLIOGRAPHY

Primary Sources

Ewart, Frank J. *The Name and the Book.* Chicago: Daniel Ryerson, 1936.

———. *The Phenomenon of Pentecost: A History of the Latter Rain.* Houston, TX: Herald, 1947.

———. *The Revelation of Jesus Christ.* Hazelwood, MO: Pentecostal Publishing House, n.d.

Haywood, G. T. *The Birth of the Spirit in the Days of the Apostles.* Portland, OR: Apostolic Book Publishers, n.d.

———. *Divine Names and Titles of Jehovah.* Portland, OR: Apostolic Book Publishers, n.d.

Urshan, Andrew D. *The Almighty God in the Lord Jesus Christ.* Los Angeles: 1919. Reprint, Portland, OR: Apostolic Book Corner, n.d.

———. "Andrew in Russia." *Witness of God* (March 1963): 5.

———. *Apostolic Faith Doctrine of the New Birth.* Cochrane, WI: N.p., 1941.

———. "The Final and the Conclusion." *Witness of God* (May 1963): 7–8.

———. "First Chapter—Story of My Life: The Assyro-Chaldean's Race, and the Life Story of Andrew David Urshan, the Assyro-Chaldean." *Witness of God* 3, no. 34 (October 1922): 2–4.

———. "The Grand and Good New Merger." *Witness of God* (May 1932): 6–7.

———. *The Life and Experiences of Andrew David Urshan.* 4th ed. N.p., n.d.

———. *The Life Story of Andrew Bar David Urshan: An Autobiography of the Author's First Forty Years.* 5th ed. Stockton, CA: W.A.B.C. Press, 1967.

———. "My Arrival in the United States." *Witness of God* (April 1963): 1–3.

———. "Republication of Our First 1918 Open Letter to All Pentecostal Saints." *Witness of God* (1941): 2–5.

———. "Scriptural Facts Concerning the Godhead Question." *Witness of God* 2, no. 19 (July 1921): 5.

———. "Second Chapter—Story of My Life." *Witness of God* 3, no. 35 (November 1922): 2.

———. *The Story of My Life.* St. Louis: Gospel Publishing House, 1917.

———. "The Story of My Life—10th Chapter—Cont." *Witness of God* 4, no. 45 (September 1923): 4.

———. "The Story of My Life—13th Chapter." *Witness of God* 4, no. 48 (December 1923): 3–4.

———. "The Story of My Life—28th Chapter." *Witness of God* 6, no. 64 (May 1925): 2–4.

———. "Third Chapter—Story of My Life: Andrew's Wonderful Conversion." *Witness of God* 3, no. 35 (November 1922): 4.

Warner, Wayne. "The 1913 Worldwide Camp Meeting." *Assemblies of God Heritage* 3, no. 1 (Spring 1983): 1, 4–5.

Secondary Sources

Baumer, Christoph. *The Church of the East: An Illustrated History of Assyrian Christianity*. London: I. B. Tauris, 2006.

Bernard, David K. *The Oneness of God. Series in Pentecostal Theology*. Vol. 1. Hazelwood, MO: Word Aflame Press, 1983.

Bettenson, Henry, ed. *Documents of the Christian Church*. 2nd ed. London: Oxford University Press, 1967.

Brock, S. "The 'Nestorian' Church: A Lamentable Misnomer." *Bulletin of the John Rylands University Library of Manchester* 78, no. 3 (1996): 35.

Brown, Raymond E. *The Epistles of John: Translated, with Introduction, Notes, and Commentary*. Vol. 30. Anchor Yale Bible. New Haven: Yale University Press, 2008.

"Christ Temple Apostolic Faith Assembly." https://christtempleac.org/church/history.

Cross, F. L., and Elizabeth A. Livingstone, eds. *The Oxford Dictionary of the Christian Church*. Oxford: Oxford University Press, 2005.

Dayton, Donald W. *Theological Roots of Pentecostalism*. Grand Rapids, MI: Zondervan, 1987.

Dugas, Paul D., comp. *The Life and Writings of Elder G. T. Haywood*. Stockton, CA: W.A.B.C. Press, 1968.

Gohr, G. W. "Franklin Small." In *The New International Dictionary of Pentecostal and Charismatic Movements*, rev. and expanded ed., edited by Stanley M. Burgess, 1075. Grand Rapids, MI: Zondervan, 2002.

Hall, J. L. "Frank J. Ewart." In *The New International Dictionary of Pentecostal and Charismatic Movements*, rev. and expanded, ed. Stanley M. Burgess, 623–24. Grand Rapids, MI: Zondervan, 2002.

"Joint Communiqué of the Second Non-Official Consultation on Dialogue Within the Syriac Tradition, Vienna February 1996." http://www.pro-oriente.at/dokumente/2SyrCons1996.doc.

Lange, Christian. *The Portrayal of Christ in the Syriac Commentary on the Diatessaron*. Leuven: Peeters, 2005.

Malech, George David. *History of the Syrian Nation and the Old Evangelical-Apostolic Church of the East*. Minneapolis: N.p., 1910.

Mar Babai the Great. Libere de Unione, I.17, quoted by Fr. Andrew Younan. http://www.kaldu.org/Theology_Course_2007/06_B_PChristology_03_Video.html.

Norris, David S. *I Am: A Oneness Pentecostal Theology*. Hazelwood, MO: WAP Academic, 2009.

Reed, David. "Aspects of the Origins of Oneness Pentecostalism." In *Aspects of Pentecostal-Charismatic Origins*, edited by Vinson Synan, 145–47. Plainfield, NJ: Logos International, 1975.

———. *"In Jesus' Name": The History and Beliefs of Oneness Pentecostals*. Blandford Forum, UK: Deo Publishing, 2008.

Robeck, C. M., Jr. "Garfield Thomas Haywood." In *The New International Dictionary of Pentecostal and Charismatic Movements*, rev. and expanded, edited by Stanley M. Burgess, 693–94. Grand Rapids, MI: Zondervan, 2002.

Segraves, Daniel L. *Andrew D. Urshan: A Theological Biography*. Lexington, KY: Emeth Press, 2017.

Smith, Robert Payne. *A Compendious Syriac Dictionary*. Oxford: Clarendon, 1903.

Taylor, David G. K. "The Syriac Tradition." In *The First Christian Theologians: An Introduction to Theology in the Early Church*, edited by Gillian Rosemary Evans. Hoboken, NJ: Wiley-Blackwell, 2004.

Urshan, A. D. *The Life and Experiences of Andrew David Urshan*. 4th ed. (N.p.: N.p.).

Younan, Andrew. Lecture: "Christology in the Patristic Period, Part III—Christ in the East." http://www.kaldu.org /Theology_Course_2007/06_B _PChristology_03_Video.html.

CHAPTER 5

The Dust District

Okies, Authority, and the Hard-Liner Transformation of California Pentecostalism

Lloyd D. Barba

The notion of the "Dust District" emerges from a quip I heard during my years of research in the mid-2010s: "The Oklahoma District is the largest district in the United Pentecostal Church, but most of its people are in California." To this day, historically white Pentecostal denominations in California's Central Valley retain similarities to their counterparts from Oklahoma, the states of the greater Western South, and those in the Deep South.[1] As a result of migration from the 1930s to the 1950s, Okie Pentecostals formed a sort of "new sacred order" in California's Central Valley, thereby challenging the existing Pentecostal and broader Protestant order. The Dust Bowl or "Okie" migration captured the attention of the nation amid the Great Depression and earned a secure place in the canon of great American literature with the publication of books such as John Steinbeck's *The Grapes of Wrath*. Readers may recall the religious air of the day that Steinbeck captured in the character of Jim Casy, a Pentecostal-preacher-turned-union-pugilist, who joined the Joad family on the journey to the Central Valley and was later martyred for his labor activism. Steinbeck's fictional account picked up on a notable feature of the migration: namely that Okie migrants brought their religion and fight with them. The extent of their influence would be realized in the decades following Steinbeck's magnum opus. And Pentecostalism is one place to examine this change.

In biographies, memoirs, periodicals, and histories, writers commonly used the terms "Okie" and "Dust Bowlers" synonymously. In reality, all "Dust Bowlers" were "Okies," but not all Okies were Dust Bowlers, as the Dust Bowlers, strictly speaking, were the migrants who fled the ecological and economic ravages of the dust storms that swept the region for much of the 1930s. The popularized "myth" of the Dust Bowl's disastrous effects clouded the categories. Generally speaking, Californians applied the term "Okie" to impoverished white migrants from the Western South and Great Plains who entered California's industrial farms. At a squatters' camp in Kern County, economist Paul Taylor observed that the 150 Okie families drove in on jalopies with license plates from "Minnesota, Missouri, Oklahoma, Arizona, California, Texas, Nebraska, Mississippi, Utah, New Mexico, Oregon, and Washington."[2] Thus, in the application of the term, the place of origin mattered little compared to one's occupational status in the state's notorious fields. As other publications have done, this chapter reserves the term "Okie" for those from the Western South.[3] Historians James Gregory and Walter Stein used the term "Dust Bowlers" with the caveat that only a few (6 percent according to Gregory) actually took refuge in California as a direct result of the dust storms. Stein listed the various economic reasons that spurred the migration of over three hundred thousand Okies into California and noted their inability to find profitable work as among the chief reasons. Nevertheless, newspapers of the day as well as the novel and film *The Grapes of Wrath* inscribed "Okie" and "Dust Bowl" migration as synonyms in the national lexicon.[4]

This chapter proposes that students of Pentecostalism examine the migratory trajectories of Oneness Pentecostal Okies in order to understand how hard-liner holiness cultures emerged more robustly in some areas over others.[5] The Oneness Pentecostals in the state who preceded the Okies hailed from a different class and cultural stock. They exhibited refined cosmopolitan qualities, hailing from various parts of the globe, and engaged in polyglot evangelism. While much more has yet to be learned about this earlier generation, a cursory overview indicates that they maintained global-minded evangelism not hampered down by the same level and kind of infighting as exhibited by Okies. Under the later Okie era, such distinguishing characteristics worked against the earlier generation. Cut from a different cloth, Okies rent asunder and restitched a sacred canopy of California Pentecostalism, pronouncing much more exclusive soteriological paradigms. This chapter begins with a profile of early Pentecostal pioneers and their characteristics, which set them at odds with the later wave of Okie Pentecostals. The latter group, as detailed in the remainder of the chapter, evangelized successfully among the state's dispossessed white migrants, establishing authority through "being tough on doctrine," "hard preaching," and confrontation.

The stories presented here are as much about migration as they are about class; furthermore, "toeing the line" on standards and expectations imported by Okie Pentecostals bore racial and gendered consequences. We will see how zealous Okie oracles projected mythologized notions of the "old paths" and handed down hard-liner teachings on how to "be separate from the world." Although this kind of rhetoric is not unique to Okie Pentecostalism in California, and the pioneers themselves would have used such language, the degree of influence and rapidity of this cultural transition in California indeed spells out a unique chapter for this tradition. Since a similar process unfolded in denominations such as the Assemblies of God (AG), this chapter will at times draw evidence from parallel AG stories in the Central Valley, inasmuch as they reflect a similar southern-inflected religiosity.[6] But it should be noted, however, that the particular "hard-liner" stances have persisted for much longer in California's Oneness Pentecostal churches than in Trinitarian ones.

The migration of Okies caused a statewide uproar and attracted years of media coverage that stigmatized them as a social problem.[7] Pentecostals, however, saw the so-called "Okie problem" as an "opportunity." Pentecostalism in the Central Valley, like few other social or religious movements, benefited most directly from the migration. After all, in a movement where the number of "souls won" acted as the measure of a congregation's success, the proof lay in the pudding of proselytism, and Okies made better pudding. The sheer numbers of migrants, their class marginalization, and their inclination toward Pentecostalism and aggressive evangelism afforded Dust District Pentecostals a numerical advantage over their pioneering predecessors. While the polyglot generation might have been able to preach sermons in German or Japanese, Okies preferred those who spoke their own southern-inflected argot, maintained their manners, and exhibited the same tough temperament.[8] Thus in California, from the 1930s to the 1950s, the migration of religiously conservative plain-folk augured well for Pentecostal evangelism. To the chagrin of Okies from Baptist and Methodist backgrounds, churches of these denominations in California largely rejected them. Their newly arrived lower-class status left few church doors open to them. But they found an alternative: Pentecostals not only welcomed them, they compelled them to come in. Beyond that, the so-called "denominal world" of established Protestant traditions proved too cold and dead for red-hot Pentecostal revivals up and down the valley.[9]

OUT OF EVERY NATION UNDER HEAVEN: PENTECOSTAL PIONEERS

The Pentecostal culture of the valley transitioned out of an older, refined, poly-glot, and more cosmopolitan strain of early Pentecostalism that emerged directly out of the Azusa Street Revival. On the heels of revival, Pentecostalism quickly expanded into the state's northern urban cities, such as Oakland, San Francisco, and Stockton. These northern California sites functioned as proving grounds for some missionaries and housed early Bible institutes of the incipient Pentecostal movement. The far-flung yet connected congregations pastored by men and women with global experiences defined the era of polyglots and pioneers from the heyday of the Azusa Street Revival through at least the World War II era. Because of the increasing migration into the state in the postwar period, the earlier generation's influence waned in places such as the Central Valley, and most rapidly in its southern portion, known as the San Joaquin Valley. Some of the earlier pioneers had grown old, but others more or less had been rooted out by their theologically stricter counterparts in their district.

While this chapter focuses on the culture of the Dust District, a brief over-view will suffice to demonstrate some of the actors of this earlier era. While attention to Oneness Pentecostalism in California often turns to the April 1913 events at Arroyo Seco and from there jumps to the Midwest, it should be noted that a robust Pentecostal revival swept through the state in many places and languages. Students of the movement would be remiss to overlook the contribu-tions of pioneers such as the Australian-born Los Angeles pastor Frank Ewart, notable for his roles as the author of *The Phenomenon of Pentecost*, publisher of the periodical *Meat in Due Season*, architect of Oneness Pentecostal doctrine in the late 1910s, and missionary supporter. This chapter briefly considers the role of overlooked figures of the state's Central Valley with whom Ewart collaborated for his missionary endeavors.[10]

Embodying this globally minded Pentecostal ethos are also figures such as Harry Morse, an Azusa Street Revival convert who initiated missions in Stock-ton and a missionary training school in Oakland.[11] Born in Appleton, Wisconsin, in 1879, Morse traveled to Stockton from Michigan in 1898. He spent his earliest ministerial days in the Holiness-based Peniel Mission. In 1908, Morse launched a Pentecostal Mission in Stockton, laying the foundation of what would later become a welcome station for Okies and one of California's most prominent Oneness Pentecostal churches: Christian Life Center. Morse's earliest converts included the ancestors of the church's current first pastoral family.[12] Some of the earlier missionaries trained at Morse's school and continued on to places

Fig. 5.1. Lodi, like several other towns in early twentieth-century California, was home to a large population of Germans, many of whom had migrated from the Dakotas. At this early 1920s Oneness Pentecostal revival, German was the primary language in which the services were conducted. Photo courtesy of Edna Francis and in author's files.

such as China, the Philippines, India, Japan, various African countries, and foreign-language missions within the United States.[13]

Just north of Stockton, the zeitgeist of early Pentecostalism suffused the German-speaking town of Lodi as shown in fig. 5.1. There, German immigrant twin sisters Ethel and Lilian Zimmer arrived after having trained at Morse's Bible school. Lodi at that time was a small town of Dakotan and upper midwestern migrants. (There, the celebrated musician and Swiss-born Oneness pioneer William Booth-Clibborn joined the twins for revivals and preached in German.[14]) In addition to the Zimmer twins, Morse later trained others who went on to found churches affiliated with the Pentecostal Church Incorporated (PCI). Foreign-language evangelism and missions shaped the views of PCI ministers in California. In nearby Modesto, PCI California pioneers Earle and Ethel Toole (neé Zimmer) founded a church, and their pastorate was succeeded in 1942 by Julius and Lilian Rode (neé Zimmer). Julius had converted in Lodi in the 1920s.

His "Germaness," nevertheless, evidently distinguished him as a man of class and refinement throughout his ministerial career in the Central Valley as he ministered among Okies in later decades. The Modesto church, near the city's airport district (the Okie area), quickly outgrew several buildings. By the 1950s, Okies filled Rode's pews. In the years ahead some of his stern-minded Okie pastor counterparts would come to paint Rode and others like him as "weak on doctrine."

OKIE EVANGELIZATION

Several studies from the 1940s on the sociological dimensions of California churches prove instructive for this chapter's historical investigation.[15] Anthropologist Walter Goldschmidt conducted fieldwork in California's Central Valley in order to show the major differences between communities built around corporate industrial-agricultural farms (e.g., Wasco) and smaller family farms (e.g., Dinuba). While the former relied on seasonal and migratory workers and generally created conditions of exploitation, the latter better facilitated family settlements. Amid his research, he picked up on palpable social and class differences between churches in industrial-agricultural communities. He labeled this phenomenon "denominational stratification," bringing to light the stark divisions between "nuclear churches" (Congregational, Methodist, Baptist, and Seventh-Day Adventists—from highest to lowest), which occupied the upper half, and "outsider churches" (Nazarene, Assemblies of God, Church of God, and Pentecostals—from highest to lowest), which occupied the lower half. He ranked these churches according to the social occupations of the members. And while the AG certainly falls within the Pentecostal tradition (as do certain Church of God congregations), its leaders and pastors in numerous places throughout California shied away from using the term "Pentecostal" because of the vast number of Okie Pentecostals who reportedly brought social ill repute to the name. Okie Pentecostals largely fell into a "sectarian" or "schismatic" camp, which included independent Pentecostals, Oneness Pentecostals, and those generally discontented with existing Pentecostal churches in California.[16]

The influx of Dust District migrants overwhelmed the kinder, gentler practices of the pioneer Pentecostals and ultimately ushered in a hard-liner Pentecostalism from the Western South. Why the overtake? For one, as with many Pentecostals, soteriological differences were at stake. And some of the pioneering Oneness Pentecostals hadn't come into the "full gospel." To put it briefly, the early Pentecostal pioneers maintained doctrines (or doctrinal emphases) that the Dust District preachers later deemed "weak." Interpretations of the New Birth (that is, Holy Spirit infilling and Jesus' name baptism), holiness standards of dress, and the fervency with which these were maintained landed one in either a camp of "weak on the doctrine" compromisers or a camp of hard-liners (in many cases a badge of honor).[17] It appears that the more capacious understanding of salvation came about from the pioneering generation that defected from the AG in 1916, as they sought ways to salvage the salvation of their Trinitarian counterparts by proposing the "light doctrine."[18] Unlike this early generation of Oneness doctrinal architects, Dust District preachers built protective walls of soteriological orthodoxy between themselves and their Trinitarian counterparts.[19] Seeing that earlier Pentecostals offered a compromised message of salvation, Okies set out to set the soteriological record straight.

The trajectory of Oneness Pentecostal churches in California followed regional as well as denominational lines. The sociological differences we can trace help us understand the contextual contingencies that influenced views on salvation, holiness, and authority. Historian Thomas Fudge demonstrated clearly the theological differences between two major and predominantly white Oneness Pentecostal denominations. The Pentecostal Church Incorporated (PCI) and Pentecostal Assemblies of Jesus Christ (PAJC) held different understandings of baptism in Jesus' name and the degree to which the infilling of the Holy Spirit and baptism were *essential* for salvation. The PCI and PAJC merged in 1945 to form the United Pentecostal Church (UPC), but subtle differences would perennially surface throughout the twentieth century. California proved to be an important battleground. In short, the PCI ministers held more flexible views with respect to salvation whereas PAJC preachers maintained an exclusivist stance. Until the 1945 merger that formed the UPC, the majority of white Pentecostal ministers in California (and much of the West Coast) hailed from the PCI.[20] In the Central Valley, tensions between the two groups loomed as Okies poured into the area.[21]

The unabashedly hard-liner PAJC preachers would often condemn PCI ministers for being too weak and "compromising," while PCI ministers would sometimes prevent PAJC minsters from speaking at their meetings. Of particular importance here are Western South migrants such as Isaac Hilliard (I. H.) "Ike" Terry, who converted to the PAJC in 1939 and moved to Bakersfield to found his own church in 1943.[22] In the early years, all his church members were from Oklahoma, and he welcomed fellow Oklahoman preachers, such as Voar Shoemake, who later established churches up north in Modesto and San Jose.[23] Terry reportedly claimed that until he arrived, "full salvation" had not been preached in the San Joaquin Valley.[24] This qualification of "full salvation" or "full gospel" has historically been leveraged as a way to partially discount the validity of the Pentecostal experiences of others. Specifically, it aimed to point out that a proper interpretation of Jesus' name baptism, the oneness of God, or holiness standards of dress had not been completely adhered to. Terry claimed that certain prominent Oneness pastors who labored in California decades before his arrival "came in under weak preaching" but eventually "came to the gospel" under his influence. These preachers include former missionary and Morse trainee David Gray and longtime Stockton pastor Clyde Haney. Terry also claimed that fellow staunch conservative Vaughn Morton of Fresno "had a PCI preacher" (referring to Julius Rode of Modesto), but that Morton eventually came to "believe in the gospel." [25] Terry, a stalwart of the most hard-liner PAJC strains of Oneness Pentecostalism, was arguably the most influential of them to arrive in California. He trained over forty preachers; many of them stayed in the Central Valley and continued to be "tough on doctrine."[26] One minister credited Terry for forging a "San Joaquin mentality."[27]

The PAJC had a strong influence in the Western South and especially in Oklahoma. Dust Bowl migrants arrived with, or encountered in places such as Bakersfield, rigid doctrinal ideas and simultaneously attempted to recapture authority from the dust of their dispossession.[28] Their uncompromising rigidity and authority rested on certitude and absolutism ("a propensity to see life in moral extremes"), both temperaments that emerged from literalism and a belief in Jesus' imminent and *soon* return.[29] Historian Grant Wacker reminds us how "Rigorous literalism—hard and unforgiving—served as an ethic for daily life."[30] Such was the case not only among Terry and his likes but also for California pastors who had attended C. P. Williams's Apostolic College in Tulsa, Oklahoma, in the 1940s and 1950s. Williams and his students followed a remarkably strict code of discipline. Stern-mindedness and no-compromise graduates from Apostolic College entered California hardly *tolerant* of their PCI counterparts. Under the hard-liner influence of preachers from the Texas-Oklahoma circuits, Okie ministers introduced more austere ideas to the Pentecostal landscape of California, largely with the support of the laity.[31]

The arrival of the Okies changed the religious landscape by creating a demand for plain-folk religion packed with intense religious experiences and high personal and social moral values akin to those upheld in the Western South. The earlier strains of Pentecostalism in the Central Valley seemed to have gained limited acceptance, leaving these open to the influence of Okie Pentecostals intent on recreating the South and reclaiming authority. Just when one reporter of the Northern California Baptist Annual Convention noted in 1927 the "marked waning of the Pentecostal and McPherson movement," the Dust Bowl migration was about to kick up.[32] Since the problem between the earlier "compromisers" and the Okie arrivals lay in soteriological differences, evangelistic competition was fair game.

The Okies' telltale vernacular English spoke louder than their actions, but it was exactly these sorts of plain-folk characteristics that granted them immediate acceptance into Pentecostal circles. The majority of Pentecostal growth in the movement's first few decades, after all, had been in the South and Western South. Dust District laity preferred preachers who had worked in the fields over those who held formal degrees. Credentials meant little for Okie Pentecostals. Cultural relatability mattered more. While "preaching" is generally conceived of as the delivery of a sermon from a pulpit, in this context it is better imagined as "proclaiming the gospel." This practice empowered the laity to take part in evangelism.[33]

Pentecostalism operated and multiplied because of the burden of urgent evangelism placed on the laity and preachers alike. PAJC Texan and Bakersfield pastor I. H. Terry recalled how one of his converts switched over the course of a weekend from the Nazarene church to Terry's congregation. By Monday the new convert was preaching the Oneness message to his coworkers.[34] Urgency and immediacy, after all, characterized many early Pentecostal conversions. Many Pentecostals did not see the need for formal training for preachers since the core gospel message could be understood and taught quickly (seemingly as quickly as one night). Good preaching conveyed certitude and toughness, even in intra-Pentecostal relations. In the shadow of looming and recently concluded world wars, the second coming of Jesus could not have seemed more imminent, and preaching that would "tell it like it is" gave people a sense of purpose and an access to authoritative discourses.

By the 1950s, much of the laity in the Central Valley was of Okie origin and so, too, were the clergy. To borrow from a proximate example, consider the migration of Okie "preachers" affiliated with the AG. Swedish American Pentecostal pioneer Arthur Osterberg bemoaned the Okies' arrival. In his capacity as the superintendent of the Southern California District (this included everything south of Fresno) he wrote to an executive at the AG headquarters in Springfield, Missouri, grumbling over the conditions in which Okies arrived, "with their broken down automobiles, their wives and large families together with their washboards and washtubs, billy goats and bedding, their chicken coops and their lice with the information that God in Heaven sent them to take up a pastorate here."[35] This influx of zealous preachers persisted through the following decade and was not unique to the AG experience. One can also detect changes in the records of the Western District's most treasured historical commemorative volume. The Western District of the predominantly white UPC published a heritage book in the early 1970s that also contained a collection of obituaries. At that time, a majority of deceased leaders hailed from PCI backgrounds. The two deceased foreign missionaries also came from PCI origin. Three of the twelve men pastored in Oklahoma prior to their arrival in California.[36] The obituaries, however, signaled a change in the offing.

RECAPTURING AUTHORITY THROUGH DOCTRINE AND HARD PREACHING

Whatever status Okies once possessed in Oklahoma seemed lost as they entered California. As the Great Depression and dust storms swept over the Western South, many erstwhile-propertied Okies now found themselves at the bottom rungs of California's social ladder and as a "problem" to state bureaucrats. Pentecostalism offered a ready avenue to recapture some sense of authority. Unlike in southern California, where plain-folk migrants influenced the political and social culture, the Central Valley's Okies wielded little political and social influence;[37] whatever limited influence they may have had was most apparent in the social spaces carved out by their fellow kind in churches. The confluence of Okie subculture and Pentecostalism in the Central Valley resulted in the formation of a new religious apparatus that sought to recapture authority. As hard as nature fought back against overzealous agribusiness farmers in the southern Plains, zealous Okie preachers combated against any contrary force. Early Pentecostals primarily looked to three overlapping sources to confirm their authority: the Bible, doctrine, and the Holy Ghost.[38] While nothing could be technically "added" to the first (a closed canon, read literally) and believers enjoyed the third as an immutable shared experience, it was the second source of authority that was the most malleable. Put differently, "doctrine" effectively became a palimpsest upon which Pentecostals for the years to come would draw, erase, and redraw the lines of salvation and its attendant rituals of the body (holiness standards). The less erasing of the lines (i.e., compromising), the better in a world of moral extremes, as less change confirmed authority. With Bible in hand and the Holy Ghost shut up in their bones, Pentecostals used the interpretively malleable idea of "doctrine" to proclaim and uphold a number of their own socially conditioned concerns. Having demarcated clear lines of doctrine and largely unwilling to bend these lines, Pentecostals accessed doctrine in order to tap into a broad sense of authority as a social group. When the Bible (because of its antiquity) or the Holy Spirit (for its immateriality) did not provide a clear-cut answer, doctrine did. (Doctrinal differences, to be sure, characterized the fissiparous nature of Pentecostalism.[39]) And herein Pentecostals developed their diverse set of characteristics, especially the peculiar ones that developed rapidly and intensely in California.

Dust District migrants turned their ascribed lower social position on its head and, in turn, nurtured a sense of pride cultivated from struggle, toughness, and down-to-earth roughness. With the upper crust of the social strata so far out of reach, Okie migrants despised that which they could not attain (class, clothes, jewelry, expensive material goods, etc.). Pentecostals pointed to their growth, despite their poverty and absence of robust social outreach programs, as evidence of their success. In fact, their poverty only reinforced their sense of eternal security, an idea historian Jonathan Ebel termed the "gospel of righteous poverty."[40] This success came about more because of (rather than in spite of) their avowed opposition to three perilous forces: a secular world, denominational Christianity, and their "weak" Pentecostal counterparts. Since Pentecostals especially sought to recapture authority in the realm of religion, the last two oppositional forces were the most common foes and consequently became the topic of many sermons and concerns.

The zealous attempts by preachers and laity to recapture authority are clearly evident in their hard-liner stances regarding behavioral and social expectations they called "Holiness." Okie Pentecostals cultivated a culture of hard-liner authority and confrontation. Rhetorical devices such "telling it like it is," "keeping the old paths," "preaching it straight," and "not compromising" constituted the bedrock of hard preaching with respect to theological nuances or behavioral expectations. With so few around them holding their Oneness beliefs in common and with a predilection to debate, Dust District Pentecostals set themselves up for many disagreements. "Hard preaching" was the term Pentecostals used to describe specific instructions formulated in order to influence individual behavior and social norms through sermons and studies. Hard preaching manifested itself in homiletical fervency, that is, the "toughness" of a stance against a perceived evil and the persistent reinforcement of familiar doctrines. A hard-liner stance could be articulated sternly in a quieter register, but such articulation lacked the expected element of toughness. The embattled world of Okies made for little room to relent or compromise.

In a world of doctrinal strife, few insults could so quickly undermine the authority and holiness of a minister other than being labeled a compromiser.[41]

One would be labeled as such for adjusting to change over time, soft-peddling new ideas, relaxing dress standards (mostly for women), or not preaching assertively enough (hammering, really) particular doctrinal points. Accepting the possibility of salvation outside the PAJC soteriology put one on the fast track to a compromiser status. The Okie culture of authority and confrontation thrived on oppositional stances and was built on behavioral disciplines and a heterodox position on salvation. Factions within the movement resulted in ministers relentlessly measuring up their holiness with and against those with whom they once shared a platform. On the one hand, Pentecostals interpreted evangelistic victories as success. Yet on the other hand, the so-called "sectarian" groups interpreted their apparent low numerical ceilings without a modicum of insecurity, for peculiarity never necessarily promised numerical prosperity. Compromisers, so it seemed, traded numbers for truth.

Okie Pentecostals ascribed a particular value to being "tough on doctrine." The honorific "preached doctrine," signified that the preacher did not back down against perceived theological enemies or larger societal threats. Maggie Terry, wife of I. H. Terry, penned her observations regarding their first service held in the newly constructed church after the 1952 tremor in Bakersfield. She recorded her thoughts with a stroke of doctrinal toughness: "On May 29, 1954, the First United Pentecostal Church pastored by Rev. Ike Terry moved to their new building on 36th St. Brother Terry kept preaching doctrine, holding revivals, loving souls, and the church kept growing."[42] The order of the actions that Terry "kept" doing likely was not haphazard. Describing a preacher as "preaching doctrine" or "keeping doctrine" boiled down to several characteristics. It signaled that one greatly emphasized several or all of the following: the Oneness of God and an unequivocal rejection of the Trinity, baptism in Jesus' name and a nullification of baptisms performed in the titles Father, Son, and Holy Ghost, and clear affirmation of specific holiness dress and behavioral standards. Ray Brown, a protégé of Terry, recalled that his mentor was "a doctrine preacher with variations of five sermons: oneness, holiness, obedience, faithfulness, and government. If I had a dollar for every time I heard oneness preached, I could make a down-payment on a nice house!"[43] Other contemporaries recalled: "All Brother Terry ever wanted to talk about was the doctrine and church government";[44] "he was a man who always had the doctrine of the New Birth, Oneness, and church government on his mind";[45] and that "Brother Terry wasn't interested in anything but teaching the doctrines of the Bible."[46]

One indication of Pentecostalism's large foothold in the area by the 1940s was the presence of a vast number of "schismatic" Pentecostal groups noted by scholars of that time.[47] Unlike the case of Methodists and Baptists, who split over differing views on major moral/political issues of the day, Pentecostal schisms existed in the mundane, everyday moral and social behavior. From small-scale arguments such as what sleeve length constituted modest attire or what color nylons were appropriate for church to larger salvific questions such as how to perform baptism, tensions boiled over to the point where families would not just merely leave but also take saints with them.[48] Churches were often a larger expression of one personality, namely the pastor, whose best saints dressed according to the prescribed standards.

Pastors set a wide range of "holiness standards." Sociologically, these could be understood as behavioral expectations set by a pastor (specifically) and/or entire denominations (generally). Holiness standards evidenced sanctification, a notion appropriated from Pentecostals' theological ancestors from the Wesleyan-Holiness tradition. According to this doctrine, a person could reach a state of perfection (a persistent or residual will to sin, notwithstanding) through consecration, that is, sustained acts of piety and a change of lifestyle.[49] Several schools of thought arose from this idea of perfection, but all schools agreed that the holiness within a believer's heart would manifest itself outwardly in comportment, speech, dress, and social engagement. The Dust District's fertile soil for new beliefs and practices allowed Pentecostals to impose various interpretations of "holiness standards." The rapid growth and saturation of sanctified folks in the San Joaquin Valley afforded Pentecostal preachers the opportunity to take bold stances without risking the loss of supporters. In reciprocation, the steady flow of plain-folk migrants ensured that the pews would stay filled despite defections. In this social soil, newer and tougher soteriological ideas took deep root and flourished.

Paradoxically, Pentecostals seeking to restore "the old paths" actually carved out new ones, demanding levels of consecration hardly heard of elsewhere beyond pockets in the greater South. Exiled from their homes by nature, it seemed that migrants built up extra safeguards to keep themselves and others from sinning while nature and improving social conditions discouraged a return to the Western South. The migration introduced change, new surroundings, and social unfamiliarity, which led religious Okies to restructure their world around religion, with the Bible as their guidebook and their raw, home-grown hermeneutics as their exegetical lenses. But in such formulations, schism broke out in the Dust District, driven by inevitable disagreements ranging from concerns over everything from theology to practical components of holy living. Historian of the Okie experience James Gregory adds that "relocation often drastically alters religious behavior, either disrupting or intensifying it." In the case of the Okie Pentecostal migration, Gregory asserts that migration did both.[50] Migration brought new ideas and sometimes intensified old ones so that "old paths" could go in a new direction.

With the exception of necessary quotidian duties, pastors strongly denounced any behavior or activity that did not promote a Pentecostal spirituality. One woman from a "Jesus Only" church in south Modesto testified, "I want to praise the Lord tonight fer this is jist another Baptist who has been baptized in Jesus' Name Only. If you want to git a thrill, git the Holy Ghost and quit goin' to shows and dances. Glory to God."[51] Farm labor camp managers picked up on their social behaviors and bemoaned that Pentecostals even refused to participate in recreational and educational activities.[52] In fact, when they participated in the one activity they cared about most (church services), they summarily met the disciplinary hand of the Farm Security Administration, which, for a short while, banned Pentecostals from conducting services. On this issue, the government camp administration joined with some private camp managers in complaining of Pentecostal-led services' "nuisance" and their "noise and excessive length."[53] In these ways, Pentecostal worship and preaching transgressed the "spirit of good neighborliness" and fell out of the good graces of the managers of these orderly camps, or what Ebel terms "New Deal Eden."[54] This sort of behavior demonstrated well the primitivist impulse of early Pentecostals who stayed relentlessly heavenly minded. The logic behind discouraging nonchurch activities was that a believer's time should be spent in consecration to the Holy Ghost, not in pursuit of leisure, amusements, and any activity remotely related to what the "world" practiced.[55] In Pentecostal parlance the "world" equated to secular and sinful society, and the term "worldly" framed issues clearly and scripturally. Inflected in an Old English–Okie argot, the preaching of Dust District evangelists took inspiration from the King James Version of the Bible to decry the ubiquitous menace of "worldliness."[56]

Holiness was the antidote to worldliness. This oppositional theology of always combating against the "world," its vices and enticements, animated social scientists' interviews with Okie Pentecostals in the 1940s. Worldliness created a binary world of either a highway of holiness or a highway to hell. One AG preacher from Live Oak defined "worldliness" as "anything that doesn't pertain to the Christian life, fer instance, playin' cards, goin' to shows, or dancin.' We don't believe in it. Our young people have parties, but no foolishness goes on."

"Anything that doesn't pertain to the Christian life" included any type of unwholesome leisure or pleasure. Time spent (or wasted) in any activity that did not "pertain to the Christian life" was believed to stymie the growth of the church and one's own spirituality. Pastors expected that instead of attending shows or carnivals saints would evangelize, spread the gospel, teach formulaic Bible studies, read their Bible, and pray (in other words, redeem the time because the days are evil).[57]

The saints who violated any of these standards often were subject to harsh pastoral correction. From public shaming to excommunication, the consequences varied in method but were bestowed with the same measure of disapproval. One Okie pastor postulated that if one of his members attended a show, he would "throw him out" of the church. That same pastor worried that if "sinners" saw him at a show, they would not hear him preach. This taboo further extended to movies and "Hellywood." Makeup and cosmetics also met condemnation in this same vein of worldliness, as some believed that "The Lord didn't teach in His Word fer us to use lipstick and rouge and finger nail polish. That's all of the devil."[58]

Hard preaching came part and parcel with aggressive "soul-winning" evangelism efforts and rested on toughness. The opprobrium accorded to Okies plagued the impoverished migrants, as the name signified second-class white citizenship. But they found ways to compensate for that which they did not materially possess in value; more crassly stated, they found ways to fight back, quite literally. On characteristics of the Okie subculture, Gregory notes how migrants valorized toughness.[59] The "cult of toughness" manifested itself in curious ways in the Dust District. Toughness became an almost necessary feature of hard preaching and an essential one of "being anointed." Hard preaching and absolutisms marked schisms and interchurch competition. Tough Okie preachers pulled no punches when it came to topics of splintered groups. Rev. Leonard Pollard, as one of many examples, opined that schisms result because "somebody wants to be boss. There's gonna be lots of preachers in hell. Positive fact."[60] His statement added a layer of absolutism to an already bold and definitive claim. I. H. Terry's own protégés described him as "not concerned with preaching pretty sermons with cute stories and funny jokes," and some remember him for his austerity, "tell it like it is" homiletic and, in some cases, offensiveness. This was the tough Pentecostal culture inculcated into him in west Texas. Terry had been converted under hard preaching in a PAJC church where evangelist C. B. Webb did not "preach anything but doctrine" and was "strong on Jesus' name, one God preaching."[61] That someone with Terry's personality traits could successfully nurture a church of seven hundred lay largely in the fact that his tough preaching enjoyed acceptance in the Okie social and cultural milieu.[62]

Verbose plain language sermons, however, contrasted to the supposed terseness of Okie argot. Maggie Terry noted in her diary how her husband (I. H.) had preached in Weedpatch for two and a half hours.[63] Tough preachers assumed that tough saints could endure tough sermons.

Just as this cult of toughness extended to boxers, brawlers, and wrestlers, it also extended to women believers who underwent "hard conversions."[64] Hard preaching wrought hard conversions. It is no easy task to gauge precisely the level of conservatism based on a group's nonparticipation, but with respect to Pentecostals we see how nonparticipation couched in terms of hard, outright rejection became part of their shared discourse and a feature of hard preaching. The boundaries of holiness attire serve as an example of how Okies intensified their practices in the Dust District. The account of one faithful saint from the small town of Hughson (south of Modesto) sheds light on the affect and effects of hard preaching: "Do you believe you could be condemned fer wearin' short sleeves? Well, you can. When I come to California I didn't own a dress with long sleeves. I was settin' right down here in church one Sunday and was condemned in my heart fer having' on a dress with short sleeves, and I had on a coat too. My arms began to hurt. . . . I was condemned fer my short sleeves. I didn't have no long sleeved dresses or money to buy any so I made me a little coat to wear over my arms and they quit hurtin.'"[65]

In Okie culture, denunciation plus toughness made for a hard-liner stance. Okies sought to compensate for their social abstinence with tough preaching and by employing forceful language when speaking against worldly things. An elderly believer from Modesto's airport community (still known today as the tough and rough part of town) attests to this toughness: "I've burned at least fifteen decks of cards since I got the Holy Ghost. My husband settin' right over there. He loves his filthy old pipe. I'm afreared its [*sic*] goints take an awful struggle to bring him to seek the Lord. . . . The devil gave me a hard blow but I want to give him a black eye."[66] The act of burning her husband's cards (symbols of profane entertainment) does not just demonstrate the force and toughness of her no-turning-back tactic of relinquishment. The rather large number of cards she had amassed marked her as an even greater sinner prior to her conversion and a more radical saint ever "since she got the Holy Ghost." Her pugilistic encounter against the devil exemplified a broader ethos of hard testimonies and confrontation. Hard testimonies captured elements of force, hyperbole, and profane things. (Terry was remembered for his defiance against the gospel in his preconvert days. He would arrive at church in Monahans, Texas, with a big cigar that he would leave on a post outside of the church and retrieve after service.)[67] Tough sinners made for tough saints. To own so many decks of cards meant that the elderly woman from Modesto was not some ordinary gambler, she was a hard gambler. Furthermore, her audacity to call out her husband in front of the congregation demonstrates how women, through the inspiration of the Holy Ghost, acted in toughness when speaking of any sin, including that of their own husbands. Women in testimony services could claim "Holy Ghost anointing" for their assertive stances, which belied notions of passive femininity. The larger congregation generally esteemed these instantiations of anointing as heroic. Pastors imposed the majority of regulations upon women, but when women had the opportunity to speak about sins of men, they did so with equal force. Such preaching, however, drew its share of criticism. The charge of a "woman acting like a man" or "usurping authority over a man" became common. But when the homiletics of preaching and testifying rested on toughness, what recourse did a woman have but to preach hell just as hot? Toughness extended from the rejection of sin to everyday living and all things that might otherwise "water down" or "compromise" faith lived out in quotidian life. At times, this even meant toughing out sicknesses.

Like other sectarian groups, Pentecostals refused medical services. This remained the rule and not the exception well past the mid-century in the Dust District. Such medical services seemed incompatible with divine healing, a pillar of Pentecostal theology. But Pentecostals from the church in Weedpatch continued to spurn human medical services to a greater extent and relatively longer than many of their fellow Pentecostals did. Rita Dawson, born in Di Gorgio (southwest of Bakersfield) in 1936 to Arkansas migrants, recounted how en route to a youth service in Carlsbad, New Mexico, she and several other youngsters sustained serious injuries resulting from a vehicle collision. She recalled how the pain in her back worsened when the ambulance that picked her up collided head-on with an oncoming vehicle. With a busted lower lip that her teeth had cut through, bruises, and swollen eyes, she, along with the injured others, refused to sign papers for admission into the hospital. They even refused aspirin. She remembered how on the following night "our battered choir was assembled. David Turk, our drummer, played with a broken collar bone and his head bandaged from an eye injury. Mike hobbled up on crutches and others wore bandages. We had not yet sung two minutes until the power of God fell."[68] Another believer from a different Jesus' name congregation in Weedpatch refused medical attention for a gangrenous leg. Her pastor continued to trust in divine healing. After weeks of prayer with no results, the believer claimed that the now rather frustrated pastor prayed once again over the phone, and finally reversed the course of the infection.[69]

Turning to medicine ostensibly undermined faith in God's healing power. Operating on a "blame-the-victim" theory, if infirm saints did not experience healing, it was because they lacked sufficient faith in God.[70] In the second half of the twentieth century, as diagnoses and medical practices became more efficient and as psychologists provided new explanations for mental condition—instead of just passing off a person as possessed—and as Pentecostals moved up the socioeconomic scale, they abandoned this practice of spurning medicine and treatment. Unlike the sustained preaching against makeup, jewelry, theaters, and ballgames, their pragmatic impulse kicked into gear, making clear that they should not resist the advancements in medical research for much longer.

As has been noted thus far, class, doctrinal, and homiletical differences shaped hard preaching in the Dust District. These preachers defined hard preaching over against the weak, soft, or false teaching of their Oneness predecessors and other Christians. Seeing themselves as embattled, Pentecostals imagined themselves as surrounded by formidable opponents, be they in the world, the larger church world, or within their own Pentecostal ranks. And no hard-liner would back down from confrontation.

AUTHORITY THROUGH CONFRONTATION

Okie Pentecostals especially forged a social identity based on what they were *not* rather than what they were. In similar manner to the lists of Torah prohibitions (some of which they sought to apply literally to their lives), preachers issued informal litanies of commandments, the majority of which were negative in nature. These negative commandments of "do nots" or denouncements were deployed in order to regulate moral and social behavior. Living as a chosen/separate people, they never decoupled the moral from the social. Dust District Pentecostals believed that other Christians erred in this decoupling of categories. Since Okies wielded very little influence over civic affairs and public social life, the conflation of the moral and social offered a convenient and tangible way of recapturing authority. Proving to others that they had a better grip on these matters afforded them a sense of authority.

Dust District Pentecostals found victories over their rivals in the everyday arena of discourse, be it evangelism, extemporaneous preaching, or debates. The spirit of these debates was captured in a sense of rigorous biblical literalism, the hermeneutic that guided Pentecostal interpretations of the Bible, which itself was the sole source of all truth. Pentecostals adapted this rather recently developed hermeneutic influenced by Common Sense Realism, a Scottish philosophical approach to texts developed in the nineteenth century.[71] The truth, in this interpretive paradigm, was clear, plain, and easily understood and thus required the least level of explanation. Inherent clarity won the day. This most apparent approach offered a special sense of understanding to even the most untrained. All explanations yielded to the easily understandable (most often, that was the literal application). Winners of such debates were decided by whose literalist interpretations could outdo the others, as little appeal was ever made to sources outside of the King James Version of the Bible.

One preacher from Oklahoma offered an account that bolstered Okies' confidence in their place at the table of theological debate. Two brothers in Oklahoma came to a theological disagreement. One was enrolled in a Baptist seminary, and the other attended a Pentecostal meeting where he felt called to preach. The two met to settle a biblical matter and, against societal expectations, the newly converted Pentecostal imparted profounder truths and "the educated Baptist couldn't say nuthin'. He tried but he jist didn't have it under his belt."[72]

Okie raconteurs could cause a righteous ruckus in a similar homiletic in which preachers could fire up a crowd to a frenzy. Storytelling and testimonies, especially epic showdowns between Low-Church preacher and High-Church seminarians, was the bread and butter of southern preaching. Expositions on the Westminster Confession would likely fall onto deaf ears, but the everyday folk preaching and singing of plain-folk preachers would almost certainly stir one into a Holy Ghost jig. A large number of men and women carved out their own careers in this profession, since prerequisites for entering the ministry were so minimal. They prized commitment over education. The enthusiastic evangelist was preferred over the erudite exegete. Whenever possible, they gloated in their victories over the educated. Pentecostals testified to trouncing their educated opponents, a victory that signaled divine inspiration and approbation.

Pentecostals found ways to create a sense of belonging, empowerment, and uplift, making the best of their condition when fighting in these social-theological wars. Pentecostal preachers prided themselves on their ability to preach despite never having attending seminary. Most Okie preachers possessed only an elementary school education.[73] They flipped the idea that seminary training produced great clergy by appealing to their down-to-earth qualities. An evangelist in Modesto appealed to his rugged, uncouth mannerisms as evidence that the Holy Spirit operated through him. The following preface to a sermon demonstrates how he wielded his Okie argot as means of relevance: "I want you good people to pray fer me as I attempt to preach. I'm not an educated man. I'm jist an old Oklahoma plough boy. I've eat about as many beans and black-eyes peas and watermelons and rose ears as anybody . . . the only [preaching] course I ever had was to bury my head in this old Book, and study. I never went a day beyond the eighth grade so if there is to be any preachin' here tonight the Holy Ghost will have to do it."[74] This raw, unedited transcription reveals how preachers esteemed themselves in opposition to trained seminarians. They posited that their lack of education offered some rawer articulation of that which God wanted to speak through the preacher. Pentecostal audiences, in turn, viewed their social shortcomings as laudable, not laughable. Less reliance on education (read: human philosophy) resulted in greater dependency on the Holy Spirit. The observations of another preacher from Modesto further demonstrated how this anti-intellectual logic appealed to pious plain-folk: "We don't go through all the stuff the regular preachers follow. We'll have a man preachin' ten years before they even git started. . . . He'll [a man ordained that Sunday] be full-fleged [*sic*] preacher in less than two weeks, jist as soon as he gits his credentials. He went to the eighth grade."[75] A quick turnaround from conversion to "full-fledged" preaching augmented the force of the Dust District's evangelism. And in a place where the number of converts functioned as the barometer of success, the overnight preachers had some room to boast over their "denominal" counterparts. Given the competitive nature of evangelism and strivings to maintain holiness standards, it should come as no surprise that Dust District Pentecostals soon sized up one another.

The culture of confrontation (possibly inspired by Peter and Paul's public debates in the Acts of the Apostles) manifested itself strongly between Oneness and Trinitarian Pentecostals. They held many doctrines in common and had a deep shared history, but the few differences that existed between them proved especially divisive for any Okie in the Dust District. These disagreements, undergirded by Okie toughness, made for public shouting matches. A brief transcript of one pastor's description is worth noting in its entirety. Reflecting on his time as a pastor in Shafter (near Bakersfield), he recalled:

> The Jesus' Name Only people are poison to the rest of the Pentecostal groups. They come to our service and testify and we can spot them the minute they open their mouth. They would like to dominate the entire service and so take it completely out of our hands. They shout right out some times that we are all going to hell if we are not baptized in the name of Jesus Only. I can usually shut them up pretty easy by starting a chorus and sit them down. Once in a while I will say, "My brother, you are out of order."

I have also said this when one has finished his testimony: "We are glad to have Brother-so-and-so of the Jesus' Name Only faith with us tonight." That burns them up. I said they are poison, and I mean poison. I've known cases where people were converted in our meetings and one of them preachers would take some of the new converts right out that very night after our service was over and baptize them in the name of Jesus Only. What is that but poison? Of course a new convert wouldn't know any difference.[76]

At this time "Jesus only" was a common way to describe (and dismiss) Oneness Pentecostals. These sorts of confrontations occasioned spirited exchanges. Ironically, this description and case are not too dissimilar with how Oneness Pentecostals themselves remember such confrontations. In 1944 I. H. Terry had recently arrived in Bakersfield and sought out converts in this manner, recalling, "One evening, I went to a Church of God service to testify. They were so glad to see me. When asked to testify, I began exhorting on the oneness of the godhead. It got real cold! The pastor called everybody to pray, and while they were praying they'd look back to see if I was still there. I sat and listened to them pray for a while. They were praying like there was a devil in the house; I guess they meant me! I finally left."[77] Terry cut to the chase, as "oneness of the godhead" represented a cornerstone theological tenet of Oneness Pentecostalism. Terry's confrontational (and reportedly successful) style, even years after his passing, continues to be embedded in the local church lore. Some recall the story of Terry, when laboring to establish his own church, setting up a sign out of the trunk of his vehicle that read: "All trinitarians are going to hell."[78]

As the minority camp in the broader Pentecostal community, Oneness preachers often took the first jab to provoke Trinitarian clergy and laity. The combative and confrontational exchanges between these groups often came to a head in formalized debates. No Okie preacher worth his salt would dare back down from a debate challenge. After all, unshakable certitude welcomed such tests. Oneness churches relied on these public debates (confrontations) in order to garner more attention and win over converts. Take, for example, Terry's recollection of founding his church in Bakersfield: "When we arrived in Bakersfield, I was ready for a fight for the gospel. I welcomed the opportunity to defend what I knew was right in doctrine. I placed a lunch board on the sidewalk in front of our storefront church. It read, 'Trinity Is The Way To Hell!' This seemed to draw attention. It wasn't long until Trinitarians came to my house, and challenged me to a debate with the Church of Christ [non-Pentecostal] preacher."[79] Debates quickly morphed into a battle of wits centered on biblical literalism. In response to a point that the Trinity manifested itself at the baptism of Jesus in three distinct forms (Jesus, the Holy Spirit as a dove, and the voice of the Father), Terry quipped, "how would you like to go bird hunting with a guy that doesn't know the difference between a dove and a person?"[80] In the battle of wits, Oneness Pentecostals articulated points seemingly so clear that they required little to no theological mulling.

Sociologist James Wilson further captured the punch that Oneness Pentecostals packed in the 1940s. A middle-aged man from a "Jesus Only" church in south Modesto made his challenge to his theological nemeses quite clear:

> I'll defy anybody to show me where it's possible to baptize in any other name. Preachers go on baptizin' in the three names of Father, Son, and Holy Ghost. They are jist deceivin' the people. In Oklahoma one of them Trinity men debated with me about Jesus' Name Only. He interrupted my sermon on the street. He said, "What are you goin' to do with Matthew 28:19?" I didn't know what to say but the Holy Ghost fell on me and give me a message. The crowd got so big the police had to clear the street. That preacher was an educated man and there I was jist a plain corn fed preacher. But he couldn't take it. I couldn't even find him after the meetin' was over and never saw him agin though I preached on the street there every Saturday night fer two years. Preachers like that can't stand up agin the Word of God.[81]

Here the unknown preacher leveraged an appeal to simplicity as just a corn-fed preacher against the educated seminarians who, in the preacher's view, spent a wealth of time learning but seemingly never understanding true riches. Okie Pentecostals were straightforward and they believed the Bible was, too. This plain-folk religion, augmented by toughness, certitude, and confrontation, appealed to many in the emerging Dust District. A successful confrontation also denoted that one had "stuck to their guns" and had not compromised. The most combative Pentecostals jumped at any opportunity to take a jab at the educated, especially when it was over a theological point. These small jabs in the larger course of debates counted as haymakers in Pentecostal preaching/storytelling.[82]

A scene in the aftermath of a vehicle accident involving the Weedpatch youth group from the local independent Oneness Pentecostal congregation merits further consideration, as it pertains to their culture of confrontation. The worst of the injured, Dearl Dawson (born in Oklahoma), husband of Rita Dawson (later pastor of the Weedpatch church), was in no condition to drive back to California from New Mexico. Dawson's insurance agent demanded that he undergo a medical examination. After much protest, Dearl consented. With a broken neck and lacerations over his head, Dearl's condition called for consultation with the doctor on duty. Rita Dawson's recollection of the story was influenced by the tendency of Pentecostal storytelling to portray doctors, lawyers, professors, and seminarians (i.e., the educated who would not join their ranks in any significant numbers) as losers in debates against Pentecostals. Just as the doctor was expressing misgivings about the Dawsons' plan for divine healing, the following exchange took place:

> [Doctor] "Just how long has there been anybody [who] believed like this?"
> [Rita] "Oh, ever since the day of Pentecost," I answered.
> "And when was that!?" he demanded.
> "'You mean, you're a doctor and you don't know that?" I said incredulously.
> "I have never met anybody so . . . ," he exploded, too angry to supply an apt description.
> "Well Doc, I'm glad you got to meet us. But I can tell you could not afford to meet very many of us. Because, from the way you're breathing right now, I can tell you'd probably die of a heart attack!"[83]

If debates ended favorably for Pentecostals, they shared these exploits with their congregations. These small victories acted as larger social reinforcements of their status as chosen and favored of God. They especially rejoiced in cases where higher education—the very product of the Enlightenment—fell flat in front of those who in some cases did not even hold a high school diploma.

CONCLUSION: UNSETTLED DUST

Pentecostals throughout the Dust District constructed an alternative system of social and religious authority. The ubiquity of Okie-influenced churches in the Central Valley stands as a testament to the region's battles in which Okies ultimately held sway over their "compromising" Pentecostal predecessors.[84] In the pursuit to find the old paths, it appears as if the hard-liners' imagined recollection of the past skipped over the generation of their immediate predecessors in California. One episode at Western Apostolic Bible College in

Stockton particularly demonstrates this doctrinal shift. The college's founder Clyde Haney would regularly invite Howard Goss, superintendent of the UPC when it formed in 1945 and longtime respected Oneness patriarch, to preach at his Bible college. Whereas Goss and the various Oneness pastors of the Stockton church had been affiliated with the PCI before the merger, over time Haney stopped inviting Goss and worked hard to correct the pioneer's more capacious views on salvation. Even former pastor Frank J. Van Buskirk, who handed over the church in Stockton to Haney in 1946, was prohibited from taking up certain topics in Western Apostolic Bible College classrooms. The turn toward a relatively tough, hard-liner stance on salvation was later cultivated by Kenneth Haney, who reportedly stated that he would not have invited Goss.[85] In this manner, holiness practices assumed more pronounced sectarian dimensions as new arrivals sought to recapture authority by ordering their new social context in alignment with the "old paths." In a culture where reasons for augmenting codes of holiness were hardly questioned, it appears that the old paths were in fact new paths, or at the very least, redirected ones.

A longer story yet remains to be told regarding the long-term effects of the hard-liner takeover. When the UPCI suffered a schism at the hands of a more conservative faction in 2007 that formed the Worldwide Pentecostal Fellowship in the following year, hard-liner strains once again surfaced. While some joined the World-Wide Pentecostal Fellowship, various churches, especially in California, opted for independent status. The long-term consequences of this stern-minded morality remain strongly apparent today in the Central Valley. From Stockton to Bakersfield, the state's mini-Bible Belt remains tightly fastened.

NOTES

1. This region includes portions of Oklahoma, Texas, Arkansas, Kansas, and Missouri.

2. Haslam, *Other California*, 106.

3. Gregory, *American Exodus*, 6–7.

4. The term "Okie" originally carried a negative connotation. Over the years, migrants and their descendants transformed that word into a source of pride, toughness, and perseverance. The term is used throughout the chapter as a signifier to describe the over one million migrants who left the southern Plains that were ecologically and economically affected by the Dust Bowl storms. "Dust Bowl Migrants" is a longer and generationally imprecise term, especially with respect to their children, who never lived in the Dust Bowl states yet they carried the various cultural nuances that Okies brought with them and bore this same stigma in their new region. Okie embodies the general ethos of migrants and articulates elements of their self-cultural awareness

as second-class citizens. James Gregory uses the term "Western South" in some cases to describe the region from which Okie migrants hailed. See Gregory, *American Exodus*. Moreover, today the term "Okieville" is still used to describe the impoverished white parts of towns throughout the Central Valley.

5. While previous studies have examined the migration of white southerners to California, none yet have specifically examined its impact on Oneness Pentecostalism. Gregory, *American Exodus*; Wilson, "Religious Leaders"; Goldschmidt "Class Denominationalism"; on the influence of plain-folk religion in southern California, see Dochuk, *From Bible Belt*.

6. Other Pentecostal churches in the Central Valley at this time included: Pentecostal Holiness Churches, The Foursquare Church, The Church of God, La Asamblea Apostólica de la Fe en Cristo Jesús, Pentecostal Assembles of the World, and various independent churches.

7. Gregory, *American Exodus*; Stein, *California*.

8. On Okie customs and temperament, see Gregory, *America Exodus*.

9. Wilson, "Religious Leaders," 251, 256, 262.

10. His periodical *Meat in Due Season*, published from 1915 to 1921, shows that Harry Morse and Ewart trained, supported, or followed at least twenty-two of the ninety-six reported Oneness missionaries; French, *Early Interracial Oneness Pentecostalism*, appendix B.2, 215–18.

11. French, *Early Interracial Oneness Pentecostalism*, 62, 206; Haney, *Man*, 42–43; Yadon Dillon, "Harry Morse," 289–90.

12. Haney, *Man*, 38–43.

13. Yadon Dillon, "Harry Morse," 291; *Pentecostal Herald* (February 1947), 7; Yadon Dillon, "Ruth Angela," 250.

14. Booth-Clibborn "Preacher's Testimony"; Booth-Clibborn, "Germany," 14; Price, "Zimmer Twins," 258–70.

15. Wilson, "Religious Leaders"; Goldschmidt, "Class Denominationalism."

16. Goldschmidt, "Class Denominationalism"; Wilson, "Religious Leaders," 251–54.

17. While the term "weak" usually refers to being "weak on doctrine" and often describes one's stance on the process of salvation behind Jesus' name baptism, it also described the rigidity or lack of enforcement of dress codes; see Fudge, *Christianity*, 171, 205.

18. Jesus' name Pentecostals taught that their Trinitarian counterparts' salvation would be judged on the basis of how they responded to the light/revelation revealed to them by God. In theory, then, those who were not baptized "in the name of Jesus" could still receive eternal salvation. This was a popular teaching among the first generation of Jesus' name believers who had suddenly witnessed a separation from their fellow spirit-filled believers. Ewart, *Phenomenon*, 105–6; Fudge, *Christianity*; Johnston, *Howard Goss*.

19. Like Morse, Goss, and many other early PCI and Pentecostal Assemblies of the World preachers, Ewart taught the "light doctrine." Regarding missionary Alfred Garr, he wrote, "When the message of the oneness of the Godhead came out, he rejected it, and this caused a very painful parting between us. But despite all these things, our love for each other survived, and this divine love will be renewed in the glory where we will all see eye to eye, and doctrinal difference will never again intrude." Ewart, *Phenomenon*, 105–6.

20. Carrier, *Man and Woman*, 60–61. Ministers from the PAJC believed that baptism in the name of Jesus and the infilling of the Holy Spirit was necessary for salvation and emphasized this point equally, if not more, than the Oneness of God. Both these points separated them from the AG, who agreed with them only on the infilling of the Holy Spirit but strongly rejected Jesus' name baptism and denounced the "Oneness Heresy."

Members of the PCI accepted the beliefs of the PAJC but did not believe that baptism and the Holy Ghost infilling were *essential* for salvation. It was welcome and they practiced it, but the absence of those two phenomena would not consign one to hell. See Fudge, *Christianity*.

21. Fudge, *Christianity*.

22. Carrier, *Man and Woman*; Leon Frost reports that Terry initially rented the "Spanish Apostolic Church" for a short time. See GBFPC 75th Anniversary Video Presentation. In 1943 Juan Rodriguez would have been pastor of the Apostolic Assembly of the Faith in Christ Jesus church in Bakersfield from whom Terry rented.

23. Carrier, *Man and Woman*, 54.

24. Fudge, *Christianity*, 172.

25. Ibid., 172n151; this does not appear to be a characterization that most would have historically maintained but speaks to Terry's hard-liner stance.

26. Carrier, *Man and Woman*, 7.

27. Fudge, *Christianity*, 173.

28. Wilson notes that many arrived as Pentecostals. Wilson, "Religious Leaders," 250.

29. Wacker offers fuller descriptions of how early Pentecostals understood "compromise," "certitude," and "absolute rightness." See Wacker, *Heaven Below*, 22–24.

30. Ibid., 74.

31. On a broader Protestant scale, Paul Harvey noted the peculiarity of "Texas Theology" among Southern Baptists. Darren Dochuk demonstrates how this brand of Texas Theology migrated from the Bible Belt to the Sunbelt. In a similar cultural vein, James Gregory noted how Okie's "stern-minded religiosity" transformed the rank and file of Baptist and Pentecostal churches. See Harvey, *Redeeming*, 151; Dochuk, *From Bible Belt*, 8; Gregory, *American Exodus*, 189.

32. *Northern California Baptist Annual Convention* (1927), 58.

33. Anderson, *Introduction*, 208–14.

34. Carrier, *Man and Woman*, 53.

35. Osterberg quoted in Dochuk, *From Bible Belt*, 34.

36. Western District, *Our Heritage*.

37. Dochuk, *From Bible Belt*. James Gregory offers some exceptions such as Bernie F. Sisk, a Texan and eventual congressman from Fresno. See Gregory, *American Exodus*, 243.

38. Wacker, *Heaven Below*, 70.

39. Sánchez-Walsh, *Pentecostals in America*; Wacker, *Heaven Below*, 76–81.

40. Ebel, "In Every Cup," 595–97.

41. Wacker, *Heaven Below*, 22.

42. Carrier, *Man and Woman*, 79.

43. Ibid., 80.

44. Carl Ballestero quoted in ibid., 35.

45. Ballestero, *How High*, 182.

46. Carrier, *Man and Woman*, 35.

47. Wilson, "Religious Leaders"; Goldschmidt, "Class Denominationalism."

48. Wilson, "Religious Leaders," 253.

49. Synan, *Holiness-Pentecostal Movement*, 5–9.

50. Gregory, *American Exodus*, 200.

51. Quoted in Wilson, "Religious Leaders," 282.

52. Conrad Reibold, manager of the Firebaugh Government Camp, attested to Pentecostals' reluctance to participate in social activities. See Wilson, "Religious Leaders," 316.

53. Ibid., 289.

54. Ebel, "Reforming Faith," 533.

55. See Grant Wacker's chapter titled "Temperament" in *Heaven Below*, 18–34.

56. On the differentiation from worldliness, 1 John 2:15–17 and Titus 2:11–12 served as key texts and refrains.

57. Grant Wacker's chapter "Temperament" offers various examples as to how Pentecostals sought to "redeem the time" of the last days. See Wacker, *Heaven Below*, 18–34.

58. Wilson, "Religious Leaders," 263.

59. Gregory, *American Exodus*, 143–49.

60. Wilson, "Religious Leaders," 253.

61. Carrier, *Man and Woman*, 28–35.

62. Ibid., 74–80.

63. Ibid., 79.

64. Gregory, *American Exodus*, 143–54.

65. Will Casey quoted in Wilson, "Religious Leaders," 263.

66. Wilson, "Religious Leaders," 284.

67. Carrier, *Man and Woman*, 32.

68. Dawson, *25 Years*, 25, 17–20.

69. Gladine Newton, interview. Newton also noted the emotional hurt that hit the pastor's family with full force when his own son died of valley fever.

70. Wacker, *Heaven Below*, 27.

71. Ibid., 75; Marsden, *Fundamentalism*, 56–62.

72. Wilson, "Religious Leaders," 255–56.

73. Goldschmidt, *As You Sow*.

74. Unnamed interviewee quoted in Wilson, "Religious Leaders," 254–55; H. C. Lafferty quoted in Wilson, "Religious Leaders," 262. Interestingly here, Wilson, a researcher from an elite institution, invariably chose to render the phonetic spelling of Okie speech in a way similar to how researchers preserved the broken English of some Mexican fieldworkers. His rendition of the word "fer" in lieu of "for" shows ways that researchers highlighted a subject's broken English. It should be noted that authors across various genres commonly employed similar practices, especially for racialized groups. Whereas cowboy talk might have been imagined as normative in the imagined American West in a similar manner that Okie speech was in the Western South, when ethnic minorities spoke broken English or mispronounced words, it served as a marker of their otherness. Columns written by Okies in the migrant labor camps passed the eye of the editors even though they were written in broken Okie English with various misspellings.

75. Ibid., 254–55.

76. Cevil Pool quoted in Wilson, "Religious Leaders," 253.

77. Carrier, *Man and Woman*, 48.

78. GBFPC 75th Anniversary Video Presentation.

79. Carrier, *Man and Woman*, 59. Terry attested to the efficacy of debates for winning over Trinitarian converts. See Carrier, *Man and Woman*, 70.

80. Ibid., 60.

81. Wilson, "Religious Leaders," 283.

82. Sánchez-Walsh, *Pentecostals in America*.

83. Dawson, *25 Years*, 17–20.

84. Fudge, *Christianity*, 90. Fudge included an entire bibliographic index on ministers and movements "weak on the message."

85. Ibid., 176.

BIBLIOGRAPHY

Primary Sources

Ballestero, Carl. *How High My Mountain*. Bloomington, CA: Self-published, 1991.

Booth-Clibborn, William. "Germany." *Latter Rain Evangel* 3, no. 7 (April 1911): 14–15.

———. "A Preachers Testimony." *Meat in Due Season* 1, no. 9 (December 1915): 4.

Carrier, Steven, ed. *A Man and Woman Passed This Way Blessed of God: The Life of Isaac Hilliard (I. H.) Terry*. N.p.: Self-published, 1996.

Dawson, Rita. *25 Years in a Place Called Weedpatch*. N.p., n.d.

"GBFPC 75th Anniversary Video Presentation." Greater Bakersfield First Pentecostal Church. https://gbfpc.org/about-us/church-history.

Goldschmidt, Walter. *As You Sow*. Montclair, NJ: Allanheld, Osmun, 1947.
———. "Class Denominationalism in Rural California Churches." *American Journal of Sociology* 49, no. 4 (January 1944): 348–55.
Newton, Gladine. Interview by author, February 2014.
Northern California Baptist Annual Convention (1927).
Pentecostal Herald (February 1947).
Western District of the United Pentecostal Church. N.p.: Our Heritage, n.d.
Wilson, James Bright. "Religious Leaders, Institutions and Organizations Among Certain Agricultural Workers in the Central Valley of California." PhD diss., University of Southern California, 1944.

Secondary Sources

Anderson, Allan. *An Introduction to Pentecostalism*. Cambridge, UK: Cambridge University Press, 2004.
Dochuk, Darren. *From Bible Belt to Sunbelt: Plain Folk Religion, Grassroots Politics, and the Rise of Evangelical Conservatism*. New York: W. W. Norton Press, 2011.
Ebel, Jonathan. "In Every Cup of Bitterness, Sweetness: California Christianity in the Great Depression." *Church History* 80, no. 3 (2011): 590–99.
———. "Reforming Faith: John Steinbeck, the New Deal, and the Religion of the Wandering Oklahoman." *Journal of Religion* 94, no. 4 (October 2012): 527–35.
Ewart, Frank J. *Phenomenon of Pentecost: A History of the Latter Rain*. Houston, TX: Herald Publishing House, 1947.
French, Talmadge. *Early Interracial Oneness Pentecostalism: G. T. Haywood and the Pentecostal Assemblies of the World, 1901–1931*. Eugene, OR: Pickwick, 2014.
Fudge, Thomas. *Christianity Without a Cross: A History of Salvation in Oneness Pentecostalism*. Parkland, FL: Universal Publishers, 2003.
Gregory, James N. *American Exodus: The Dust Bowl Migration and Okie Culture in California*. New York: Oxford University Press, 1989.
Haney, Olive. *The Man of the Hills—Served in the Valley: The Biography of Clyde J. Haney*. N.p., 1985.
Harvey, Paul. *Redeeming the South: Religious Identities and Racial Identities Among Southern Baptists, 1865–1925*. Chapel Hill: University of North Carolina Press, 1997.
Haslam, Gerald. *The Other California*. Reno: University of Nevada Press, 1993.
Johnston, Robin. *Howard A. Goss: A Pentecostal Life*. Hazelwood, MO: Word Aflame Press Academic, 2010.
Marsden, George. *Fundamentalism and American Culture*. New York: Oxford University Press, 2006.
Price, Alyce. "The Zimmer Twins." In *Pioneer Pentecostal Women*, edited by Mary Wallace, 1:258–72. Hazelwood, MO: Word Aflame Press, 1981.
Sánchez-Walsh, Arlene. *Pentecostals in America*. New York: Columbia University Press, 2018.
Stein, Walter. *California and the Dust Bowl Migration*. Westport, CT: Greenwood Press, 1973.
Synan, Vinson. *The Holiness-Pentecostal Tradition: Charismatic Movements in the Twentieth Century*. Grand Rapids, MI: William B. Eerdmans, 1997.
Wacker, Grant. *Heaven Below: Early Pentecostals and American Culture*. Cambridge: Harvard University Press, 2001.
Yadon Dillon, Jewel. "Harry Morse." In *Profiles of Pentecostal Preachers*,

edited by Mary Wallace, 2: 289–300.
Hazelwood, MO: Word Aflame
Press, 1984.
———. "Ruth Angela Scott Yadon."
In *Pioneer Pentecostal Women*,
edited by Mary Wallace, 1: 243–57.
Hazelwood, MO: Word Aflame
Press, 1984.

CHAPTER 6

The Braziers

Three Generations of Apostolic Activism

Rosa M. Sailes

Historical and theological studies of Black Apostolic Pentecostalism have settled, until recently, for discussions of pioneering leaders like Garfield T. Haywood and Robert C. Lawson and have generally abandoned the story at the moment of racial fragmentation in Oneness Pentecostalism.[1] Anthropological studies have highlighted local and congregational dimensions to Apostolic life and culture.[2] While historian Wallace Best's study presents a discussion of Chicago's religious ecology, this study fleshes out an understanding of congregational leadership on the ground and offers a view of Apostolic social commitment and ministry.[3] The remarkable story of the Brazier family's holistic ministry in Chicago can be understood as a multigenerational legacy, framed at one end by Robert and Geneva Brazier during and after the Great Migration and at the other by the current ministry of Dr. Byron T. Brazier. The central figure, Bishop Arthur Monroe Brazier, pastored the Apostolic Church of God in Chicago's Woodlawn community for forty-eight years. A look back to his parents, Robert and Geneva Brazier, reveals much of the source of his character and drive. An overview of the ministry of his son, Dr. Byron T. Brazier, provides a glimpse of the family's continuing influence on the civic and religious life of Woodlawn and Chicago (see fig. 6.1).

Fig. 6.1. On June 15, 2008,
presidential candidate Barack
Obama delivered an admonitory
Fathers' Day speech at the
Apostolic Church of God in
Chicago. Bishop Arthur M. Brazier
and Dr. Byron T. Brazier usher him
into the sanctuary. Photo by David
Banks via Getty Images.

THE BEGINNING

Near the end of World War I, Robert Stengstacke Abbott's newspaper, the *Chicago Defender*, sparked a campaign that became known as the Great Migration. This Black-owned weekly encouraged southern African Americans to move north where they could "get the wrinkles out of their bellies and live like men."[4] By 1918, Chicago's Black population nearly tripled.[5] It was on the wave of the Great Migration that Robert Brazier came to Chicago.

Robert Brazier was born in 1873 in Mobile, Alabama, but little is known about his parents and early life. Robert married Geneva Scott Green, who was born in Montevallo, Alabama, in 1885. Geneva, whose father was a Baptist minister, was one of the younger children in her family of nine. Robert and Geneva wed with two children each from previous marriages. The family eventually moved to Birmingham, Alabama, where Robert found work in the coal mines. When a mining accident almost took his life, Robert promised God that if he was spared, he would never return to the mines. In 1917 the mines reopened, but Robert moved to Chicago.[6]

Like many other young men, Robert left his wife and family in Birmingham while he looked for work and housing in Chicago. Robert found work as a maintenance man at a laundry. Maintenance was one of four similar domestic occupations held by 45 percent of the Black men in Chicago. Geneva and the family joined Robert in 1920. Like 63 percent of Black women in Chicago, Geneva found work as a domestic, doing laundry in her home for white families.[7]

Despite Chicago's exploding population, Blacks, Jews, and other minority populations were forbidden from living in areas designated for whites. Whereas in the South, segregation was accomplished through de jure or legal structures, in Chicago and other northern cities, de facto policies that lacked lawful authority enforced racial isolation. Chicago's de facto segregation and restrictive housing covenants kept 78 percent of Chicago's Black population in the southside Black Belt.[8] Efforts to move beyond the Black Belt were often met with riots, beatings, and bombings by mobs of whites. Eventually a few white clergy and neighborhood newspapers called for a cessation to the violence that had precipitated situations like the Red Summer of 1919 with riots and lynchings across the United States. In Illinois, Red Summer race riots occurred in Springfield, East St. Louis, and Chicago. By 1921, there had been "58 racially-inspired bombings" in Chicago.[9]

Arthur Monroe Brazier was born in the Brazier's Black Belt apartment in 1921, when very few African Americans were admitted to hospitals.[10] When their building was demolished in a city scheme to make room for the privately developed Lake Meadows complex, the Braziers found a large, old house at 3168 South Ellis Avenue. This allowed family members coming from the South to stay with Geneva and Robert. Arthur Brazier vividly recalled the living arrangements: "We lived in a ten- or eleven-room house. My mother and father, my sister and her husband, and their three children, my aunt and her two children, a cousin, another couple whose names I have forgotten.... The eleven rooms were filled to capacity at all times. I can never remember coming into the house and finding it totally and completely empty."[11]

PASTOR GENEVA BRAZIER

The Great Migration had seen the growth of storefront and house churches among Holiness congregations. As migrants redefined worship spaces and styles, these structures became typical of the migration era. In 1920, there were twenty storefront Holiness churches in Chicago, and by 1938, storefronts made up 66 percent of the Holiness churches in the city. Geneva Brazier was converted in 1920 at the Merciful Church of Christ, a Oneness Pentecostal house church located at 30th and Dearborn Streets. The church was founded in 1915, but within two years, the prayer band that had organized the Merciful Church of Christ realized the need for a leader. They called Elder A. R. Schooler, a Pentecostal Assemblies of the World (PAW) minister who had already established a church in Ohio. Schooler split his time between Chicago and Cleveland, spending two Sundays a month at each.[12]

Geneva Brazier did not remain at the Merciful Church of Christ. In 1927, she became one of the charter members of the Universal Church of Christ located at 58 East 30th Street. Urban renewal forced the church to relocate to 3107 South Wentworth Avenue.[13] A doctrinal conflict with its pastor caused the congregation to ask Geneva to accept the pastorate of the thirty-member Apostolic Pentecostal storefront church located by then at 4107 South Michigan Avenue.[14]

Most female pastors headed missions or small churches. While several Pentecostal denominations restricted the ministry of women and denied the legitimacy of their work,[15] Geneva Brazier was a member of the PAW, which had always ordained women and allowed women to pastor.[16] While Geneva remained active in the PAW for the rest of her life, there is no evidence that she was officially ordained. The PAW issues several categories of licenses. Its national license essentially affords holders, male and female, permission to conduct marriages and funerals and pastor churches while withholding the ordination documents and rights.

Theologically, Geneva evidenced a strong adherence to Fundamentalism and Holiness, which were the foundations for her belief in the inerrancy of the Bible, the reality of the Virgin Birth, the certainty of the miracles of Jesus, and the faith in Jesus Christ's return. Her religious practices, traditions, and strength of faith were undergirded by Apostolic Pentecostalism.[17] While Geneva's theology was grounded in the strict doctrines of Oneness and Holiness, she was driven by her passion for helping people surrender their lives to God while acknowledging the struggle that decision could present. The Universal Church of Christ was known to accept all who wanted to be "saved" without judgment. In her own diocese, her church was sometimes referred to as a "garbage can church" because her congregation welcomed everyone despite their rejection from other churches for past behaviors or failure to live up to Apostolic standards. According to her son Arthur, Geneva Brazier did not turn people "away from church because of some human weaknesses they may have had, such as wearing earrings or smoking cigarettes. The church had no artificial walls; anybody could attend. She had strong convictions and tried her very best to help people who had what Pentecostals referred to as 'weaknesses' and 'carnality.'"[18]

While Robert Brazier is described by family as gentle and quiet, Geneva was seen as the disciplinarian and the person her family and older siblings looked to for guidance.[19] She was determined to keep her household and church operating despite the economic and social structures that inhibited the progress of African Americans. The Social Gospel of the early twentieth century was seen as a "religious movement that applied a liberal theology to a range of social reforms."[20] Its influence was evident in northern Black churches. In larger African American churches, social programs were often organized by educated Blacks as an extension of their professional work. In storefronts and house churches, pastors like Geneva Brazier addressed the emotional, physical, and economic hardships of recent migrants as their commitment to social justice.[21] Her generosity and ability to encourage others despite the obstacles they faced were grounded in her sense of religious responsibility. As her son Arthur recalled, "Very often some of the families that she worked for when they wanted to get rid of some of the clothes and shoes that they had; they would give (them) to her. She'd bring them home and would give some of it to some of us, but the vast majority would go to the poor families outside that she knew. And she was very, very concerned for the spiritual welfare of people, really wanted children to grow up in school, grow up in Sunday school, and spent a lot of time picking up kids and taking them to church."[22] Pastor Geneva Brazier led the Universal Church of Christ in Chicago from 1937 until her death in 1949. Like other churches established as part of the Great Migration, her church was subjected to the hardships of the Great Depression, racism, and poverty, yet Geneva steadied its course. By the time she died, she had built a small but well-established congregation. Its members navigated the struggle to identify a new pastor and set a course for the church's future. Geneva Brazier's life and pastoral work became the bridge to the ministry of her son, Arthur M. Brazier.

BISHOP ARTHUR M. BRAZIER

Growing Up Brazier

Like many children raised in urban ghettos, Arthur Brazier was unaware of the inequities impacting his life. He described how "There was no talk of racial conflict in my home. . . . My parents never expressed any bitterness or animosity toward white people at all. Consequently, I was not raised to harbor bitterness."[23] But Chicago's racist history was the fabric of his life.

> My earliest recollection of school [in the 1920s] was going a half a day. We either went from nine to twelve, or from one to four. I do not recall going to school full time until I got to the third grade at Stephen A. Douglass Elementary. I remember very clearly that the schools themselves were segregated. There were no white kids in the school at all. All the black kids west of Lake Park went to either Doolittle or Douglass, and of course, in those early days, I always wondered where the white kids went to school because they did not go to Douglass or Doolittle, which were in walking distance.[24]

While life for the average child in a PAW home was restrictive, Geneva Brazier circumvented denominational practices she felt were unnecessarily harsh. While the PAW denounced Christmas trees, saying the tradition was steeped in paganism, Geneva chose to decorate a Christmas couch instead.[25] She also refused to accept PAW restrictions against baseball or marbles as sinful activities, leaving Arthur to enjoy such games. Throughout his life Arthur Brazier was a voracious reader, an ability encouraged by his father, who read all of the daily papers with Arthur at his side.[26]

Despite being an avid reader since early childhood, Arthur Brazier disliked school and often got into trouble for talking. During the Great Depression, he left high school after one year, determined to work to help his family. In 1942, Arthur was drafted into a segregated United States Army. He served on the Burma and India fronts, where he learned the intensity of poverty and injustice in other parts of the world.[27] When he was stationed in South Carolina, he had several personal encounters with overt racism and segregation. In one situation, while in uniform, Arthur attempted to pick up a package at the local post office. He was angrily told by a postal worker to go to the colored entrance even though the package was visible from the window. When he complied with the demand, the package was cheerfully handed to him.[28] This and other experiences brought an added perspicuity about Chicago's restrictive covenants, unequal allocation of city services, and crowded conditions in the Black Belt. Upon his return from military service, Brazier became acutely conscious of how government funds were used to demolish slum property and acquire the land for corporations looking to use federal housing legislation for their own benefit while maintaining the most restrictive and confining conditions for

African Americans. While the Great Depression and World War II shaped
his worldview, Arthur Brazier's Holiness/Apostolic Pentecostal background
anchored his life. Several times he faced near-death situations, but he always
attributed his miraculous deliverances to God's grace and never wavered from
his understanding of the intervention of the Holy Spirit in human lives.[29]

After his military service, Chicago's nightlife became Arthur's major pas-
time. His mother's attempts to have him attend church were generally resisted.
He finally agreed to attend a church picnic. Since "unsaved" young men could
not court girls in the church, he declared that he was going there "to find a wife,"
thinking that would discourage his mother. Instead, he met Isabelle Holmes
and was immediately smitten. Arthur started attending services and reading his
Bible. While reading the Book of Revelation, Arthur asked his mother to pray
with him for conversion.[30] Arthur and Isabelle were married in February 1948.
Housing, however, was so difficult to find that families often rented rooms in
their homes. Whether she realized it or not, when she found the couple a large
room to rent in the home of Elder Ahart Medders, Geneva Brazier set events
in motion that led to her son's involvement in civil rights and his pastorate of
her church. Ahart Medders was the assistant pastor of the Apostolic Church
of God. Elder Walter Clemons, the church's founder, lived in the same building.
The two men provided early and key mentorship for the young Brazier.[31]

Chicago's restrictive covenants created deplorable living conditions as more
Blacks were forced into limited space within the Black Belt. Realtors and home-
owners associations threatened whites if they considered selling properties to
Black families. Once a property was sold, the entire block changed rapidly.
Woodlawn presented a new opportunity for ownership and tenancy for Black
families, but by the time neighborhoods were relinquished to Black families, the
buildings were deteriorating. Between 1940 and 1945, Woodlawn's population
changed from 80 percent white to 100 percent Black.[32] In 1948, the covenants
were struck down by the court; by the 1950s, Chicago's neighborhoods were
changing rapidly from white to Black. Despite "four civil rights bills, dozens of
court decisions, and thousands of brave words about Negro rights," the restrictive covenants persisted until 1966.[33] According to Bishop Brazier, "You couldn't
get a loan until the Supreme Court outlawed [restrictive covenants].... You
could never move out of the ghetto into a white neighborhood. If the ghetto
moved at all, it moved *en masse*. It moved block by block. [Realtors would] find
one white who would sell to a Black.... [W]ithin three months, every house
in the block had a 'for sale' sign on the lawn. It wasn't long before that block
was totally black."[34]

The Ministry and the Movement

In 1948, at the age of twenty-seven, Arthur Brazier recognized "the call" to preach. Nevertheless, he resisted the pull toward ministry, finally deciding to enroll in Moody Bible Institute. Even though the school denounced such Pentecostal practices as speaking in tongues, Brazier sought formal, systematic theological education.[35] His mother's death in 1949 meant a change in the leadership of the Universal Church of Christ. Elder Stephen Lucas succeeded Geneva Brazier as pastor but died only three years later. In 1952 Arthur Brazier became the pastor of the congregation his mother had led. In 1959, the storefront Universal Church of Christ was condemned by the city to make way for construction of the Dan Ryan Expressway. Brazier's small congregation began to share facilities with the Apostolic Church of God. While each church had its own schedule, the two groups often worshipped together in both services. In 1960, following the death of Elder Walter Clemons, founder and pastor of the Apostolic Church of God, and the resignation of Clemons's handpicked successor Elder Ahart Medders, Arthur Brazier was asked to become the pastor of the Apostolic Church of God. He agreed only if they could combine the congregations and retain the more well-known name. In May 1960, Arthur Brazier was installed as the pastor of the newly reconstituted Apostolic Church of God.[36] He was thirty-nine years old.

When he assumed his new pastoral duties, Brazier had already committed to community activism. Saul Alinsky, founder of the Industrial Areas Foundation, an organization that trained communities to fight injustice, worked with Brazier and a consortium of pastors and community leaders to develop what was then called the Temporary Woodlawn Organization (TWO) to address "dilapidated housing; unscrupulous merchants and landlords; overcrowded, segregated schools; [and] the expansion of the University of Chicago."[37] In 1959, Brazier became the official spokesperson (and later president) of TWO. "I felt that it was very important for ministers to become involved in the civil rights movement. I believe that God is interested and concerned about the whole person, not just the soul, but also the conditions under which people have to live, conditions that can mar or scar the soul, conditions that can destroy the person. These conditions do not make the mind a fertile ground for receiving the preaching of the gospel."[38] In July 1960, the University of Chicago announced its intent to enlarge its land ownership by developing a south campus in Woodlawn. Brazier's church lay directly in the path of the proposed expansion. The community vocalized its opposition to the expansion on the basis of the plan's failure to provide any benefit to the residents of Woodlawn while serving the interests of the city's power structure.[39]

TWO had begun its battle against the city's housing policies, but they soon decided to take on the issue of public-school segregation, realizing that the plight of schools as a civil rights issue could rally communities in the struggle for self-determination.[40] Brazier also had a personal desire to save the schools. His children were just entering school when the United States Supreme Court ruled in the 1954 *Brown v. Board of Education* case, which outlawed segregation. In May 1955, the *Brown II* decision by the Supreme Court demanded that schools be desegregated "with all deliberate speed." The violence that erupted in direct response to the *Brown* decision included the kidnapping and murder of fourteen-year-old Emmett Till as he visited relatives in Mississippi. Emmett Till lived on the west end of Woodlawn. His funeral service at the Roberts Temple Church of God in Christ galvanized Black America; among other effects, it steeled the resolve of Rosa Parks months later when she sparked the Montgomery Bus Boycott.

In April 1962, Edmund C. Berry and Arthur Brazier founded the Coordinating Committee of Community Organizations (CCCO), an alliance of Chicago's civil rights organizations, including the NAACP, the Urban League, Teachers for Integrated Schools, and the Woodlawn Organization.[41] This positioned the civil rights groups to take on Mayor Richard J. Daley and school superintendent Benjamin Willis, whom the *Chicago Defender* called the "Governor Wallace of Chicago standing in the doorway of an equal education for all Negro kids in the city."[42] Although the Black schools had twice as many students, the white schools had over three hundred unused classrooms that were not accessible to Black students. Furthermore, Black schools were on double and triple shifts. When double shift (half days) proved insufficient, Willis ordered classes to meet in auditoriums and cafeterias, a practice referred to by civil rights activists as "triple shift." When Chicago stopped its double-shift policy, Willis offered an alternative.[43] As Bishop Brazier explained:

> In order to have the kids get off the double and triple shifts, the schools entered into a program of building portable classrooms which was not anything new. When I went to Frances E. Willard [in the 1920s], they had portable classrooms, even then. But this . . . new thing was a ruse to keep black kids in the black community. . . . Schools in the black community started mushrooming almost everywhere. You had schools almost in two or three blocks of one another. The whole effort was to keep black kids in the

black community. . . . The Board of Education said they were not segregated. The kids just went to school in the district where that school was located.[44]

Left with few options, the civil rights groups took to the streets. The CCCO called a one-day boycott at Carnegie School in Woodlawn. Ninety percent of the students stayed home. After that, African American elementary and high school students across the city participated in boycotts and marches on City Hall. The *Chicago Sun-Times* reported that 224,770 students boycotted on October 23, 1963. On June 21, 1964, Dr. Martin Luther King Jr. came to Chicago and led a march of 10,000 people from Grant Park to City Hall in protest over the school situation. Benjamin Willis finally stepped down August 31, 1966.[45]

Dr. King and members of the Southern Christian Leadership Conference (SCLC) felt that the issue of fair housing would provide a better platform for national debate and litigation since de facto segregation was an issue in many of the large northern cities. As they had in the South, the leadership of SCLC wanted to use churches in Chicago as Action Centers where enthusiasm for the protests could be rallied. King, however, had not expected the loyalty of Blacks to Daley. Black pastors felt that hosting a rally or being an Action Center could lead to alienation from the mayor they had come to depend upon. Additionally, they feared for themselves, their families, and their churches more of the violence that King had already met in Chicago. While pastors across denominations refused to support the movement, Arthur Brazier was one of the few who invited Dr. King to preach at his church. King's presence encouraged members of the Apostolic Church of God, many of whom lived in Woodlawn, to engage even more in civil rights work. When King and other civil rights leaders met with Daley in August 1966, Arthur Brazier was there.[46] The fight for Chicago's streets and schools was attracting national civil rights leaders and organizations who would continue incursions toward justice.

Despite his involvement, Bishop Brazier sought to separate his civic work from his pastoral ministry and personal life. His commitment to nightly family dinners and activities remained firm. However, his involvement in the civil rights campaign made him the target of violent opposition. Byron Brazier recalled answering the telephone during those times: "I do remember very vividly when [my father] had bodyguards [when] I was about 16. It was dangerous. The white people would call the church. . . . They said, 'I'm gonna kill your pastor tonight.' So we got a lot of threats."[47]

There were also other struggles that took their toll on Bishop Brazier. TWO undertook the development of the Youth Demonstration Project to make positive change in Woodlawn, which was caught in the crossfire of two rival and violent gangs. The Project received more than $900,000 in a federal grant. Trainees were to receive a $25 per week stipend for participating in the training program. However, it was found that one gang had committed fraud and there were claims that one of the churches in the TWO network had become a haven for the gang. The ensuing IRS investigation and Senate hearings called Brazier and others to testify in Washington, DC. TWO and the accused church and pastor were exonerated as the charges were deemed unfounded.[48]

Bishop Brazier often spoke of his parents' disappointment in his decision to leave high school to work, but he made up for it. He completed his studies at Moody Bible Institute in 1960. He received his degree in 1961. Despite his graduation from Moody, Arthur Brazier was largely a self-taught man whose intellect led him to read the works of theologians, philosophers, and scientists. He also read and spoke French fluently and preached in France on several occasions. Nevertheless, his own experiences left him determined to educate youth. In 1996 Bishop Brazier admitted that he was "torn between creating a school in our own Christian tradition and supporting the existing public-school system." He determined that it was better to work with the public schools.[49] In 1969, his work with TWO led to the creation of a "tripartite collaborative" between TWO, the Chicago Board of Education, and the University of Chicago. The resultant but short-lived Woodlawn Experimental Schools District funded reading-readiness programs throughout Woodlawn but primarily targeted the curriculum and instructional plans of two schools in east Woodlawn: Hyde Park High School and Wadsworth Elementary School.[50] In 2008, he again partnered with the University of Chicago and the Chicago public schools to create the Woodlawn Children's Promise Zone. This initiative sought to connect all of the schools in Woodlawn with all stakeholders having a voice in every aspect of the educational program.[51]

In 1960, Bishop Brazier took to the pulpit of the Apostolic Church of God, which had fewer than one hundred members and was $50,000 in debt. When he retired in 2008, the Apostolic Church of God was debt-free, had a twelve-acre campus with four buildings, and twenty thousand members. Each year, the Apostolic Church of God gave thousands of dollars in scholarships to graduating seniors in the congregation as well as to the students of Hyde Park High School. He built the Arthur and Isabelle Brazier Youth and Family Center to provide programs for children of all ages. The Arthur and Isabelle Brazier Veteran's Resource Center attracted veterans from across Chicago and garnered international recognition for its work. He and his wife Isabelle also instituted a successful violin program at the church and replicated it to provide a string performance program in Woodlawn's Carnegie Elementary School. The church also supported national and international organizations such as the NAACP and Doctors without Borders, as well as missions' projects that provided food and medical help to children in Africa and India.

Bishop Brazier never stopped doing the work of social justice and civil rights. In 1970, he took a position with the Citizen's Crusade against Poverty before working for the Center for Community Change (CCC) where, as vice president of major projects, he provided technical assistance nationally to communities seeking to revitalize.[52] (The CCC was located in Washington, DC, but Brazier never missed Wednesday night Bible class or Sunday morning worship service at his church in Chicago.) In 1987, Bishop Brazier helped found the Woodlawn Preservation and Investment Corporation and fought for the removal of the elevated train tracks in order to attract housing and business investments in Woodlawn. It was a bitter community fight that lasted several years.[53] In the end, middle-income homes, apartments, and commercial spaces were built. Bishop Brazier also served on the Public Building Commission and the Chicago Housing Authority, both unpaid, voluntary positions. Until his death on October 22, 2010, he was an adviser to Mayor Richard M. Daley, the son of his 1960s nemesis.

Denominational Grit

Not surprisingly, Brazier faced a measure of opposition from elements within his own denomination that adamantly rejected the thought that Pentecostal ministers should involve themselves in the political and civic lives of the communities where they served and usually resided. Despite his plea, this predominantly African American organization refused to declare its support for the rights of Black people.[54]

Nevertheless, Arthur Brazier rose through the ranks of the PAW. In 1976, he became bishop of the Sixth Episcopal Diocese (Illinois). As the diocesan over eighty churches, Brazier focused on training pastors, organizing the diocese, and helping churches obtain economic stability by leveraging the financial power of the diocese to secure loans for building improvements. In 1977, Brazier was elected to the PAW Executive Board and eventually became chair of the powerful finance committee. He gained popularity among the clergy and lay membership based on his demonstration of integrity and wisdom as a senior statesman. Brazier publicly supported PAW policies even when he disagreed with organizational decisions and traditions. He believed that the Apostolic Church of God must "exercise whatever influence it may have in encouraging the P.A.W ... to explore new dimensions and directions.... [T]his does not mean that [large churches] should withdraw from the denominational alliance and relationship, but because of independent financial resources at its disposal, one should continue to help build other churches of like faith."[55] Like Geneva Brazier before him, Arthur Brazier embraced the PAW but did not fully accept its soteriological teaching. As Brazier put it, "In my earlier Christian experience, I heard about the doctrine of eternal security, but I didn't believe in it because it wasn't taught to us." However, as he began to "read not only the Holy Bible, but the masterful works of other men—both pro and con," he questioned the Arminian theology of the PAW, which "taught that once you were saved, you had to be very careful because you could commit some kind of sin and still end up in hell."[56]

Bishop Brazier developed a Calvinist theological perspective that differed from the PAW Arminian position. This led to a contentious denominational debate on Eternal Security; Bishop Brazier voiced the affirmative position. In the end, the PAW published a positional statement that offered five points designed to discount Eternal Security.[57] Bishop Brazier was disappointed but undaunted. He also made every effort to engage PAW leaders in respectful dialogue on the godhead and pressed the denomination on its exclusivist policy of permitting none but Oneness ministers to preach at PAW conventions. In the end, he found the hostility and personal attacks to be alarming and disconcerting.[58] Bishop Brazier withdrew his membership and his church from the PAW in 2007. The Apostolic Church of God remains an Apostolic Pentecostal congregation.

Arthur Brazier recognized the integral relationship between civil rights work and ministry as one of power to be used in accordance with biblical mandates for justice. He was clear about the civic responsibility of the church. "For the Church, which is the strongest, most honored organization in the black community, to close its eyes to the injustices that were being perpetrated on black people, in my mind is not consistent with the mission that God prescribed for the Church. I felt that working in the Movement to alleviate the evils of segregation and discrimination was just as important as preaching against personal evils. Social evils are just as much a sin as are personal evils."[59] In quintessential Pentecostal fashion, though, Bishop Arthur Monroe Brazier felt that his legacy would not be his work with economic and educational justice and fair housing. Instead, his legacy lies in the Apostolic Church of God's commitment to sharing the message of God's grace toward people.[60]

DR. BYRON T. BRAZIER

Byron Brazier is the second of Arthur and Isabelle Brazier's four children. A graduate of Chicago's public schools, Roosevelt University, and McCormick Theological Seminary (MTh, DMin), he joined the staff of the Apostolic Church of God in 1995 as general administrator after a career at IBM and other business and consulting ventures. For the next thirteen years, he brought his business and managerial expertise to the growing church complex. He became one of the assistant pastors before being elected pastor in 2008.[61]

By the time Byron Brazier was installed as pastor, very few of the congregants lived in the Black Belt or in Woodlawn. The post–civil rights expansion meant that church members lived across the city, suburbs, and neighboring states. While continuing his grandmother and father's salvation-centered vision, he understood that society had become more secular, individualistic, and materialistic. It was obvious to him that newer members needed to understand their spiritual identity as people of faith. He immediately focused on helping congregants develop personal character and vision consistent with their call to salvation and life as Christians in a changing world.[62]

One of Byron Brazier's first acts in response to community need was to develop the Arthur M. Brazier Foundation. Building on his father's concerns for education and economic empowerment as well as addressing the violence that still permeates Woodlawn, the Brazier Foundation has envisioned solutions that address the education, economic development, health and human services, and public safety needs of Woodlawn. The Brazier Foundation works to continue Bishop Brazier's "legacy of equality and empowerment" in the Black community.[63]

In 2010, Byron Brazier created the Network of Woodlawn (NOW), which partners with organizations such as the Urban League to "develop the vital infrastructure that creates a vibrant, thriving community that can sustain itself."[64] Since Chicago's identification as the future home of the Barack Obama Presidential Library, the Brazier Foundation has also established an initiative to educate community members about how to assess large-scale real estate and economic projects in their community. This second major initiative is called "1Woodlawn" and is designed to give Woodlawn residents a voice in the project.[65] Through these organizations, Dr. Brazier's leadership of the Apostolic Church of God continues his father's vision for Black self-determination and empowerment.

Concerned with the dwindling ability of African Americans to prepare for a drastically changing workforce, the Brazier Foundation created BSD (Building Self Determination) Industries, a social enterprise manufacturing company that provides training for residents in the area of robotic controls. BSD Industries began by creating the infrastructure to produce plastic cutlery but has expanded to include the production of cleaning products. Early in the training of BSD students, job offers were extended and company requests for the products grew. A specific aim of BSD is to produce enough revenue to support the schools of Woodlawn with a proposed $250,000 annually. BSD has received $3.5 million in grant funds, and Chicago State University is now giving college credit to those who enroll in the robotics classes. Part of the grant pays the tuition of Chicago Housing Authority residents. The Apostolic Church of God pays the tuition for church members who are accepted into the program.[66]

Just as Arthur Brazier mobilized members and residents for self-determination during the civil rights era, Byron Brazier has mobilized church members to address their own self-determined concerns. One of the newest programs of the Apostolic Church of God is "The Evangelism of Grace," which is "spiritual in nature but civic in execution."[67] It incorporates elements of Liberation Theology and extends the work of the church into communities across the city. The design allows members of the congregation to assume leadership in their neighborhoods (via zip codes) as they join with other church and community members to identify the most pressing needs in their areas. Since the church has staff who can assist with identifying resources, Evangelism of Grace groups can access the resources of the church to meet those needs that are unique or common across neighborhoods and families. Evangelism of Grace is aimed not at proselytizing but at challenging the oppressive and systemic issues that continue to beset the Black community. At the same time, these efforts help build relationships among neighborhood stakeholders and extend the arm of Grace, which is the focus of the church.[68]

CONCLUSION

Pastor Geneva Brazier ministered to the spiritual and natural needs of Black people in the throes of the segregated world of migration. Arthur Brazier's activism reflected his understanding of the power of God's grace to confront racism and economic injustice. Byron Brazier's understanding of the Holy Spirit undergirds his commitment to economic empowerment and social justice. Together the Braziers represent three generations of Apostolic Pentecostal pastors who took seriously the mandate of Matthew 25 to care for the hungry, the thirsty, the stranger, the prisoner, the sick, and all who need comfort through the power and guidance of the Holy Spirit.

NOTES

1. Goff, *Fields*; Wacker, *Heaven Below*; Jacobsen, *Reader*; Jacobsen, *Thinking*; Tyson, *Early Pentecostal Revival*.

2. Casselberry, *Labor*.

3. Best, *Passionately Human*.

4. Wycliff, "Founding the Chicago Defender," 84.

5. Rice, *Images of America*, 7.

6. Dortch, *When God Calls*, 8.

7. Spear, *Black Chicago*, 29.

8. Cohen and Taylor, *American Pharaoh*, 31.

9. Grossman, *Land of Hope*, 179; Spear, *Black Chicago*, 211.

10. Dortch, *When God Calls*, 7.

11. Crowe, "Bishop Arthur Brazier," tape 1, story 6.

12. Smith, *Apostolic Faith Church*, 16; Best, *Passionately Human*, 44.

13. Apostolic Church of God, *AMB: 25th Anniversary*, 21.

14. Dortch, *When God Calls*, 11.

15. Alexander, *Black Fire*, 24.

16. Sims, *Telling Our Story*, 12.

17. Spear, *Black Chicago*, 175.

18. Dortch, *When God Calls*, 9, 11; Best, *Passionately Human*, 60.

19. B. Brazier, Interview on Family History.

20. Evans, *Social Gospel*, 2.

21. Dortch, *When God Calls*, 10; Best, *Passionately Human*, 60, 72.

22. Crowe, "Bishop Arthur Brazier," tape 1, story 3.

23. Arthur Brazier quoted in Dortch, *When God Calls*, 8.

24. A. Brazier, Interview, 2002.

25. Dortch, *When God Calls*, 10.

26. Ibid., 19.

27. Ibid., 29.

28. Crowe, "Bishop Arthur Brazier," tape 3, story 1.

29. Dortch, *When God Calls*, 30.

30. Ibid.

31. E. I. Brazier, Interview.

32. Drake and Cayton, *Black Metropolis*, 187.

33. Spear, *Black Chicago*, 224.

34. A. Brazier, Interview, 2002.

35. Dortch, *When God Calls*, 32.

36. Apostolic Church of God, *Bishop Arthur Brazier*, 1.

37. Ibid., 5.

38. Apostolic Church of God, *AMB: 25th Anniversary*, 22.

39. A. Brazier, *Black Self-Determination*, 52.

40. Fish, *Black Power*, 48.

41. Cohen and Taylor, *American Pharaoh*, 285.

42. Ibid., 308.

43. A. Brazier, *Black Self-Determination*, 46–47; Crowe, "Bishop Arthur Brazier," tape 4, story 2.

44. A. Brazier, Interview, 2002.

45. Arthur M. Brazier Foundation, *Black History Month Video Series*.

46. A. Brazier, Interview, 2002.

47. B. Brazier, Interview: Son of a Civil Rights Leader, 1999.

48. A. Brazier, *Black Self-Determination*, 82–125.

49. Dortch, *When God Calls*, 102.

50. A. Brazier, *Black Self-Determination*, 66–67.

51. Chicago Community Trust, *Woodlawn's Children's Promise Community*.

52. Pentecost in Perspective, *Ministry Beyond the Gates*.

53. Apostolic Church of God, *Bishop Arthur Brazier*, 10–11.

54. A. Brazier, Interview, 2002; Pentecostal Assemblies of the World, *Organizational Manual*, section IV, section 18, 121–22. Until a 2018 revision, the annual PAW Minute books included its 1967 response to Bishop Brazier's request for a statement in defense of the civil rights movement, "Reaffirmation of the Position since 1919.... In Regard to Civil

Rights and Human Dignity." The statement ends with the declaration that "this
statement is not a result of the present
unrest in our society."

55. Apostolic Church of God, *Bishop
Arthur Brazier*, 18.

56. Dortch, *When God Calls*, 72.

57. Pentecostal Assemblies of the World,
2015 Organizational Manual, section IV,
section 18, 123–24.

58. Dortch, *When God Calls*, 97.

59. Apostolic Church of God, *AMB:
25th Anniversary*, 22.

60. Crowe, "Bishop Arthur Brazier," tape
5, story 4.

61. Apostolic Church of God, *About
Our Pastor*.

62. Ibid.

63. Arthur M. Brazier Foundation,
About Us.

64. Ibid.

65. Gousman, *Woodlawn's Renaissance*.

66. B. Brazier, Interview on Family
History, February 25, 2020.

67. L. Smith, Interview.

68. Apostolic Church of God, *Evangelism of Grace*; L. Smith, Interview, 2020.

BIBLIOGRAPHY

Primary Sources

Apostolic Church of God. *About Our Pas-
    tor: Dr. Byron T. Brazier*, Apostolic
    Church of God, 2020. https://www
    .acog-chicago.org/about/our-pastor.
———. *AMB: 25th Anniversary of Bishop
    Arthur Brazier*. Chicago: Apostolic
    Church of God, 1985.
———. *Bishop Arthur Brazier: A Man
    with a Vision, 35 Years*. Chicago:
    Apostolic Church of God, 1995.
———. *Evangelism of Grace*. Apostolic
    Church of God, 2020. https://www
    .acog-chicago.org/about/our-pastor.
Arthur M. Brazier Foundation. *About Us*.
    Arthur M. Brazier Foundation, 2013.
    https://www.brazierfoundation.org
    /about.
———. *Black History Month Video
    Series*—Tape 2. Arthur M. Bra-
    zier Foundation, 2013. http://
    brazierfoundation.org/legacy.
Brazier, Arthur. *Black Self-Determination:
    The Story of the Woodlawn Organiza-
    tion*. Grand Rapids, MI: William B.
    Eerdmans Publishing Company,
    1969.
———. Interview by Rosa Sailes, 2002.

Brazier, Byron. Interview on Family His-
    tory by Rosa Sailes, February 25, 2020.
———. Interview: Son of a Civil Rights
    Leader by Rosa Sailes, May 23, 1999.
Brazier, Esther Isabelle. Interview by Rosa
    Sailes, 2018.
Chicago Community Trust. *Woodlawn
    Children's Promise Community*.
    Chicago Community Trust, 2008.
    https://www.cct.org/what-we
    -offer/grants/woodlawn-childrens
    -promise-community.
Crowe, Larry. "Bishop Arthur Brazier."
    The History Makers, January 7, 2005.
    https://www.thehistorymakers.org
    /biography/bishop-arthur-brazier.
Gousman, C. "Woodlawn's Renaissance:
    Chicago Neighborhood Poised
    to Bloom in Time for the Obama
    Presidential Library." WGN-TV.com
    video, May 24, 2017. https://wgntv
    .com/news/cover-story/woodlawns
    -renaissance-chicago-neighborhood
    -poised-to-bloom-in-time-for-obama
    -presidential-center.
Pentecostal Assemblies of the World,
    Inc. *2015 Organizational Manual*.
    Indianapolis: Pentecostal Assemblies
    of the World, 2015.

Pentecost in Perspective. "Ministry Beyond the Gates." Pamphlet, n.p., n.d.

Sims, Jane. *Telling Our Story: A Brief History of Women in the Pentecostal Assemblies of the World.* Self-published, 2003.

Smith, Lanyaird. Interview on Evangelism of Grace by Rosa Sailes, January 16, 2020.

Smith, Susan Davenport. *Apostolic Faith Church: One Hundred Years, One Hundred Stories.* Chicago: Apostolic Faith Church, 2015.

Secondary Sources

Alexander, Estrelda Y. *Black Fire: 100 Years of African American Pentecostalism.* Downers Grove, IL: IVP Academic, 2011.

Best, Wallace D. *Passionately Human, No Less Divine: Religion and Culture in Black Chicago, 1915–1952.* Princeton: Princeton University Press, 2005.

Casselberry, Judith. *The Labor of Faith: Gender and Power in Black Apostolic Pentecostalism.* Durham: Duke University Press, 2017.

Cohen, Adam, and Elizabeth Taylor. *American Pharaoh: Mayor Richard J. Daley—His Battle for Chicago and the Nation.* Boston: Little, Brown and Company, 2000.

Dortch, Sammie M. *When God Calls: A Biography of Bishop Arthur M. Brazier.* Grand Rapids, MI: William B. Eerdmans, 1996.

Drake, St. Clair, and Horace R. Cayton. *Black Metropolis: A Study of Negro Life in a Northern City.* Chicago: University of Chicago Press, 1970.

Evans, Christopher H. *The Social Gospel in American Religion: A History.* New York: New York University Press, 2017.

Fish, John Hall. *Black Power White Control: The Struggle of the Woodlawn Organization in Chicago.* Princeton: Princeton University Press, 1973.

Goff, James R. *Fields White unto Harvest: Charles F. Parham and the Missionary Origins of Pentecostalism.* Fayetteville: University of Arkansas Press, 1988.

Grossman, James R. *Land of Hope.* Chicago: University of Chicago Press, 1989.

Jacobsen, Douglas G. *A Reader in Pentecostal Theology: Voices from the First Generation.* Bloomington: Indiana University Press, 2003.

———. *Thinking in the Spirit: Theologies of the Early Pentecostal Movement.* Bloomington: Indiana University Press, 2003.

Rice, Myiti Sengstacke. *Images of America: Chicago Defender.* Charleston: Arcadia Publishing, 2012.

Spear, Allan. *Black Chicago: The Making of a Negro Ghetto (1890–1920).* Chicago: University of Chicago Press, 1967.

Tyson, James. L. *The Early Pentecostal Revival: History of Twentieth-Century Pentecostals and the Pentecostal Assemblies of the World, 1901–1930.* Hazelwood, MO: Word Aflame Press, 1990.

Wacker, Grant. *Heaven Below: Early Pentecostal and American Culture.* Cambridge: Harvard University Press, 2003.

Wycliff, N. Don. "Founding the Chicago Defender." In *Chicago Days: 150 Defining Moments in the Life of a Great City*, edited by Stevenson Swanson, 84. Chicago: Chicago Tribune, 1997.

CHAPTER 7

Bossed and Bothered

Authority and Gender in the Pentecostal
Assemblies of the World

Dara Coleby Delgado

Since 1906, the Pentecostal Assemblies of the World (PAW) has provided
women a platform for leadership and ministry. As a predominantly Black
Pentecostal organization, this means that Black women have been recognized
preachers, teachers, missionaries, pastors, and auxiliary heads for generations.
Still, even as the organization provided leadership opportunities for *godly
women*, it also created near-impenetrable barriers to prevent women from doing
the unthinkable, namely, usurping authority over a man.

Using the PAW as a critical historical lens to examine race and gender
among Black Apostolic Pentecostals, the following will show that although the
PAW is a primitive Pentecostal community with progressive policies toward
women in ministry—recently solidified by the promotion of several women
to the bishopric—it is also challenged by a stubborn gender politic set on rei-
fying ecclesial authority as the prerogative of PAW men. Moreover, because
this challenge is often obscured by the organization's overarching gender and
sociopolitical demographics, the following will (re)vision the ministerial lib-
erties afforded to Black Apostolic women affiliated with the PAW beyond the
limitations of institutional pragmatism.

By (re)visioning PAW's Black women preachers and leaders as cosmological
disturbances capable of upsetting the patriarchal preference for the subordination of women, I assert that when Black Apostolic women religionists assume

positions of authority—whether behind the sacred desk or on the rostrum—they critically disrupt ecclesial hegemony and all concomitant attempts to keep them *bossed and bothered*.

UN/BOSSED AND UN/BOTHERED: BLACK WOMEN DARING TO BE THEMSELVES

In the foreword of the Fortieth Anniversary edition of Shirley Chisholm's autobiographical book, *Unbought and Unbossed*, political strategist and major news network contributor Donna Brazile recalled the words of Chisholm, the first Black woman elected to Congress and to seek the Democratic nomination for president. Chisholm: "I want history to remember me . . . as a black woman who lived in the 20th century and dared to be herself."[1] Proud to be both Black and a woman, Chisholm made it clear that whether in her politics or her personal life, she was nobody's pawn. While seeking the Democratic nomination, she ran as the people's president. Refusing to allow her race or gender to be essentializing, Chisholm's commitment to serving all American people was not a political gimmick. Instead it was a testament to her way of being, a way of being that was by all accounts fiercely and unapologetically unbought and unbossed.

"Unbought and unbossed," Chisholm's presidential campaign slogan–turned–book title, signified her tenacity to self-define and etch out new inroads into territories thought to be the sole prerogative of white America and/or Black men. Chisholm having to assert that she was both unbought and unbossed evinces America's long-standing and widespread proclivity toward dehumanizing Black women. As an act of resistance, Black women have had to make such assertions to halt, or even just slow, this country's insatiable commodification of their existence. In the hands of Black women living during the current era, trying to survive the multilayered terrain of classism, racism, and sexism, Chisholm's words take a new form. Over the last few years, young Black women have modified and culturally adapted Chisholm's former campaign slogan. As if tipping their proverbial hat to their foremother in the struggle, young Black women have chosen to define their experience in the United States as being "unbossed and unbothered."

Like the original, the contemporary slogan is a declarative statement. For many, it is shorthand for being so acutely focused on doing the work their souls must have[2]—activism, building community wealth, and dismantling oppressive systems—that they give little space or time for destructive people, politics, and powers set on either determining or destroying their Black lives. Moreover, like the original motto, the contemporary slogan names a particular reality while asserting hope. In other words, inherent to its message is a painful truth that every day Black women are bossed and bothered, and every day they are voluntarily and involuntarily forced to engage in efforts set on disassembling and disempowering hegemony.

The overarching idea is that Black women everywhere, no matter their lot in life, are given to the overall survival and the welfare of their community. And whether on Capitol Hill or in the Black Church, the community's survival depends on Black women's ability to make a way out of no way.[3] Black women in the Black Church, specifically, often found that entrepreneurship, innovation, and agentive activism paired with quotidian acts of empathy, gratitude, and righteous discontent was the difference between life-giving self-actualization (communal and individual) and soul-killing systematic oppression (communal and individual).[4]

With this reality in mind, recent works in twentieth-century Black religious studies have included examinations of major denominations through the vantage point of Black churchwomen.[5] During the late nineteenth and early twentieth centuries, women's departments were ubiquitous. The PAW boasted not one but two women's auxiliaries: the International Missionary and Women's Workers Auxiliary and the International Minister's Wives. Although each auxiliary maintained a distinct ministerial focus, together they, like their Black Baptist and Church of God in Christ counterparts, supported the broader organization in its effort to attend to everything from the parameters of acceptable womanhood to community outreach.

PAW women differed, however, because they were part of an organization that readily and openly ordained and recognized women as preachers and pastors. Ultimately, this means that PAW women have had a different relationship with religious patriarchy. The version of limited liberty doled out to them includes ministerial credentials served with a side of misogyny. In short, women can preach and pastor, but only within the predetermined constraints of womanhood defined by the PAW's male-dominated executive board. Prior to 2015, constraints included, but were not limited to, promotions within the organization, as women were refused positions that might put them in chief positions of authority over men, or make them equal to their male counterparts.[6]

Soon after its founding in 1906, the PAW became one of the more racially integrated Pentecostal denominations. However, time, doctrinal disputes, and the adoption of an episcopal polity that included a Black bishop made becoming a predominantly Black Pentecostal organization inevitable. Because of its racial make-up, racism proper was/is not a critical issue for ordained PAW women.[7] Unfortunately, that honor goes to sexism, leaving ordained PAW women to feel the soul-killing blows of what Black feminist scholar Audre Lorde called "the many varied tools of patriarchy."[8]

Lorde's statement, originally published in "An Open Letter to Mary Daly," addresses "how those tools are used by women without awareness against each other," and how they serve "the destructive forces of racism" and facilitate "separation between women." [9] Here, however, Lorde's words amplify the breadth and width of patriarchal oppression—namely, how the many varied tools of patriarchy constitute the inherent tensions of the PAW's gender politics. Thinking about the PAW's progressive patriarchalism as one of the many varied tools of patriarchy provides a useful theoretical framework to critically examine what it means for a faith community like the PAW to be so *double-minded in all its ways* about the woman question. Such that, on the one hand, it can see women as freely called by God but on the other, be so resolute in dominating women that it is willing to go to absurd lengths to bring to a full-on stop women trying to go beyond socially constructed ways of being.

Within the predominantly Black PAW, this means that while the Blackness of a woman's skin draws little feeling of ire, her feminine form does. In response to this, Black PAW men make it their business to ensure that liberated PAW women are never *too* liberated. To be bossed and bothered within the PAW means that women are free to grow and secure the successful future of the organization, but individual aspirations that can potentially make them forget their place and strive to become equal to men are an abomination.[10] From the earliest denominational reports, it is clear that PAW men felt that fully liberated women were abhorrent, especially married religious women who seemingly preferred the altar over the hearth. These women required explicit rules of conduct, so as to preserve the facade of respectability.[11]

Black women and men know better than anyone else that it is duplicitous at best to try to restrict Black women religionists on the pretense of respectability. Historically, Black women were not extended the right to claim the privileges of womanhood. Even more, as the proverbial mules of the world,[12] Black women have been neither feminine nor masculine. In fact, in the hierarchy of humanness, Black women fall dead last. The anti-Black misogyny, better known as misogynoir, suffered by Black women in the United States began with chattel slavery when Black women birthed and nursed babies while carrying out some of the same grueling tasks as men. The dehumanization and de/hypersexualization of the Black woman's personhood continued throughout the nadir of race relations in the United States. During this period of grotesque race-based cruelty, Black women were vulnerable to rape and sexual assault and were also beaten or lynched as were Black men. The terror precipitated in reaction to the civil rights movement impacted women as well as men. Images from the period show Black women being hosed down like rubbish in the street and assaulted with a brute force typically reserved for men.[13]

Given this history, it is fair to assert that any effort to prevent the full equity and inclusion of women in religious leadership on the pretense of respectability is little more than thinly veiled resentment toward the Black *feminine mystique*. That Black PAW men insisted on preserving gendered respectability politics is telling. Ultimately, it suggests the perceived fragility of their own claims to manhood and masculinity. Arguably, as a tool, respectability was a way to remedy their precarious state. It allowed them to tighten the strictures on Black womanhood and control whatever modicum of liberty Black women enjoyed. To their chagrin, even the most beloved *daughters of thunder*[14] in the PAW could not perform all of the rights and responsibilities of their calling without the impositions of bossy and bothersome men.

ANSWERING THE QUESTION: ARE WOMEN CALLED BY GOD TO PREACH?

The proliferation of opinions around the woman question has been no small matter among Apostolic Pentecostals.[15] Because the PAW answered in the affirmative, it also had to address chauvinistic inquiries about a woman's proper place. At the root of such queries—masked as regard for the safety, security, and stability of the (Black) family—were narrowed concerns about preserving an androcentric hierarchy. Unsurprisingly, PAW men who had not fully embraced women religionists pejoratively determined that a preaching woman was synonymous with a liberated woman and (rightly discerned) that a liberated woman was a woman who dared to be herself. Because *this* was unconscionable, for generations the PAW's all-male executive boards continued to actively delimit the institutional authority of women.

In 1920, during the PAW's annual General Assembly, the executive leadership team met to vote on previously submitted motions. The details of the annual meeting were included in the following issue of the denominational newsletter, the *Voice in the Wilderness*. Along with a general overview of what happened at the annual meeting, the newsletter included excerpts on how the board voted on ordinations, ministerial licensing, and missionary support. The details provided in the *Voice* were to preview the forthcoming and more formal "Advanced Report on the General Assembly." Still, it seems that it was important to Garfield T. Haywood, then an executive board member of the not yet racially splintered PAW and editor of the *Voice*, that decisions on these motions be made public.

Along with the above motions, the board also voted on whether to purchase property for an official headquarters. Haywood's coverage of that September business meeting gave significant attention to the property proposal. In many ways, the property—slated to provide "adequate and appropriate central offices for the proper conduct of [PAW] business"—represented a broader conversation around order and respectability. According to the *Voice in the Wilderness*, the PAW was working toward getting their "office matters on a good sound basis." The decision to purchase property, therefore, signified an intentional effort to update policies, streamline existing procedures, provide more structure for affiliate ministers, and to help the executive team keep "proper record of each minister holding papers in the future."[16]

Reading this report from Haywood's vantage point, one gets the sense that he was particularly anxious about allegations that the then fourteen-year-old PAW was planning to institutionalize. Reflecting an early Pentecostal affinity for anticreedal autonomy and revivalism, Haywood denied the claims and insisted, "We are not trying to build an institution, but endeavoring to build up the cause of Christ. The Name of Jesus must be upheld[,] and we expect to be upheld by it. We are going on in Jesus' name." However, he did offer a formal defense of the recent changes on behalf of the executive leadership: "Many seem to think that the Pentecostal Assemblies of the World have "organized" in order to get half-fare on railroads, but that is a mistake. The missionaries who go to the foreign field must be connected with some recognized body with a mission board back of them, and we have endeavored to meet the demand. They are going forth!"[17]

If property acquisition framed the conversation on order and respectability, and processes toward becoming a more formal organization furnished it, then it is no surprise that the woman question was the evaluative tool for whether the PAW was a communion of so-called proper race men and race women.[18] Before 1920 and its deliberate efforts to become a "recognized body," women had preaching rights. However, it seems that as PAW men grew in their concerns about their reputation, they also became disquieted about how PAW women's rights impacted their own, both in the church and at home. On these grounds, section 2 of the resolution adopted by the executive board during the General Assembly in September 1920 determined that "on the motion; the following resolution was adopted: That this Body go on record as not endorsing any woman leaving her husband and going out into the work of the ministry without her husband's consent; and any mother leaving her children and going out into the work of the Lord, in a capacity, without leaving her children in the hands of reliable persons who shall properly care for them. And at no time should her absence from her children be longer than thirty days at one time, except by consent of her husband—if she is married."[19]

Evincing their general unease with the possibility that women might disrupt gender norms in the home and ultimately usurp male authority, PAW men in 1920 established a gender politic that remained fixed well into the contemporary era. Following in the footsteps of their forefathers, later generations enacted similar patriarchal discursive practices. Typical tactics included: (1) relegating women to determinative physical spaces during the preaching moment to publicly reify their inferiority to male clergy, (2) affirming the legitimacy of women preacher-pastors while dredging up old and damaging doctrines on women and "original sin," and (3) preventing the elevation of women to the bishopric, despite years of work and service constitutive to the demands of the office.

In 1977, some fifty-seven years later, the late Bishop Morris E. Golder published *The Life and Work of Garfield Thomas Haywood (1880–1931)*. In the third chapter, Golder submits a small treatment on the "godly women" in the PAW. Because Golder's presentation focuses on a few members from Haywood's Apostolic Faith Assembly church in Indianapolis, it is neither an ambitious nor a comprehensive analysis. Nevertheless, Golder identifies the women selected for his text as being exemplary both in their love of God and in their service to the local church. For Golder, the universal fulcrum for discussing these women as "godly" was their commitment to consecrated living. Here, Golder discloses a very Pentecostal epistemological underpinning in his line of thinking and subsequent conclusions—specifically, that a life consecrated to God made "godly women" in the PAW competent and trustworthy, and therefore, fit to be evangelists, teachers, and church planters. For Golder, part and parcel to the fitness of these women, and by far their most praiseworthy attribute, was that they "knew their place in God and in no case, did one of them seek to 'usurp authority over a man.'"[20]

Centering "godly" womanhood on whether women refrain from usurping male authority unveils the patriarchal influences in Golder's gender ideology and a well-established gender politic within the PAW; specifically, one in which some leaders circled their wagons to safeguard the male prerogative and prevent women from traversing beyond their designated sphere of influence. Even when pastors complied with the PAW's position on the woman question and allowed them to preach in their churches, they developed passive-aggressive techniques to prohibit their full equity and inclusion. For example, on more than a few occasions, Golder notes that these so-called *godly men*, "[who] did not look favorably toward having women in their pulpits," forced women to minister "to the saints standing down on the floor." In his account, Golder is so preoccupied with celebrating the women for "following custom" and "knowing their place" that he failed to question the practice as contrary to the Spirit of Christ.[21]

Although Golder's treatment raises essential questions about women at the altar, as a whole his project relegates them to the background almost entirely. By producing more of a hagiography than history, Golder's presentation on PAW women misses significant opportunities to critically engage not only the contribution of women to the denomination's history but also the denomination's contribution to women's religious history. More importantly, he does not consider how the PAW as a primitive community with progressive ideological tendencies was stifled by its proclivity toward patriarchalism. Ironically, the same year that Golder offered his "history" of PAW women, the PAW boasted nearly 180 women pastors, an impressive number that did not quell the organization's internal struggles with sexism.

Despite its ongoing efforts to negotiate the fault lines of gender equality within its own ranks, in 1977 the PAW showed a fascinating interest in how other denominations and religious traditions were tackling the woman question. In the "National H-O-T Newsline" section of the *Christian Outlook*, the PAW's official organ, a nameless contributor shared a national story on the Episcopal Church titled, "Are Women an Obstacle?" The short write-up summarizes a report on the presiding bishop of the Episcopal Church who believed "'that God's Spirit is moving in efforts to reunite,' and that Catholics and Anglicans may establish intercommunion 'within our lifetime.'" It goes on to say that besides a host of other differences, the Episcopal bishop felt that women priests were "a 'real obstacle' to this eventual reunion."[22] The timeliness of the report coincides with the ordination of Jean Means, the first woman formally ordained an Episcopal priest.

In a similar article published in August, another unnamed contributor to the "National H-O-T Newsline" included a piece titled "Orthodoxy and Women." The contributor reports, "For the first time, the women's liberation movement has been discussed formally by the Rabbinical Council of America." The brief write-up provides few details. Still, the report does note that at the annual meeting a speaker, presumably the plenary speaker, proposed that Orthodox Judaism include women on the all-male board of directors of synagogues, nonprofit institutes, and policy-making positions in education "from which they have traditionally been excluded." [23]

The final write-up of this kind appeared in November 1977. In this short treatment featuring Cliff Baptist Church in Dallas, Texas, the contributor reported that the church voted not only to accept women deacons but also to ordain women to the ministry. Although this was good news for the women of Cliff Baptist, the decision generated no small controversy. According to the report, upon hearing the news "across town, the pastor of the denomination's larges[t] congregation in that city, Rev. W. A. Criswell, said that his church would 'never ordain women.'"[24]

Undoubtedly, 1977 was a year of notable "firsts" that helped bolster the women's rights movement.[25] Given that the *Christian Outlook* from years prior did not include such opinion pieces on women religious leaders in the United States, it seems that the PAW via the *Christian Outlook* was taking a new and different interest in women and the church. As such, it is arguable that between the growing number of PAW women pastors and its sizable and influential women's auxiliaries, the organization was looking to something outside of itself to (1) measure the import of this "trend" and (2) quell internal rumblings about women's liberation. In later editions neither the H-O-T Newsline section nor the interest in the ordination of women appear ever again. The closest the PAW comes, at least via the *Christian Outlook*, is a two-part series published in March and April 1983 titled "Are Women Preachers Called of God?"

At the time of the publication, the author, Bishop Earl Parchia, was the auxiliary bishop of the then Missionary and Women Workers Auxiliary. Seemingly on his own volition and not on behalf of either the presiding bishop or the executive board, Parchia claims the two-part series was "especially prepared" for PAW women.[26] Part 1 of "Are Women Preachers Called of God?" is overtly collegial and supportive of "the elimination of sex discrimination." Here, Parchia asserts that in the economy of salvation everyone is given liberty under grace, and that God's redemptive plan has always included women. For this reason, Parchia rhetorically asks, "How can you forbid the woman to tell the very story that she is an integral part of?" Closing with the biblical exhortation, "'Where the Spirit of the Lord is, there is liberty,'" Parchia is emphatic that women are free in Christ to minister, and "to serve under God as the Lord sees fit."[27]

Throughout, however, Parchia peppers this essay of endorsement with some puzzling ideas and phrases. For one, he opens with the parenthetical statement,

"God's second choice" but does not explicate. Then, his position on women in God's redemptive plan is qualified by his treatment of them as mere "portals" of both sin and salvation. He writes, "without [the woman] there would be no sin, and neither would there be Salvation. The whole story of the Gospel is centered around the woman. Jesus was born of a woman, of course, not born of a man. Gen. 3:15."[28] This is a unique position, seeing as how before this conclusion, Parchia submitted that "the flesh (male and female) profit nothing."[29]

In part 2, he continues his project, though this time with subheadings to organize his main ideas. The first, "The Various Social Orders of Men," includes a brief comment on the physical separation of men and women in the Bible during times of worship, which Parchia bridges to a traditionalist exposition on gender heteronormativity, all of which qualifies his previous position on gender equality and the elimination of sex discrimination. He writes, "I wish to make it abundantly clear that our spiritual order and total equality in worship and in service to God does not set aside God's natural order nor the natural function of the woman as a wife in submission to her husband, childbearing and guiding her house. A woman may be a Pastor of a church in which her husband worships; at church, she is his spiritual leader, but in all natural matters regarding their relationship as husband and wife, she should submit to him. This is God's order for the natural family."[30]

The second heading, "Veils," includes both a brief historical treatment on why women in scripture wore veils and an interpretation of Pauline household codes vis-à-vis "the natural order of God and the Human family." According to Parchia, even though modern women affiliated with the PAW do not wear veils as a sign of modesty or to honor their husbands, how they dress still matters. Moving away from Paul's main point about women preaching and prophesying with heads uncovered, Parchia chides any woman who wears a "low cut dress so as to expose her breast and, or a dress so short so as to reveal her thighs." For Parchia this is a matter of great import because such women threaten to dishonor their husbands *and* their "God as well" (a peculiar ordering in a treatment about God-ordained hierarchy). Ultimately, he wants to stress that although women are liberated to preach and pastor like men, they are not liberated *from* men. For this reason, there must be "a traditional restriction" to ensure that women remain within the predetermined boundaries of the natural order.[31]

Parchia's final discussion, titled "Customs and Tradition of Men," concludes his work and admonishes women against even the inclination of using their "sex to impress God" or men.[32] Without so much as a clear explanation, he swiftly returns to his earlier point on the centrality of women in the economy of salvation. As if citing his work in part 1, Parchia writes, "Is it reasonable to indict the woman for the sin that fell upon the whole family without also recognizing that through the woman came salvation also?" Once again, however, Parchia fails to expound on his point. Instead, he randomly lists the names of women preachers in the Bible and encourages contemporary preaching women to "consider" them.[33] In the end, Parchia closes with one final thought: "If you want to know the will of God, you'd better not reject His spokesman regardless of race, class or sex."[34]

Although there is so much that needs to be said about Parchia's think-piece within the theoretical frameworks of Black feminism and womanism, suffice it to say that his ambivalence toward women as *people*, theological conclusions on the economy of salvation, and position on the woman question are consistent with the PAW's distinct brand of progressive patriarchalism. Haywood, Golder, and Parchia reveal the organization's propensity to promulgate and normalize disparate messages. These accounts show that male leaders were incapable of imagining a world where the societal thrust did not cater to their fulfillment or prerogative. Moreover, while they recognized the Spirit as having made itself available to women to exist as God's empowered prophetic daughters, they could not see how the self-same Spirit made women their equals. The unwillingness to see women as equals made it easy to dismiss as silly girlish ambition serious requests to pair prophetic ministry with priestly authority.

Within the PAW, priestly authority, or better the chief seats of institutional authority, are the prerogative of the bishopric. The patriarchy's propensity to liberate and limit, free and constrain, prevented PAW women from being elevated to the office of bishop, bearing all of the rights and responsibilities of a diocesan without qualification or prejudice. Sadly, qualification and prejudice are all ordained PAW women have ever known. "Women evangelists shall be permitted to officiate at a marriage ceremony, funeral service, baptismal service, and the Lord's Supper, in case of emergency. All credentials given to women in this body shall be written to read 'Missionary' or 'Evangelist' or said title in authority shall be designated by the general assembly. Ordination: That women applying for ordination must give cause for ordination (either) whether giving all time to evangelistic work or pastoring a commendable work. That the commendability of her work be decided by the bishop of the diocese and the district elder."[35]

In the subsequent decades very little changed within the PAW. Ordained women and men maintained the status quo, with minimal interruption over the woman question pertaining to the bishopric. In 2015, that changed when the

PAW ordained Aletha J. Cushinberry as its first female bishop. The solemnity of the occasion bowed to the hard truth that this was long overdue, and that it happened on the backs of women for whom ordination meant subjecting themselves to humiliating forms of gender bias and cruelty.

PAW—A TIME FOR CHANGE: ELEVATING WOMEN TO THE BISHOPRIC

The PAW is not oblivious to its history of gender inequality. Although it has not issued a formal addendum to previous statements on "natural order" and gender hierarchy, in 2008 it began to address its sins of sexism related to women in ministry. That year, the PAW appointed an Apostolic Manifesto Critical Issues Committee to address the matter of elevating women to the bishopric within the organization.

Choosing to form such a committee indicated that, as an organization, the PAW was ready to prioritize this aspect of the woman question. In doing so, it hoped to course correct past efforts that also began the process but left the matter unresolved. Within the guidelines of their assignment, the committee purposed to work on settling the question of whether to elevate women "in the PAW, Inc. without any more legislative delays and tablings, and vote the matter up or down in 2009." The committee's overall goal was "[to recommend] action from the Executive Board of the PAW, Inc., to promote women into the bishopric as early as [the] summer's convention in Atlanta, in 2009."[36]

To achieve this goal, the committee agreed to meet six times. During these meetings, they planned to debrief eight corresponding tasks, some of which included examining (1) the PAW's history of women leaders, (2) the PAW bylaws and constitution on gender and the bishopric, (3) the amendment ratification processes for changing said bylaws and constitution in favor of elevating women to the bishopric, (4) Pauline theology in 1 Corinthians 14:33–35, 1 Timothy 2:9–15, and 1 Timothy 3:1–7, and gender roles and pronouns in both Greco-Roman culture and modern culture, and (5) the elevation of women in other denominations.

The directive to perform a comparative study on other denominations is particularly interesting. Assigned to Suffragan Bishop Ruben Graham, the task was to submit "an in-depth study on other denominations who promote women into the bishopric." According to the manifesto, Graham's findings were to include insight about impact—for example, (1) how denominations fared after elevating women to the bishopric, (2) how faith communities respond, and (3) what measures toward damage control they took to prevent schism. Furthermore, Graham was to determine whether said denominations experienced growth and revitalization as a direct result of consecrating women bishops.

It is important to note that the proposal does not indicate whether the comparative study was inclusive of all of the Christian traditions (sacramental, sanctified, and mainline Protestant) or restricted to denominations within the sanctified tradition.[37] In 2008–9, had Graham delimited his research to denominations affiliated with the sanctified tradition, his findings would have been minimal at best, as many of the PAW's most noteworthy peers were "still struggling to have a national conversation."[38] Whatever the prescribed stipulations, it appears that Graham went beyond Holiness-Pentecostal denominations to draw data from the entire Christian tradition.

Motivated by the reality that women, especially Black women, in the contemporary era are "being promoted to the ranks of CEOs and COOs of Fortune 500 companies and women are serving as prominent and powerful political leaders in nations around the world," the committee determined that it was time for the church to boast similar claims. Beyond the biblical mandate that *both sons and daughters shall prophesy,* the committee determined that the PAW's stability and future depended on qualified women leaders. On January 1, 2009, they completed their proposal and submitted it to Dr. Horace E. Smith, the presiding bishop. On January 22 in Detroit, the document, officially titled, "Securing Our Future: An Apostolic Manifesto on the Issue of WOMEN IN MINISTRY: Elevation of Women to the Senior Ranks of the PAW, Inc.," went before the Executive Board Committee (EBC) and was formally adopted.[39]

From the executive summary of the proposal, it is clear that the committee recognized the seriousness of its assignment and the long-term impact of this "most controversial" work. The final vote included not only institutional consequences but spiritual consequences as well, as their decision would ultimately "shape the way [the PAW] read and interpret[ed] scripture" going forward.[40] Potential challenges to biblical interpretation aside, the manifesto affixed itself to the PAW's Pentecostal fundamentalist identity and employed scripture as its primary weapon in defense of gender equality.

Beginning with the book of Genesis, the committee made its case for gender equality by arguing from a qualified egalitarian position defined by a theological definition of purpose. In sum, the committee asserted that God created two genders, male and female, and called them both "man," as a testament of their being "a complete picture of God Himself." The committee added that because of this, the distinctive qualities that make men and women who they are should not be "a source of discord or inequality, but a beautiful complement to each other," fitting them for the shared "task of *overseeing* and ruling His creation."[41]

Essential to this reading of Genesis 1–3 was an understanding that God commanded men and women to share not only in the workload but the rights and responsibilities of equal authority as well. According to the committee, the fact that this has not been the case is the result of (original) sin. Here, the committee asserts, and in no uncertain terms, that patriarchalism is part of the curse that distorted human relationships and negatively impacted all of created order. Defining the solution in quintessential evangelical terms, they affirmed Christ's redemptive work as the only means for restoring the original Edenic model, wherein men and women are equal colaborers in the body and Christ is the head.[42] Having established Christ as the head of all those born of the Spirit, the committee advanced to the New Testament to employ Paul's letter to the church at Galatia. Citing Galatians 3:28, they contended that everyone in the Kingdom of God is a new creature and that within the Kingdom, there is "neither male nor female." The message to the executive board was deferential but clear: from the biblical perspective, God's will is that men and women are both to rule and have dominion without unjust distinctions in authority between the genders.[43]

Along with scripture, the committee appealed to history, beginning with women leaders in the New Testament and progressing to the 1906 Azusa Street Revival. In addition to scripture and history, the committee reflected theologically on the woman question. Although the executive summary offers a comparatively thin account of the committee's theological argument, it does put on record their overarching claim: "Scripture cannot be interpreted by traditional or personal prejudices. While it is important to depend upon the Holy Spirit, one must also consider the accurate translation of words, dates, and circumstances under which the passage was written." Consequently, the committee placed before the executive board a challenge to disregard those who opposed women leaders and sought "to undermine authority [instead of] undergird[ing] the truth."[44]

The executive summary also offers a keen sense of the PAW's response to the Apostolic Manifesto Critical Issues Committee's recommendation to elevate women to the bishopric:

> The initial presentation of the Apostolic Manifesto stirred the hearts of many constituents across rank and status. Such a response indicates a corporate passion for right and meaningful change in the PAW in order to

secure the future of this great organization. Continuing to operate with outdated internal infrastructures and programs induces corporate "atrophy" and flies in the face of the constituents' response and concern. Based on the research conducted by this committee, we believe that continuing the tradition of full support and participation of women, as begun in the PAW in 1906, gives credence to right and meaningful change, and justifies any discussion to promote women into ecclesiastical positions beyond the ranks of Lay Leader and District Elder. Furthermore, it must be noted that several religious organizations have successfully accomplished elevating women to the Bishopric to the betterment of their organizations.[45]

In the end, the executive board adopted the manifesto and began the long arduous process toward transition:

We must recognize the time for change. There are some within the PAW who, believing that only men are qualified to lead, will choose to defend the traditional position of restricting women from ecclesiastical leadership in the church. Those who choose to defend this traditional practice must recognize that such a position is stagnant and closed to the move of God within our ranks. In the spirit of healthy debate, it must be recognized that everyone may not be pleased with a position of change; however, we can and we must have reasoned discussion from the basis of truth. The truth is that the governing documents of the PAW are both legally open to and have no restrictions against the elevation of women to the Bishopric.[46]

Recognizing the potential for schism, the leaders concluded that it "must not fail to act or decide based on fear ... and elevating women to the bishopric is the right thing."[47]

The board's decision to support the Critical Issues Committee's proposal to elevate women to the bishopric came six years after it decided to appoint women to the rank of district elder. Although many thought that the 2003 decision would lead to women bishops, the proverbial stained-glass ceiling of the PAW remained stubbornly fixed. Even worse, the stained-glass ceiling that denied "access to women into the ranks of the Bishopric" remained fixed after the manifesto was adopted, and the EBC resolved to take action. It was not until August 2017, some eight years later, that the first two women were ordained diocesan bishops in the PAW.[48]

Fig. 7.1. On August 4, 2017, at the PAW annual convention, Mona Reide (second from left) and Gwendolyn Weeks (third from left) assumed their roles as the first female bishops in the PAW. Photo courtesy of the Pentecostal Assemblies of the World.

PAW—WOMAN AT/ON THE ALTAR: CHANGING THE IMAGE OF GOD

"Never has a woman led one of the Pentecostal Assemblies of the World's more than 60 dioceses, but that's about to change,"[49] was the first line in the story covered by the *Tennessean* about the two soon-to-be women bishops, Mona Reide and Gwendolyn Weeks (see fig. 7.1). The highly anticipated moment, birthed some eight years prior, had finally arrived. For the first time in PAW history, women were going to be elevated to the office of diocesan bishop with the full rights and responsibilities of the position.

Although the initial decision approving the installation of women to the bishopric came about under Horace Smith's term as presiding bishop, his successor, Bishop Charles H. Ellis III, oversaw the services. In an interview with the *Tennessean*, just one month before, Ellis echoed the sentiments of the manifesto adopted nearly a decade earlier: "I think it again continues to move us in the direction that we feel our organization should be moving in." [50] Confirming that Reide and Weeks were going to "be the first [women bishops] with dioceses," having charges in West (the Republic of Sierra Leone) and South (the Eastern Cape)

Africa, Ellis confirmed the religio-social significance of this historic moment when he said, "That means that they will actually oversee and they will govern male pastors."[51] If ever there was a shot heard around the Black sanctified world, that was it. *The PAW, a historically male-led and dominated Pentecostal organization, planned to put "godly women" in chief positions of authority over men.*

Interestingly, while the PAW was celebrating a historic step forward, one of the candidates appeared eager to take a step backward to somewhere between 1920 and 1983. During her interview with the *Tennessean* Reide said, "I clearly understand that in a home, God has established differences. . . . But in the work of God, it is an opportunity for men and women to see that gender does not determine God's call on your life or the type of call that God places on your life."[52] Reide's comment was little more than a positive spin on the patriarchally defined gender politics instantiated by Haywood's generation and reified by Golder's and Parchia's. Consequently, Riede's comment cuts two ways.

First, it reinforces the same gender politics that kept women like her and Weeks from ever imagining that such a day would come. Second, the comment normalizes a particularly damning religio-cultural binary that essentializes gender and bifurcates feminine identities and ways of being. Based on Reide's words, the logical conclusion is that gender equality matters, but *only* in the pulpit. In other words, when the "work of the Lord" ends and the anointing lifts, like Cinderella when the clock strikes twelve, women are to step back into their place to preserve the natural order of androcentric gender hierarchy. Reide's words attest to the unforgiving tensions between the altar and hearth that women leaders *have to* maintain if they are going to preach and pastor. Having to maintain the tension between altar and hearth is rightly understood as another one of the many varied tools of the patriarchy. Its insidious goal is to preserve the male prerogative by trying to divide a woman against herself so as to force her to abdicate her power and silence her voice.

Nevertheless, the altar and all of its concomitant parts—for example, intonation, posturing, and sartorial choice/vestments—remains a critical site of liberation. When a woman ascends the altar, she is free to transverse its breadth and width. Moreover, when a woman ascends the altar, she finds a distinct performative space of play that gives license to a transgressive liminality that is exclusive to the ministerial moment. Before the PAW decided to do what was right and elevate women to the bishopric, women stood at the altar week after week and subverted natural order and redefined the boundaries of gender hierarchy. These women, in a kaleidoscopic display of brilliance and defiance, hollered and whooped, twisted and turned, contracted and extended as acts of liberation and resistance. Unquestionably, theirs was the most profound cosmological disturbance.

Finding freedom at the altar, therefore, means that women leaders have a place/space where they can escape, in plain sight, the patriarchal gaze. At the altar, enveloped in the euphoria of their call, PAW women dare to be themselves. More importantly, they dare to alter the image of God by changing the predominant sex at the altar.[53] The connection that the theological imagination has drawn between patriarchal claims about the maleness of God and the socially constructed masculinity of proper churchmen is a critical part of why Black churches struggle with the woman question and wrestle with whether there should be a woman at the altar. Yet, as other denominations struggle with whether a woman should be *at* the altar, the PAW struggles with whether to allow women *on* the altar. Integral to this particular struggle of whether women ought to stand *in persona Christi*, is the question of what it means when a Black woman sits in the chief seat of institutional authority.

Unquestionably, when men and women ascend the altar as mediators of grace, they participate in its inherent sanctifying power and authority. The preaching moment aside, the altar is a symbol of authority not only because it houses the pulpit but also because, often, it is where the clergy sits. Seated *on* the altar, elevated above the people in the pews, the message to the congregation is clear: *These* are your leaders; *these* are the people in charge. Before 2015, when the PAW consecrated Aletha Cushinberry as the first female bishop, all of the senior seats on the altar were unabashedly filled by men. Since her consecration, the episcopacy is still predominantly male. Sadly, progress toward full equality has been slow and unimpressive. Why is this the case? Or, as Wallace Best asked, "What is threatened by a [B]lack woman in the position of church leadership?"[54]

While a perfectly acceptable response to this inquiry might be that "women in [chief positions of] church leadership challenge religious convention and American culture,"[55] something more needs to be said, especially when the female subject in question is a Black woman. Stating emphatically that a Black Pentecostal woman on the altar is one of the most threatening illustrations of a cosmological disturbance, arguably, is a good start. Such a claim recognizes that the lived experience of Black women by virtue of being, disrupts the status quo. As prophets without honor everywhere they go, the altar, as intimated above, reclaims Black women in an extraordinary way. Graciously, the altar extends to them its liberation, authority, and power and elevates them and their peculiar performative discourse. The altar therefore becomes a space for their marginalized bodies to provoke a new theology[56]—one that goes beyond the rigidity of propositional faith or the subjectivism of experiential faith. By invoking an authority *given to them from above*, Black women, through their Black female bodies, simultaneously preach justice and indict their offenders.

So again, what is threatened by placing Black women in the position of church leadership? The short answer is male dominance. The long answer is the dissolution of the unjust quid pro quo established by progressive patriarchalism. Within the PAW, this arrangement allows for the Black female body to figuratively provoke a new justice-oriented theology, but it does not allow that same body to carry out that message with executive decision-making powers absolutely. Black women in leadership, therefore, threaten to shift and ultimately dismantle the centrality of power in male headship, in favor of greater democratization of the work and antisexism at/on the altar.

CONCLUSION: A FINAL WORD AND THEOLOGICAL REFLECTION

The cosmological disturbance caused by Black female bodies both at and on the altar is a divine interruption. Since 1906 Pentecostal women in the PAW have upended the preferential option for the status quo that disregards men and women as cocreated equals in the image and likeness of God. Consequently, they have reprioritized the inviolable importance of recognizing God with us, *through us*. Here, intimation to incarnation emphasizes the with-*ness* of God's presence being represented in and through all—whomever God chooses, and whomever God wills. In representing God on Earth in a way that reveals the real and living Jesus who is both in full solidarity with and intimately touched by the *pathos* of the human condition, mediators of the divine-human encounter must reflect even in their bodies the differences and pluralities that make up humanity. Ergo, this cosmological disturbance, via a social and theological interruption, unsettles prescribed gender norms by (re)visioning women beyond the constraints of the patriarchy altogether.

Undoubtedly, anchoring attempts to (re)vision Black women at/on the altar in the metaphysical framework of cosmological disturbance exposes deep theo-political assumptions about divine representation. Within Apostolic Pentecostalism, in particular, this is no small issue, especially given its adherence to a form of Modalistic Monarchianism that rejects Trinitarianism and (re)visions the Triune God as both radically one and fully revealed in the historically male Jesus. Critically, it is a doctrine that *proves* that God is male. Such a hard-line masculinist view of God is part and parcel of an ideological stance that favors the superiority of males and therefore spurns the presumption of gender equity (at least on this topic). The argument is simple: A woman cannot be Christ's representative because a woman does not "'look like' God."[57] Or, from the Apostolic Pentecostal perspective, a woman cannot be Christ's representative because a woman does not look like Jesus, the full revelation of God.

Nevertheless, every time PAW women ascend the altar, with their bodies they argue to the contrary. Indeed, by merely standing at or sitting on the altar they are unequivocally asserting that like their male counterparts, they represent Christ "in everything, including [their] physicality."[58] As such, God is not only represented but also encountered through their Blackness and femaleness. In doing so, PAW women have fundamentally expanded the notion of the functional and ontological nature of religious leadership in general and the bishopric in particular. Smartly, in wanting institutional affiliation, Black PAW women chose an organization so committed to its Apostolic Message that when they said they were called by God to preach and lead, the PAW believed them and entrusted them to do the work. Sadly, affiliation with the PAW also meant abiding within a restrictive and frustrating form of progressive patriarchalism that ensures that even when elevated to the chief seats of authority, they will be perpetually bossed and bothered.

NOTES

1. Brazile, "Foreword," xiv.

2. Walker, *In Search*.

3. Williams, "Sisters in the Wilderness."

4. Frederick, *Between Sundays*, 65.

5. Higginbotham, *Righteous Discontent*; Butler, *Women in the Church*; and most recently Casselberry, *Labor of Faith*. These texts include other aspects of Black Pentecostal women's agency, history, and feminist/womanist politics beyond ordination, namely, their quotidian acts as homemakers, pastors'/ministers' wives, Sunday School teachers, missionaries, evangelists, and church mothers. For an additional resource that does not explore Black Pentecostal women, see, "Women in Ministry" in Poloma, *Assemblies*, 101–21.

6. The PAW was founded in 1906, but the first iteration did not adopt an episcopal polity until 1925 with the election of its first bishop, Garfield Thomas Haywood.

7. This does not mean that race or its equally destructive sibling colorism/shadeism were not issues that Black women within the PAW had to face, it just means that of the multilayered oppressions that plague Black women, race was not primary.

8. Lorde, *Sister Outsider*, 67.

9. Ibid., 67, 69.

10. Growing up in the PAW, I can recall hearing such women described as "mannish" as they have taken on qualities and traits most constitutive of patriarchal masculinity instead of the socially acceptable notions of womanhood.

11. Respectability, and later "respectability politics," are moralistic discourses referred to by Evelyn Brooks Higginbotham. The term refers to the classist practices of racial uplift among Black Americans. According to this philosophy,

if Black Americans eliminate socially
unacceptable aesthetics, behaviors, family
structures, gender roles, politics, sexual
identities/practices, etc., they will receive
better treatment and be seen as equals in
the so-called dominant culture. Among its
many faults, the philosophy fails because
it does not hold racists accountable for
racism but rather the victims. See Higginbotham, *Righteous Discontent*.

12. Hurston, *Their Eyes*.

13. For additional works on the dehu-
manization of Black women in the United
States, see Collins, *Black Feminist Thought*;
Giddings, *When and Where*; Hine, *Hine
Sight*; Guy-Sheftall, *Words of Fire*.

14. "Daughters of Thunder" is a
Black colloquial term for Black women
preachers, made popular with the 1998
publication of Bettye Collier-Thomas's
groundbreaking text by the same name.
The phrase is derivative of the biblical
"Sons of Thunder," the nickname given to
James, the son of Zebedee, and his brother
John in Mark 3:17.

15. In 1919 Robert C. Lawson (Church
of Our Lord Jesus Christ of the Apostolic
Faith) and Garfield T. Haywood (Pentecostal Assemblies of the World, Inc.) split
over the matter. Casselberry, "Politics of
Righteousness," 75.

16. Haywood, "Some Important Acts," 15.

17. Ibid.

18. "Race man" and "race woman" refers
to Black Americans who are exceptionally
loyal to the health and well-being of the
Black community. A proper race man or
race woman is committed to confronting
and disabusing others—whether within
or without the community—of ideas, ste-
reotypes, and politics that threaten Black
people's betterment.

19. Haywood, "Some Important Acts," 15.

20. Golder, *Life*, 18.

21. Ibid.

22. Parchia, "Are Women an Obstacle?,"
12.

23. "Orthodoxy and Women," 7.

24. "Ordination of Women Disputed in
Dallas," 14.

25. Besides Jean Means, the Chicago
White Sox hired Mary Shane as its first
female announcer; Bette Davis was the
first woman to receive the American Film
Institute's Life Achievement Award; Eva
Shain was the first woman to referee a
heavyweight championship.

26. Parchia, "Are Women Preachers
Called of God?," 7.

27. Ibid.

28. Ibid., 10.

29. Ibid., 7.

30. Parchia, "Are Women Preachers
Called of God? Part 2," 7.

31. Ibid.

32. For contemporary works on the
Black church, the hypersexualization of
the Black female body, and misogynoir,
see "Juanita Bynum No More Sheets
Part 2."

33. Parchia, "Are Women Preachers
Called of God? Part 2," 7.

34. Ibid., 9.

35. As quoted in Williams-Jones,
"Minority Report," 39.

36. Apostolic Manifesto Critical Issues
Committee, "Overview."

37. The sanctified tradition refers to
an amalgamation of Black Holiness
and Pentecostal congregations. The
sanctified tradition emerged during the
Post-Reconstruction era of the American
South in response to the more Eurocentric
worship practices of more established
Black congregations—that is, those
founded before the Civil War. Theologically, the tradition embraces the Holiness
message, and religio-racially, it consists of
a multifaceted Black American spirituality
that includes but is not limited to the
slave religion of enslaved Africans. The
distinct articulations of the sanctified
tradition happen within the context of the
Black American experience in the United
States and stress communal kinship,
racial consciousness, and spiritual power/

empowerment. See Gilkes, "Together in Harness"; Crumbley, *Saved and Sanctified*; Coulter, "Holiness, Folk Culture."

38. In a Facebook post commenting on an article written about the PAW's decision to ordain two female diocesans, theologian Keri Day wrote, "Meanwhile, COGIC [is] still struggling to have a national conversation. But let's remember: Seymour had his experience through his pastor, Pastor Lucy Farrow and it is well recorded that Mason owes his experiences to the preaching and pastoral ministry of various women. At a point where I am no longer engaging institutions who just want to persist in old wine skins," https://www.facebook.com/keri.day (July 27, 2017).

39. Apostolic Manifesto Critical Issues Committee, "Overview."

40. Executive Summary, "Securing Our Future," 1.

41. Ibid.; emphasis added.

42. Ibid.

43. Ibid., 2.

44. Ibid.

45. Ibid., 2–3.

46. Ibid., 3.

47. Ibid.

48. The first bishop ordained within the organization after the 2009 decision was Aletha J. Cushinberry in 2015. Cushinberry died a few months later in December of that year. Unlike Mona Reide and Gwendolyn Weeks, she did not oversee a diocese. Hers was honorary, although she was given voting power during her short tenure. The distinction of overseeing a diocese also separates these women from those appointed suffragan bishops after the 2009 decision.

49. "2 Women Picked."

50. Ibid.

51. Ibid.

52. Ibid.

53. Grant, *White Women's Christ*, 78.

54. Best, "'The Spirit,'" 102.

55. Qualls, *God Forgive*, 4.

56. Copeland, *Enfleshing Freedom*, 7.

57. Best, "Spirit," 110–11.

58. Ibid., 112. Also see, Douglas, *Black Christ*, specifically chapter 5, "The Womanist Approach."

BIBLIOGRAPHY

Primary Sources

Apostolic Manifesto Critical Issues Committee. "Overview." March 2009.
Executive Summary. "Securing Our Future: An Apostolic Manifesto on the Issue of WOMEN IN MINISTRY: Elevation of Women to the Senior Ranks of the PAW, Inc." March 2009.
Haywood, G. T. "Some Important Acts in the General Assembly." *Voice in the Wilderness* (1920).
"Ordination of Women Disputed in Dallas." *Christian Outlook* (November 1977): 14.
"Orthodoxy and Women." *Christian Outlook* (August 1977): 7.

Parchia, Earl. "Are Women an Obstacle?" *Christian Outlook* 53, no. 6 (June 1977): 12.
———. "Are Women Preachers Called of God?" *Christian Outlook* 59, no. 3 (March 1983): 7, 10.
———. "Are Women Preachers Called of God? Part 2." *Christian Outlook* 59, no. 4 (April 1983): 4, 7.
"2 Women Picked as First Female Bishops to Lead Pentecostal Denomination's Dioceses." *Tennessean* (July 27, 2007). https://www.tennessean.com/story/news/religion/2017/07/27/2-women-picked-first-female-bishops-lead-pentecostal-denominations-dioceses/470135001.

Secondary Sources

Best, Wallace. "'The Spirit of the Holy
    Ghost Is a Male Spirit': African
    American Preaching Women and
    Paradoxes of Gender." In *Women
    and Religion in the African Diaspora:
    Knowledge, Power, and Performance*,
    edited by R. Marie Griffith and
    Barbara Diane Savage, 101–27. Bal-
    timore: Johns Hopkins University
    Press, 2006.

Brazile, Donna. "Foreword." In *Unbought
    and Unbossed*, by Shirley Chisholm,
    Expanded 40th Anniversary ed.
    2nd ed. Washington, DC: Take Root
    Media, 2010.

Butler, Anthea D. *Women in the Church
    of God in Christ: Making a Sanctified
    World*. Chapel Hill: University of
    North Carolina Press, 2007.

Casselberry, Judith. *The Labor of Faith:
    Gender and Power in Black Apostolic
    Pentecostalism*. Durham: Duke Uni-
    versity Press, 2017.

———. "The Politics of Righteousness:
    Race and Gender in Apostolic
    Pentecostalism." *Transforming
    Anthropology: Journal of the Associ-
    ation of Black Anthologists* 21, no. 1
    (2013): 72–86.

Collins, Patricia Hill. *Black Feminist
    Thought: Knowledge, Consciousness,
    and the Politics of Empowerment*.
    New York: Routledge Classics, 2009.

Copeland, M. Shawn. *Enfleshing Freedom:
    Body, Race, and Being*. Minneapolis:
    Fortress Press, 2009.

Coulter, Dale M. "Holiness, Folk Culture,
    and the African-American Expe-
    rience." *First Things* (February 13,
    2014). https://www.firstthings
    .com/blogs/firstthoughts/2014
    /02/holiness-folk-culture-and-the
    -african-american-experience.

Crumbley, Deidre H. *Saved and Sancti-
    fied: The Rise of a Storefront Church
    in Great Migration Philadelphia.*

Gainesville: University Press of
    Florida, 2013.

Douglas, Kelly Brown. *The Black Christ*.
    Maryknoll, NY: Orbis Books, 1994.

Frederick, Marla F. *Between Sundays:
    Black Women and Everyday Struggles
    of Faith*. Berkeley: University of
    California Press, 2003.

Giddings, Paula. *When and Where I
    Enter: The Impact on Black Women
    on Race and Sex in America*. New
    York: Perennial, 2001.

Gilkes, Cheryl Townsend. "'Together in
    Harness': Women's Traditions in the
    Sanctified Church." *Signs* 10, no. 4
    (Summer 1985): 678–99.

Golder, Morris E. *The Life, and Work of
    Garfield Thomas Haywood (1880–
    1931)*. N.p., 1977.

Grant, Jacquelyn. *White Women's Christ
    and Black Women's Jesus: Feminist
    Christology and Womanist Response*.
    Atlanta: Scholars Press, 1989.

Guy-Sheftall, Beverly. *Words of Fire:
    Anthology of African American
    Feminist Thought*. New York: New
    Press, 1995.

Higginbotham, Evelyn Brooks. *Righteous
    Discontent: The Black Women's Move-
    ment in the Black Baptist Church,
    1880–1920*. Cambridge: Harvard
    University Press, 1993.

Hine, Darlene Clark. *Hine Sight: Black
    Women and the Re-construction of
    American History*. Bloomington and
    Indianapolis: Indiana University
    Press, 1997.

Hurston, Zora Neale, and Cheryl
    Wall, eds. "Their Eyes Were Watch-
    ing God." In *Zora Neale Hurston:
    Novels and Stories*. New York:
    Library of America, 1995.

"Juanita Bynum No More Sheets Part 2."
    Feminist Wire. https://thefeministwire
    .com/tag/no-more-sheets.

Lorde, Audre. *Sister Outsider: Essays and
    Speeches*. New York: Crossing Press,
    1984.

Poloma, Margaret M. *The Assemblies of God at the Crossroads: Charisma and Institutional Dilemmas.* Knoxville: University of Tennessee Press, 1989.

Qualls, Joy E. A. *God Forgive Us for Being Women: Rhetoric, Theology, and the Pentecostal Tradition.* Eugene, OR: Pickwick, 2018.

Walker, Alice. *In Search of My Mother's Gardens: Womanist Prose.* New York: Harcourt, 1983.

Williams, Delores S. *Sisters in the Wilderness: The Challenge of Womanist God-Talk.* Anniversary ed. Maryknoll, NY: Orbis Books, 2013.

Williams-Jones, Pearl. "A Minority Report: Black Pentecostal Women." *Spirit: A Journal of Issues Incident to Black Pentecostalism* 1, no. 2 (1977): 39.

CHAPTER 8

Trust God to Provide for the Difference

The Economic and Opportunity Costs
of Being Female and a Preacher

Andrea Shan Johnson

In 1915, Howard Goss, one of the founders of the Assemblies of God and one of the men responsible for issuing ministerial credentials in that organization, posted a notice to female ministers in the periodical *Word and Witness*. He suggested that they should not apply to the Clergy Bureau for the book that would authenticate their ministerial credentials, as these books would not be issued to women who in the organization were bestowed only with the title of missionary. The rank of missionary indicated to bureau officials that the female clergy did not have a guaranteed salary unless they were serving in a foreign field. Women serving the church in America, in whatever capacity, all bore the unfortunate label of a temporary worker. Lacking the proper recognition of their ministerial credentials, they were no longer entitled to reduced railroad fare, not an insignificant detriment in an era when the train was a major form of transportation. By contrast, men, who could apply for ordination, would be granted this discount by the railroads. Goss's proposed solution was that women "trust God for full fare." He gave no indication that the organization would attempt to remedy this by issuing women credentials that reflected their true levels of service.[1]

Early women ministers, the denial of transportation discounts notwithstanding, often exercised independence from traditional family structures, embraced adventures in pulpits often far from home, and enjoyed a high degree of agency in their ministry. At the same time there were both economic and opportunity costs for the women pursuing callings to the pulpit. Women were often denied equal means of financial support and felt they had to turn down opportunities that would have meant clearly violating traditional norms of the American family. They would often find a welcome in smaller churches or on the mission field where their work might be considered temporary, but where they might be able to exercise more control of the daily work.

These women became key participants in the formation of Oneness denominations, including those that eventually became part of the United Pentecostal Church International (UPCI). One might imagine that as the organization came to allow women among the ranks of the ordained, their clerical numbers would have grown over the ensuing decades. However, such is not the case. In a 2016 news blog entitled "A Pentecostal Statement on Women in Ministry," the UPCI promoted recent efforts to recruit women to the ministry while considering their historically low numbers of female clergy. The author of the blog noted that several leadership offices, mostly those at the district level, were open to men only. The author attributed (without documentation) the decline of women in ministry to displacement by men who sought out leadership positions in a religious movement that became more socially accepted. The author also attributed this decrease of women in ministry as part of a "backlash against the women's liberation movement of the 1960s and 1970s, as Pentecostal women did not wish to be identified with the attitudes and mannerisms of worldly women who fought against biblical morality." Additionally, the author cites the influence of fundamentalists who opposed women in ministry as a reason for this decline.[2] In many ways, this 2016 narrative on women in ministry revealed that the church had not advanced much further from the church of the era of Howard Goss over one hundred years ago. While the author asserted that women could hold the highest offices in the organization, they did not acknowledge that without being able to establish a record of district leadership, women were unlikely to be considered for national office. Like Goss, the modern leadership offered no meaningful remedy. In addition, this report of the struggle to rebuild the numbers of women in ministry miscontextualizes women, ignoring the rise of household containment trends of the late 1940s and 1950s.[3] The hope that American households with distinct gender roles would stand as a bulwark against communism was a phenomenon that occurred while the UPCI was forming. This narrative also calls for the reader to assume that these women were displaced rather than examining why women of different eras may have decided that their calls lay in other areas. The author of the news blog does not consider the economic and opportunity costs paid by these women in ministry and how their testimonies, or portrayals of their lives, may have encouraged or discouraged the participation of women in the field. To understand why Oneness women may have left the ministry, it is important to develop a historically accurate narrative as to why women entered the ministry in the beginning of the movement. These stories matter.

It is difficult to document a distinctive early Oneness position on women in ministry. Historian Grant Wacker asserts that Oneness Pentecostals did not differ from their Trinitarian brethren here.[4] Extant sources, such as *Word and Witness* and the *Weekly Evangel* (which later became the *Christian Evangel*), are mostly associated with the Assemblies of God, but between 1913 and 1916, they also represented some of the views of Oneness adherents. Andrew Urshan contributed missionary reports to both, and the editor of these papers, E. N. Bell, temporarily supported Jesus' name baptism. In these papers, the general view is the one settled on by the 1914 General Council of the Assemblies of God.[5] Bell responded to a question about women in ministry in his "Questions and Answers" column in the *Weekly Evangel* explaining his view that "if she is able to build up the assembly in the Lord and in peace, many brethren hold she is 'not usurping authority' if this privilege is granted her as temporary needs may require."[6] Frank Ewart's newsletter *Meat in Due Season* is essentially the earliest newsletter devoted to Oneness theology and missions. The June 1916 edition reprints a 1913 article that references women's suffrage as an "abnormal condition" identifying it not with voting rights but rather with women in authority. The author of the piece believes that there is a place for women in ministry as long as they, like a good wife, do not usurp authority over men. The boundaries of such authority are conveniently undefined.[7]

After Oneness ministers left the Assemblies of God in 1916, they formed several Oneness organizations. The two dominant ones came to be the Pentecostal Assemblies of the World, which was interracial until 1924 with some (albeit ultimately failed) efforts continued until the late 1930s, and the United Pentecostal Church, which in 1945 formed from a few smaller predominantly white organizations that emerged after the racial split. As a result, the story of Oneness Pentecostal women in ministry is complicated by organizational fracturing and the racial history of the United States. Despite Wacker's contention that there is little difference between Trinitarian and Oneness positions on women in ministry among early Pentecostals, as a whole, Oneness women— Black, white, and Latina—have been understudied. Oneness adherents lack a strong academically sourced narrative explaining the rise and decline of women ministers in their movements. Members of the Trinitarian Church of God in Christ (COGIC) and those in the Sanctified churches can look to scholars such as Cheryl J. Sanders and Anthea D. Butler.[8] Both Black and white Trinitarian groups are heavily represented in recent edited volumes such as *Philip's Daughters: Women in Pentecostal-Charismatic Leadership* by Estrelda Alexander and Amos Yong[9] or *Women in Pentecostal and Charismatic Ministry: Informing a Dialogue on Gender, Church, and Ministry* by Margaret English de Alminana and Lois E. Olena.[10] There has been little published academic work on the experiences of women in the Oneness Movement, the exceptions being perhaps folklorist Elaine Lawless's works from the 1970s and 1980s, which rely on her observations of independent Oneness church women and Judith Casselberry's more recent work on Black women in the Church of Our Lord Jesus Christ of the Apostolic Faith, Incorporated.[11] This lack of scholarship is particularly glaring in light of the current move of the UPCI to build numbers of women in ministry.

ECONOMIC IMPACT

The organizational history of Oneness Pentecostal denominations reveals the ways in which the structures of these groups resulted in systems of inequality for women. As World War I began, it became important for ministers to hold credentials with a denomination recognized by the federal government as holding a conscientious objector status, so that Pentecostal men, the majority of whom held pacifist beliefs, could avoid being drafted.[12] Because of this, in 1918, the Pentecostal Assemblies of the World (PAW), an organization that authorized ministers mostly in the western United States, was joined by the General Assemblies of the Apostolic Assemblies, one of the groups that had formed after the split from the Assemblies of God. The latter was too recently organized to gain exemption from military service for its ministers and needed to borrow the more established PAW name. In the January 1918 conference where the merger and first bylaws were created, the ministers of the new organization affirmed that a woman could be an evangelist or missionary but not a pastor or an elder, a stance that mirrored that of the Assemblies of God. The following year, the organization more explicitly defined the roles of women in ministry. Women evangelists could perform marriages, funerals, baptisms, and communion, but only in an emergency. In a policy similar to that of COGIC, women who had charge of an assembly were not referred to as pastors, although essentially they were, and were reminded that they could "maintain oversight thereof . . . until a man is raised up in their midst," and that the General Assembly had the power to "adjust such matters." This meant that female pastors never had the same ministerial independence that men did and could be removed from their pulpit for reasons of their sex.[13]

Since the boundaries of women's authority were not clearly delineated, and at no point were men required to undergo a rigorous formal vetting process as women's replacements, women in ministry were subject to the whims of the leadership of the congregations and denominations. This was part of the economic cost of being a woman in ministry. In many organizations, male leaders barred women from pastoring sizable congregations. Thus, a woman could never expect to have financial stability from her ministry in a way that a male minister moving up through the ranks might, and her pastorate would always be susceptible to challenges from ambitious men. Such women were then doubly susceptible to having their authority within a church questioned. When Oma Ellis, a pioneer of early church planting and evangelism, attempted to establish a church near Tulare, California, she faced two such significant challenges. She recalled one man with ministerial ambitions who would ambush testimony services, waiting until the end of that portion of the service, then, rising to his feet, deliver an hour-long sermon rather than a testimony. Ellis recalled that in previous churches, she would have relied on the men of the church to handle the situation, but she lacked such support in Tulare. She believed that her church was more often the target of this behavior because it had a female pastor. She also recalled a revelation from God that a man would come into her congregation and try to control more recent converts by speaking against women ministers. This man appeared and was successful in swaying the congregation, and rather than have a church split, and because his doctrine was otherwise sound, she turned the church over to him and left. Later, while evangelizing in 1941, Ellis recalled that rather than give her the expected offering from the evening service, the local pastor decided to use it to pay the church payment, proclaiming that he would not have deprived anyone else in such a manner, adding that he and his wife would provide Ellis with food and shelter for the week. Ellis, who was by then estranged from her husband and who had children to support, had borrowed money and needed the cash to pay her debt. She felt resentment, knowing that he would probably have not done the same to a man. Fortunately for her, one of the men in attendance that night had not liked how she was treated. He saved his offering for her, an amount greater than what had been taken up in the service.[14] Ellis's sex and the rules about women in ministry directly contributed to her inability to maintain economic security.

In addition, to maintain a position in ministry, women would often have to defer other professional and personal opportunities. The Davis twins, a pair of sisters who established churches in Maine and New Brunswick, are significant examples of this. When Carro Davis decided to preach the gospel, she left her profession as a schoolteacher. Although orphaned at a young age, Davis had been raised by an aunt on a Georgia plantation staffed by servants. She graduated from normal school in 1903 and taught school in her hometown of Macon, Georgia. She had been exposed to Pentecostalism in Georgia but did not convert until she attended services at a Pentecostal mission in Chicago on a summer trip. When she had not received the Holy Ghost by the time she was scheduled to return to Georgia, she sent a message resigning as the principal of the school and stayed in Chicago. Her sister Susie was less willing to abandon all in Chicago and returned to Georgia to teach at the high school. In 1911, shortly after converting, Carro embraced ministry full-time; her sister Susie soon followed. In 1923, after nearly a dozen years as itinerant preachers, they moved to Bangor, Maine, and established a church there, as well as churches in Fredericton and Saint John in New Brunswick, Canada.[15] The sisters never married. Carro Davis had apparently been a favorite of the Persian Evangelist A. D. Urshan but had decided not to marry him because she did not want to go with him to Persia.[16] To build and maintain her ministerial career, Carro Davis abandoned a career as an educational administrator and turned down marriage, believing it impossible to maintain either in conjunction with her ministerial calling.

The Davis sisters developed a career in ministry that allowed them to establish churches and gain recognition as church leaders, but this too came with a cost. Like many Pentecostal women in ministry, they mentored younger male leaders, perhaps, because, as argued by Linda Ambrose and Leah Payne, these early women in ministry often realized that in a patriarchal culture, men would have the most success as ministers.[17] One of their mentees, Stanley McConaghy, recalls that early in his own ministry he and Howard Hatt had been holding a series of revivals when the Davis sisters brought them food, preached for them, and taught them how to hold prayer meetings. He also recalled that the Davis sisters had bought a large circus tent that had been seized by the city from a failed circus. Other ministers were able to use parts of the tent to hold their own revivals in the region.[18] While these practices contributed to their influence, the sisters were able to do this because they at least paid tribute to the notion that women were to take a lesser role within church leadership, finding male ministers to perform the rites of the church when needed. T. Alton Stewart, who pastored near the Davis sisters for some years, recalled that he performed both baptisms and funerals for the congregants of the sisters.[19] Dolores Northrup, who was converted by the Davis sisters, recalled that on her wedding day in Saint John, New Brunswick, the Davis sisters came by to see the couple and signed the required documents but left it to Howard Hatt to conduct the marriage ceremony, as they neither conducted marriage ceremonies nor served communion.[20] There was an economic cost to this decision as well. Ministers usually were paid at least a token amount for conducting funerals and weddings, and so women who abided by this policy lost another economic opportunity. The beneficiaries were often some of men they had mentored.

OPPORTUNITIES ON THE MISSION FIELD

When women found themselves restricted from pastoral ministry, they began to compensate in other ways. If women desired to work in full-time ministry, they might choose to go to a mission field. A. G. Jefferies estimated in 1916 that more than half of the missionaries in the early broader Pentecostal Movement were women whom God had "pulled" to the position.[21] Women in the mission field were less likely to face gendered challenges to their attempts to preach the gospel. Work on the mission field also offered these women a chance to work with native populations they perceived as needing help. In this way, these Progressive era missionaries were not unlike the Settlement House workers of their time. Kept from using their skills and education in traditional leadership capacities, white women, often educated, found ample opportunities on mission fields and among nonwhite populations.

The missionary career of Alice Kugler Sheets illustrates some of the challenges for women missionaries in the early days of Oneness Pentecostalism. Born Alice Sarah Kugler in 1883, she was a schoolteacher and later taught at a Holiness school in Iowa before receiving the Holy Ghost in Kansas in 1910. She was ordained to the ministry by E. N. Bell in 1912 and received further training in evangelism and obstetrical work. She moved to China to serve as an evangelist in 1914 and lived through the rise of Sun Yat-sen and the growth of communism in the region. Her diary from 1917 records times of loneliness and isolation, particularly as she recovered from small pox. She mourned the loss of a cat and prayed that God would punish the woman who had taken the pet until it was returned. But she also had a high degree of control over her situation. She maintained charge of teachers and workers at the local mission and settled conflicts between staff, intervening when one female worker reported that a male worker had been watching her bathing. There is some evidence that she debated the Oneness theology with other missionaries, as she recorded on April 26, 1917, that one of the women stationed near her had returned to believing in "three persons," a prospect that upset her. In May 1917, she attended a meeting with a group of seventeen missionaries in which they debated baptismal formulas. Seven attendees wanted to use Jesus' name, while others were open to both Oneness and Trinitarian forms of baptism, and a third group wanted to use only the titles "Father," "Son," and "Holy Ghost." In this same meeting, they came to agreements on salaries for local teachers and decided that no one should live alone at a station, although there seemed to be no way to ensure that policy was followed. She furloughed in the United States between 1919 and 1921 and then returned to China until the United States government asked her to leave in 1926 due to the unrest in the region.[22]

After returning to the United States in 1926, she met and married her husband, Daniel Sheets (see fig. 8.1). For a few years, they pastored in Arizona, but by May 1934, she was once again on a boat to China, bringing with her Daniel, who had not previously served as a missionary. Although she took her husband's name after their marriage, their business card shows her name styled as Alice Kugler Sheets. She maintained a reference to her maiden name and the recognition that it brought of her previous missionary work.[23] Within three years, events that would lead to World War II began in Asia, during which she hid from raiding Japanese soldiers and survived several months in captivity, essentially a prisoner of war.[24]

Elizabeth Stieglitz, who also served as a missionary to China, exercised similar agency in her ministry. Converted by William Durham in 1908, she attended a few months of Bible school in Ohio before traveling to China as a missionary in 1910. In China, she regularly made decisions such as where to start new points of outreach. When the Japanese invaded the region during World War II, she kept them out of the mission and pushed Japanese military officials to keep their soldiers out of the mission gardens until she was forced to leave, taken prisoner, and exchanged for Japanese prisoners of war in 1942. She also provided the impetus for her missionary group's conversion to the Oneness doctrine after she found part of Frank Ewart's *Meat in Due Season* in a Christmas box. After the war, she partnered with Kathryn Hendricks, another woman who had briefly served in China, and returned to the region, only to find they would have to start the work all over again, as Mao Zedong's communist forces now occupied their mission.[25] The role of such women in establishing Pentecostalism in China needs further examination. Much of the

Fig. 8.1. Alice Kugler Sheets
with her husband Daniel on
their wedding day, September 25,
1926. Photo courtesy of Flower
Pentecostal Heritage Center.

current scholarship focuses on the rise of the True Jesus Church but does not
always take into account the impact of these early women religious workers.

Men might have been more accepting of a woman in leadership if that leadership position was in missions. To some degree, the work of Kugler Sheets and
Stieglitz illustrates this, as they ran mission stations, controlled and paid local
workers, and were involved in the growing debates over the doctrine. This trend
was also evident among postwar missionaries serving in other regions, including
Georgia Regenhardt and Gladys Robinson, who were assigned to Liberia by the
newly merged United Pentecostal Church. Regenhardt, born in 1902, had been
widowed with three young children in 1933. She worked in a factory to support
the family until her children left the house. In 1945, she attended the Pentecostal
Bible Institute in Tupelo, Mississippi, before being appointed to Liberia in 1946
to run a mission station there while the L. E. Haney family was on furlough.
After they left, she supervised the clearing of land for crops and settled disputes

over funding within the local church.[26] She was joined by Gladys Robinson in 1947. Robinson, born in 1907, had been married three times, two of which ended in divorce. In 1942, she acknowledged a call to missions. For the next few years she preached revivals and established churches in the United States until attending Apostolic College in Tulsa, Oklahoma, in 1946, and then she joined the missions team in Liberia.[27] Together in Liberia the two women established a household, with Robinson taking charge of an orphan whom Regenhardt had taken in, buying half of the hens, and assuming part of the grocery debt.[28] In 1948, the women reported that the church had obtained twelve acres of land from an American mining company, on which they were establishing a station and a day school. Robinson lived there and supervised the local workers in the new facility. Meanwhile Regenhardt supervised the production of rice and cassava crops on which the mission relied for financial support, meaning that the two women, assigned together, would have to be separated.[29]

Many of these trends of women in leadership extended to Black Oneness churches. For example, Hilda Reeder, an Indianapolis elementary schoolteacher and member of the Pentecostal Assemblies of the World, was one of the only women to hold a national office in that organization. She was appointed by G. T. Haywood as the secretary-treasurer of the Missions Department. She was the only woman to appear in the leadership portraits of the 1940s.[30] In her case, as long as the cause was missions, her role was not challenged.

At this same time, the opportunities for Hispanic Oneness women were being constricted. It is likely that Jesus' name baptism was first taken into Mexico by a woman, Romana Carbajal de Valenzuela, who returned to Mexico during the Mexican Revolution of the 1910s, risking her life to travel home with the news of the gospel. However, she often showed deference to male leaders, once even escorting a converted Methodist minister over the border into El Paso to be baptized by a Black Oneness minister there.[31] Her example was not to be later equaled. As Daniel Ramírez has found, women in the predominantly Hispanic Apostolic Assembly of the Faith in Jesus Christ chartered in 1930 were licensed, often under the label "deaconess," with the prohibitions found in the PAW documents of former years. Gradually, however, the office of deaconess disappeared as the women in the position died and were not replaced. This was complicated by the repatriation issues of the 1930s, as many who were Mexican citizens were sent back to Mexico during the Great Depression, a historical trend that both complicated and facilitated missionary attempts.[32]

In addition, it should be noted that white women might also seek out opportunities to minister in nonwhite communities domestically, an arena in which they would also exercise a fair amount of authority. The Davis sisters began their ministry in Georgia and seem to have had more success there among Blacks than with whites.[33] When stationed in Somerton, Arizona, in the early 1930s, Oma Ellis and the wife of another pastor in the region decided to preach to Native Americans in the region.[34] In 1948, the Texico District of the United Pentecostal Church endorsed the work of Carrie Eastridge, who had moved to Gallup, New Mexico, to evangelize among tribes in that area. She connected with reservation welfare workers and began to try to navigate the process of building a mission near reservation lands.[35]

It would be negligent not to acknowledge that in such cases white women's agency was possible only because they were able and willing to exert authority over nonwhite male locals in a way that they did not exert over white men at home in the United States. Women on the mission field were not as careful to maintain gendered boundaries and seem to have received fewer challenges from the North American churches. Women such as Oma Ellis or the Davis sisters felt reluctance to exert authority over white men in America and avoided doing so even to a loss of income, but women on the mission field felt no such qualms about managing local workers. While these women might submit to white, male missionaries, such as when Alice Kugler Sheets deferred to another missionary's decision not to baptize a particular local, they showed no such tendency to submit to local or national men the same way.[36]

THE WORD OF THEIR TESTIMONY

Clearly, early Oneness Pentecostal women were willing to push the boundaries of behavior deemed desirable for faithful women of their time. They trod a careful path as they supervised men in their ministry and often were either single or in marriages that were fractured, meaning that while they upheld the gender norms of the day, they themselves often led lives that challenged such norms. In reality, to be a woman in ministry, one would have rejected the most conservative interpretations of women's roles in the church. However, a woman preaching or raising money for her missions work still needed to appease the more conservative laity in the congregations, and they often did so by developing more socially acceptable testimonies. When folklorist Elaine Lawless studied independent rural Pentecostal churches in Indiana and Missouri in the 1970s and 1980s, she found several women active in a preaching ministry. She noticed several common elements in their interviews, including being horrified at the call to preach when they first received it, a tendency to vilify the feminist movement even though they themselves had chosen a nontraditional path for women, a feeling that they were different from other youth, an ability to recount their calling with detail, and a calling to revival or missionary work.[37] The themes that Lawless identified were not new, and some, particularly the internal tensions over being a woman called to do what some considered a man's work, can be seen among earlier Pentecostal women ministers. Alice Kugler Sheets recalled that when she first repented at the age of twelve, she told her cousin that she might someday be a missionary, thus identifying a call at a young age.[38] Oma Ellis, who converted in the early 1920s, recalled for her biographer that her grandfather had received the Holy Ghost in 1896, and on his deathbed had prayed over her pregnant mother that the child would be a preacher. Relatives had scoffed when she was born a girl, but her cousin pointed out that she could still fulfill her grandfather's prophecy. The cousin also proclaimed that as God had healed her grandfather, God could help Oma recover from tuberculosis. Her call to preach was also confirmed by a male figure. Although she had felt the call to the pulpit prior to conversion, as she lived in a rural area, she had been unable to attend regular services. Upon her first visit to a church, the pastor called her up to preach, saying he had seen her in a vision. Thus began her ministry.[39]

Unlike Pentecostals later studied by Lawless, these early women did not decry the suffrage or women's movements, but they did proclaim conservative views of the home. This was the case even as their religious commitments and ministries might contribute to the destruction of their own homes. Grant Wacker has pointed out that many early female Pentecostal leaders never married, but those who did had a high marriage casualty rate.[40] Oma Ellis defied her husband's orders during her first Pentecostal service when she interrupted the service to demand that the pastor baptize her in Jesus' name before her husband arrived to take her home at the end of the service. Although unsure that a woman should preach, she eventually answered the call. As her husband had not converted, they were in conflict, and eventually he gave the children, including a seven-month-old, to his mother to raise and told Ellis to support herself. He retained control of the children, deciding when they would live with her and when they would be with his mother. She believed he made three attempts to kill her, but she herself would not file for divorce, and eventually he initiated proceedings. Once divorced, she determined not to remarry, a stand she maintained until at the age of sixty-one she remarried her former husband.[41]

Elaine Lawless also noted that many of her subjects from the late 1970s could recall a woman preacher from a key revival. These women, many from rural areas, had few women as role models other than perhaps their mothers or teachers, none of whom led the life of adventure and independence of the woman preacher or missionary.[42] Those women of the 1970s would have remembered the women from the early days of the Pentecostal Movement: women such as Alice Kugler Sheets, Oma Ellis, the Davis sisters, Elizabeth Stieglitz, Georgia Regenhardt, and Gladys Robinson. These were women who had led lives of adventure and who also had exercised a high degree of agency in their ministerial lives.

The women of early Pentecost were products of the Progressive era and the 1920s, a time when the New Woman was on the rise. These women, many of whom had worked as teachers, found ways in which to use their hard-earned skills for the work of God. There were consequences, to be sure: the economic insecurity of a domestic pulpit, or the isolation of a life overseas. But within their ministries they were able to exercise a high degree of agency, provided they paid some heed to church restrictions on women. Postwar women, the ones Lawless studied, were not of the New Woman era. While they may have been inspired by the early women ministers, they had come of age in a postwar world in which the home and the country were to be saved by strong families with specific gender roles.[43] Instead of reading about women such as Alice Kugler Sheets, who survived the Japanese takeover of China, they read about women such as Shirley Cole. William H. Cole, a missionary to Thailand, wrote an article for the May 1963 *Pentecostal Herald*, which exemplifies some of these changes. He intended the article to promote the work of the UPCI Ladies Auxiliary, which had sent funds to buy a stove and refrigerator. Cole was thankful that his wife could cook almost as she had in America and described his wife as having faced the changes in their life, "perhaps with tears, but always with courage in her heart," and as a woman who mourned the loss of the kitchen in the parsonage in their previous pastorate. These appliances are seen as having freed Sister Cole, whose first name is never given in the article, from having to shop on a daily basis, and as her husband wrote, "Cooking is now a relaxation instead of a burden."[44] Perhaps Cole was being dramatic in his attempts to praise the Ladies Auxiliary, but in this article, his wife's role is that of a cook whose days consist of shopping for dinner and crying over missing appliances rather than as an essential leader in ministry. A younger woman reading this article in 1963 would have seen little in this piece to encourage her to see herself as a potential minister or missionary. If she desired adventure and independence, the wife whose days consisted of shopping was hardly an example of that. If she desired a traditional home, replete with the appliances and middle-class hallmarks of American life, sacrificial missionary work would not offer a reasonable path in that direction. This was, after all, the era in which Richard Nixon used the plethora of available kitchen appliances meant to ease the life of the American housewife as evidence of the rightness of American capitalism and democracy. The 1959 kitchen debate in the Soviet Union connected American household consumerism with American virtues. While women of the Progressive era and the 1920s had been able to make ministry work for them, manipulating economic and social opportunities for their betterment, women of later years did not want the same lives and were perhaps unwilling to make the same economic and social sacrifices as earlier women. These women were not merely displaced by men, nor were they only reacting to second wave feminism of the 1970s. While folklorist Elaine Lawless observed Oneness Pentecostal women in ministry in the 1970s had derided feminism, they had not abandoned the pulpit because of such connotations. Women of the Cold War did not seek the same opportunities in the same numbers as their earlier counterparts, perhaps because the narrative testimonies had shifted, but also perhaps because they wanted different lives.

Oneness Pentecostal women of the early years pastored smaller churches, paid higher rail fares, and passed on income-producing opportunities to men they had trained, but ministry still provided fairly independent women with the adventure and agency they desired. Over time, these women faded from the view of those on the pews, to be replaced by the Shirley Cole–style figure of the pastor's wife as the woman in ministry. This was not a lifestyle that many of the early female ministers could have related to, and it has failed to attract a generation of women who, like the earliest women, might be willing to answer a call to a smaller pulpit or an international location and find ways to work around the limitations that male clergy place upon them in exchange for agency and adventure. These women are likely to find a more comfortable and emotionally rewarding home in secular careers where barriers to women have decreased over time. The doors open matter. The stories told matter. The women of the early days of the movement provide an understanding of what their stories and their opportunities can mean to women who hear a call.

NOTES

1. "Notice to Women Missionaries," 5.

2. United Pentecostal Church International, "Pentecostal Statement on Women in Ministry."

3. See May, *Homeward Bound*, for a discussion of containment trends.

4. Wacker, *Heaven Below*, 168.

5. See, for example, Bell, "Women Elders," 2.

6. Bell was consistent in his argument that women were only to serve as pastors as a temporary measure. Bell, "Questions

and Answers," January 29, 1916; Bell, "Questions and Answers," February 5, 1916, 8; Bell, "Questions and Answers," September 2, 1916, 8.

7. Morse, "Woman's Place in the Body," 3.

8. Butler, *Women in the Church*; Sanders, "History of Women." See also Gilkes, "Together and in Harness," 678–99.

9. Alexander and Yong, *Philip's Daughters*.

10. English de Alminana and Olena, *Women*.

11. Lawless, "Rescripting Their Lives," 53–71; Lawless, *Handmaidens*; Lawless, *God's Peculiar People*; Casselberry, *Labor of Faith*.

12. Alexander, *Peace to War*.

13. Minute Book and Ministerial Record of the Pentecostal Assemblies of the World, 1918 & 1919, Indianapolis, Indiana, and Minute Book and Ministerial Record of the General Assembly of the Pentecostal Assemblies of the World, 1919 & 1920, 287–314.

14. Ellis and Smelser, *Oma*, locations 2549–817, 2985–3013.

15. Paynter to Pickard, June 17, 1988; Obituary for Carro Davis, September 3, 1976; "Presbyterian Aristocrats Become Pentecostal Preachers."

16. Pickard, Notes on Group Meeting.

17. Ambrose and Payne, "Reflections," 45–63.

18. McConaghy, "Down Memory Lane."

19. Stewart to Pickard, letter, n.d.

20. Northrup, *Unlimited God*, 68–69.

21. "Limit of Divine Revelation," 6–7.

22. Ministerial Credentials; Sheets, *Perilous Paths in China*; 1917 Diary of Alice Sarah Kugler.

23. Business card, Papers of Daniel K. and Alice Kugler Sheets.

24. Sheets and Sheets, "Returned from Captivity."

25. Freeman, "Story of Elizabeth Stieglitz," location 4483–897.

26. Freeman, "Story of Georgia Regenhardt," locations 2392–422, 2661–90.

27. Freeman and Ross Wallace, "Story of Gladys Robinson," location 2952–3326.

28. Freeman, "Georgia Regenhardt," location 2705.

29. Regenhardt and Robinson, "Missionary Progress in Liberia, Africa."

30. Sims, "Telling Our Story," 16–19.

31. Ramírez, *Migrating Faith*, location 62–65.

32. Ibid., 53–54.

33. Paynter to Pickard, June 17, 1988.

34. Ellis and Smelser, *Oma*, locations 1745, 1871–912.

35. Eastridge, "Indian Problem," 15.

36. 1917 Diary of Alice Sarah Kugler, May 10, 1917.

37. Lawless, "Rescripting Their Lives," 53–71.

38. Sheets, *Perilous Paths in China*, 7.

39. Ellis and Smelser, *Oma*, location 249–524.

40. Wacker, *Heaven Below*, 175.

41. Ellis and Smelser, *Oma*, locations 328–43, 693–909, 3486–553.

42. Lawless, "Rescripting Their Lives," 65–66.

43. For further discussion along these lines, see May, *Homeward Bound*, and Self, *All in the Family*.

44. Cole, "Ladies Change the Picture," 10–11.

BIBLIOGRAPHY

Primary Sources

Bell, E. N. "Questions and Answers." *Weekly Evangel*, January 29, 1916, 8.

———. "Questions and Answers." *Weekly Evangel*, September 2, 1916, 8.

———. "Women Elders." *Christian Evangel*, August 15, 1914, 2.

Business card. Papers of Daniel K. and Alice Kugler Sheets, Center for the Study of Oneness Pentecostalism.

Cole, William H. "The Ladies Change the Picture." *Pentecostal Herald* 38, no. 5 (May 1963): 10–11.

Davis, Carro. "Presbyterian Aristocrats Become Pentecostal Preachers." *Pentecostal Testimony* (May 1936): 1. Clippings file, Pickard Papers, Folder S.1 Pentecostal, Fuller Theological Seminary.

Eastridge, Carrie. "The Indian Problem." *Pentecostal Herald* 23, no. 10 (October 1948): 15.

Ellis, Oma, and Georgia Smelser. *Oma: The Story of Oma Ellis, a Woman Whose Tough Faith Emerged in the Face of Conflict and Heartache.* Kindle ed. Hazelwood, MO: Word Aflame Press, 1981.

Freeman, Nona. "The Story of Elizabeth Stieglitz." In *Profiles of Pentecostal Missionaries*, edited by Mary Wallace, location 4483–914. Kindle ed. Hazelwood, MO: Word Aflame Press, 2011.

———. "The Story of Georgia Regenhardt." In *Profiles of Pentecostal Missionaries*, edited by Mary Wallace, location 2392–947. Kindle ed. Hazelwood, MO: Word Aflame Press, 2011.

Freeman, Nona, and Marie Ross Wallace. "The Story of Gladys Robinson." In *Profiles of Pentecostal Missionaries*, edited by Mary Wallace, location 2952–3358. Kindle ed. Hazelwood, MO: Word Aflame Press, 2011.

"The Limit of Divine Revelation." *Weekly Evangel*, March 18, 1916, 6–7.

McConaghy, Stanley. "Down Memory Lane." *U.P.C. Home Missions News* 14, no. 2 (September 1966): 1. Pickard Papers, Folder S.1 Pentecostal, Fuller Theological Seminary.

Ministerial Credentials. Papers of Daniel K. and Alice Kugler Sheets, Center for the Study of Oneness Pentecostalism.

"Perils and Thrills in South China," transcription of newspaper clipping. Papers of Daniel K. and Alice Kugler Sheets, Center for the Study of Oneness Pentecostalism.

Minute Book and Ministerial Record of the Pentecostal Assemblies of the World, 1918 & 1919, Indianapolis, Indiana, and Minute Book and Ministerial Record of the General Assembly of the Pentecostal Assemblies of the World, 1919 & 1920, Indianapolis, IN. Reprinted in *The Early Pentecostal Revival: History of Twentieth-Century Pentecostals and the Pentecostal Assemblies of the World*, by James Tyson, 287–314. Hazelwood, MO: Word Aflame Press, 1992.

Morse, H. "Woman's Place in the Body." *Meat in Due Season* (June 1916): 3.

1917 Diary of Alice Sarah Kugler. Papers of Daniel K. and Alice Kugler Sheets, Center for the Study of Oneness Pentecostalism.

"Notice to Women Missionaries." *Word and Witness* 12, no. 6 (June 1915): 5.

Obituary for Carro Davis, September 3, 1976. Clippings file, Pickard Papers, Folder S.1 Pentecostal, Fuller Theological Seminary.

Paynter, Matilda, to Patricia Pickard, June 17, 1988. Pickard Papers, Folder S.1 Pentecostal, Fuller Theological Seminary.

Pickard, Patricia. Notes on Group Meeting in St. Paul, Minnesota with Rev. Benjamin Urshan, October 14, 1995. Pickard Papers, Folder S.1 Pentecostal, Fuller Theological Seminary.

Regenhardt, Georgia, and Gladys Robinson, "Missionary Progress in Liberia, Africa." *Pentecostal Herald* 23, no. 9 (September 1948): 11.

Sheets, Alice Kugler. *Perilous Paths in China.* Houston, TX: The

Herald Publishing House. Papers of Daniel K. and Alice Kugler Sheets, Center for the Study of Oneness Pentecostalism.

Sheets, Alice Sarah Kugler. 1917 Diary. Papers of Daniel K. and Alice Kugler Sheets, Center for the Study of Oneness Pentecostalism.

Sheets, Dan, and Alice Sheets. "Returned from Captivity." *Apostolic Herald* 19, no. 2 (February 1944): 1, 9, 13. Papers of Daniel K. and Alice Kugler Sheets, Center for the Study of Oneness Pentecostalism.

Sims, Jane. "Telling Our Story: A History of Women in the Pentecostal Assemblies of the World." Spiral bound, in the collection of Fuller Theological Seminary.

Stewart, T. Alton, to Patricia Pickard. Letter, n.d. Pickard Papers, Folder S.1 Pentecostal, Fuller Theological Seminary.

United Pentecostal Church International. "A Pentecostal Statement on Women in Ministry." https://www.upci.org /statement-archive/article/2016/04 /women-in-ministry.

Secondary Sources

Alexander, Estrelda, and Amos Yong, eds. *Philip's Daughters: Women in Pentecostal-Charismatic Leadership.* Eugene, OR: Wipf and Stock, 2009.

Alexander, Paul. *Peace to War: Shifting Allegiances in the Assemblies of God.* Telford, PA: Cascadia, 2009.

Ambrose, Linda M., and Leah Payne. "Reflections on the Potential of Gender Theory for North American Pentecostal History." *Pneuma* 36, no. 1 (2014): 45–63.

Butler, Anthea D. *Women in the Church of God in Christ: Making a Sanctified World.* Chapel Hill: University of North Carolina Press, 2007.

Casselberry, Judith. *The Labor of Faith: Gender and Power in Black Apostolic Pentecostalism.* Durham: Duke University Press, 2017.

English de Alminana, Margaret, and Lois E. Olena. *Women in Pentecostal and Charismatic Ministry: Informing a Dialogue on Gender, Church, and Ministry.* Boston: Brill, 2017.

Gilkes, Cheryl Townsend. "'Together and in Harness': Women's Traditions in the Sanctified Church." *Signs* 10, no. 4 (Summer 1985): 678–99.

Lawless, Elaine J. *God's Peculiar People: Women's Voice and Folk Tradition in a Pentecostal Church.* Lexington: University Press of Kentucky, 2005.

———. *Handmaidens of the Lord: Pentecostal Women Preachers and Traditional Religion.* Philadelphia: University of Pennsylvania Press, 1988.

———. "Rescripting Their Lives and Narratives: Spiritual Life Stories of Pentecostal Women Preachers." *Journal of Feminist Studies in Religion* 7, no. 1 (Spring 1991): 53–71.

May, Elaine Tyler. *Homeward Bound: American Families in the Cold War Era.* New York: Basic Books, 2008.

Northrup, Dolores. *The Unlimited God: Stretch Your Expectations, God Has Not Changed.* N.p.: Xulon Press, 2008.

Ramírez, Daniel. *Migrating Faith: Pentecostalism in the United States and Mexico.* Chapel Hill: University of North Carolina Press, 2015.

Sanders, Cheryl J. "History of Women in the Pentecostal Movement." Cyberjournal for Pentecostal-Charismatic Research PCCNA National Conference, 1996, Pentecostal and Charismatic Research Archive, Series 2, Box 2 Folder 1, Center for African American Church History and Research, Dallas, Texas. Digital version USC Libraries Pentecostal and Charismatic Research Archive.

Self, Robert O. *All in the Family: The Realignment of American Democracy Since the 1960s*. New York: Hill and Wang, 2012.

Wacker, Grant. *Heaven Below: Early Pentecostals and American Culture*. Cambridge: Harvard University Press, 2001.

CHAPTER 9

Women in the Luz del Mundo Church

A Transnational Study

Patricia Fortuny Loret de Mola

Most feminist scholars hold that Christian religions are patriarchal and therefore male dominated. Scholars who see only the patriarchal side in any religious organization employ a definition in which power is located at the apex of the institutional structure (or *on the emperor's head* in Michel Foucault's words), and not as a power that flows throughout the whole structure from bottom to top, reaching the most hidden and marginal places of the structure. If we just observe the higher echelons within a religion, we would often find that formal power is taken up by males in the hierarchy of the church. However, if we look beyond formal power and focus on the informal types of power, then we will see a predominant female presence. Stressing only the patriarchal side prevents us from looking at the other side of religious power and denies the agency that women execute within a Pentecostal tradition, as in the cases studied here.

Furthermore, to get a better picture of women acting through faith we must look at "marginal, non-mainstream religions, [where] women often have more power and autonomy than in the major religion found in their society."[1] Mexican historians and anthropologists like Isabel Lagarriga,[2] Silvia Ortíz,[3] and Noemí Quezada[4] have noted in their studies that in Mexico, since colonial times, it has been mostly women who have participated in religious or spiritual activities, both in number and intensity. These scholars confirm that in both the

Old and the New Worlds, in order to stand out and play leading roles, women have turned to peripheral religious expressions outside or inside institutions but always far away from mainstream creeds and traditions, such as occurs in the Luz del Mundo (LDM) Church in Mexico. It is there, in marginal spaces, that women both historically and in the present have achieved greater acknowledgment as well as better access to social spaces otherwise unattainable.

In this chapter I focus my analysis on the quotidian life of three Mexican migrant women belonging to the Oneness Pentecostal Church (LDM) in Mexico and the United States. The study is based on fieldwork carried out during the summers of 1999 and 2000 with transnational members on both sides of the US-Mexico border: Houston, Texas, and Guadalajara, Jalisco; theoretical interpretation of the empirical data is grounded on the paradigm of "transnational migration," which centers on mobility across nation-state borders.[5]

In Mexico, this church and all the other non-Catholic churches comprise a religious minority and therefore hold a lower social and political position than that of the Catholic institution. Although I am dealing here with the US branch of the LDM (in Houston), the character of a subordinate tradition integrated with "second-class Mexican status" is still imprinted on it. I look at power as informal that has as its central point human agency rather than only social structure. I see these three women as individual subjects with their own experiences, interests, projects, and choices, and all of these not just as the result of cultural norms and expectations. These case studies explain how some female believers of LDM manage to succeed within a male-dominated Pentecostal institution embedded in a social context that is also controlled by men.

In their article on "The Ironic Role of Women in Immigrant Religious Institutions" migration scholars Helen Ebaugh and Janet Chafetz have stressed that "in the process of 'doing gender' and recreating gender through nurturing activities, women typically also contribute to the recreation of the class and ethnic (sub) cultures in which their families are embedded."[6] Immigrant women are also capable of taking advantage of the US multicultural environment where new and different opportunities exist, and they can develop gender consciousness to better perceive and resist systemic gender inequality.

In the following section I give a brief description of the LDM and the norms and rules that women have to abide by. The following three sections include the case studies of women from three different generations. The description and analysis of the case studies presented here were originally written sometime in 2002. Consequently, the narrative has been rewritten to account for inevitable changes in perspective, given the twenty-year gap, together with necessary verb tense adjustments. Finally, I outline and analyze the three women's achievements and limitations within their particular social contexts.

A FEW WORDS ABOUT THE CHURCH

La Luz del Mundo Church was founded in the late 1920s by a Mexican man of peasant origin and military experience as a common soldier. This religious movement started in Guadalajara, Jalisco, located in the western-central region of Mexico, which is characterized by a powerful and belligerent Catholicism. After the Revolution (1910–20), many poor Mexican migrants left the United States and returned to their home country. Eusebio Joaquín González (later on called the Apostle Aarón),[7] founder of LDM, recruited his first followers from among poor displaced people, and like most Pentecostal leaders, he did not enjoy any previous legitimation; he propagated a Bible-based Protestant religion in a context dominated by an all-embracing, intransigent, anti-Protestant Catholicism that did not favor lay biblical literacy. He represented a counterideology attractive to people who possessed little and were dissatisfied with their social conditions. The exportation of Pentecostalism via returned migrants from the United States to Mexico in the 1920s and 1930s also contributed to the rise of LDM. One of the main attractions of Aarón's new faith was to break the Catholic clergy's monopoly over the "production and distribution of sacred goods" as Bourdieu would say.[8]

Aarón died in 1964 and his son Samuel succeeded him. The religion's origin and development centered around these two charismatic figures until the death of Samuel in December 2014, when his son Naasón became the next living Apostle. The international headquarters are located in a district of Guadalajara called Hermosa Provincia (see fig. 9.1).[9] LDM constitutes a transnational church because it is a "a religious system whose organization transcends frontiers and weaves over and above national, political and cultural specificities a network of ideologically unified communities linked to a single seat of government."[10] Its doctrine and practice combine Pentecostal norms and theology with regional Catholic culture. It is a loosely Oneness Church where baptism is administered "in the name of Jesus Christ,"[11] rather than in the Trinitarian formula "in the name of the Father, and of the Son, and of the Holy Spirit." Devotees consider their faith to be the restoration of the primitive Christian Church; thus they are the "chosen people." God had elected the Apostles Aarón, Samuel, and Naasón to restore his religious belief in the modern world. They are Christians

Fig. 9.1. The LDM's grand headquarters temple (built from 1983 to 1991) lies at the heart of and towers over the Hermosa Provincia neighborhood. The temple seats approximately twelve thousand with standing room for thousands more. Photo: Wikimedia Commons / Cesar Rodriguez Mejia (CC BY-SA 4.0).

who follow the Bible and accept Jesus Christ as the savior of humanity. Nevertheless, salvation will be achieved only by following the living Apostle.[12]

Women do not have access to the priesthood, which includes bishops, pastors, and deacons, all of whom are anointed in a special ceremony in the presence of the Apostle. Women can only be *encargadas* (in charge)[13] or *obreras* (workers). These positions are equivalent to evangelizers or missionaries, and they are at the bottom of the hierarchy. Women are also granted broad roles in the administration, coordination, and organization of their communities. The women adhere to a number of norms regarding attire; women wear long full skirts or dresses, maintain long hair, wear veils or shawls on their heads during religious services, and do not wear jewelry or makeup as adornment. In contrast, male members do not have to change as much of their appearance as women do upon conversion. During religious services, women sit on the left side of the temple and men on the right. Since its very beginning, an exclusively female prayer service directed by women was established. The ritual is generally held during the morning from Monday to Saturday in every congregation throughout the world. Instead of standing at the center of the altar like laymen do when they deliver a sermon, women preach from a special place at floor level.

THE CASE STUDIES

The cases selected are not necessarily representative of all women belonging to LDM in the United States. However, the different ages of each (Antonia, sixty-four; Isabel, thirty-six; and Amanda, twenty-seven) give a good idea of the type of life led by many female members of similar ages within the congregations studied. I met these three women first in Guadalajara around the days of the Holy Supper celebrations in 1999,[14] and I interviewed them in 2000 a few months later in Houston, where they were living. The church is a common denominator of all the cases, though women always translate, adjust, and reinterpret the norms and limitations demanded by their religion. Of the three cases, the last two women were born within the LDM, and the first one was converted when she was a child, and thus did not receive much of a Catholic education. These case studies allow us to see how women reinterpret religious, educational, economic, and domestic domains. In wielding their agency, female members use their knowledge and experience and adapt themselves to their own personal circumstances.

First Case Study: First Generation

Antonia has trusted me since I met her, perhaps because most of her nuclear family members do not belong to the Luz del Mundo, and this makes her feel more familiar with outsiders like myself.[15] She phoned me early one morning to let me know that she was going to prepare *pozole*,[16] and that she was expecting me at five o'clock in the afternoon to have lunch at her home in the Magnolia barrio,[17] located in Houston, where she lives with her husband Joaquín, their eldest daughter, and four grandchildren. Her three children bought the house for her, so she could stay in Houston with them.

The first time I saw Antonia she was sixty-four years old during the women's religious service in May 1999. She conducted a very impressive service because of the way she delivered the gospel with her rich vocabulary and self-assurance during the ritual. Antonia was born in 1935, in a little village called Villa Purificación located in the region of Autlán, Jalisco, Mexico. She finished only elementary school in Mexico, as her family was very poor. Her father worked his own land, and Antonia remembered that as a child she used to help him pick cotton and peanuts in the fields. She is part of the second generation of converts. She was very young when evangelizers went to her little village to spread the Word and her parents converted. Later on, they all migrated to Guadalajara to be close to their church. When Antonia's family moved to the city, they initially lived near downtown, where LDM had its first temple in the late 1930s, and then in the 1950s, they moved again to what it is today Hermosa Provincia.

As a young woman Antonia migrated from Guadalajara to a northern-border city. On this occasion, Antonia recounted that she left home at this time in order to leave the city because she wanted to secure a better job. She then stayed with one of her sisters in Ciudad Juárez. Once there, she frequently crossed the border to clean houses in El Paso, Texas. While living in Ciudad Juárez she met and married Joaquín, despite the fact that he was not a member of the church. Joaquín and Antonia had their three children in Ciudad Juárez.

At the beginning of the 1980s, Antonia revealed again her strong agency and also her self-made way of being and decided to leave Ciudad Juárez in order to go to Houston. Her idea was to look for a better job and salary in order to attain a higher standard of living for her family. Even though she knew that this would be a sacrifice that would separate her from her children and husband, it was worth it as it would mean a benefit for all in the long term. Although Joaquín was a carpenter, he was also a man of many vices, and she hoped to give her children a better life. When Antonia started her process of settling down in Houston, she was on her own, but she was able to find a place to live and a job, thanks to her church networks. She became a babysitter in a government nursery. Later on, she sent for all her children to come to Houston and started the years-long process of facilitating their legal immigration. The eldest daughter Maria, like her father Joaquín, never joined the church. Maria worked in a disco in the evenings and returned home late. Antonia and her husband looked after their grandchildren while Maria was at work. Antonia also had a son who lived in Houston but rented a room closer to his job and did not seem to be very close either to the family or to the church. Karla, Antonia's youngest daughter, was twenty-one years old. She attended middle school in Mexico and high school in Houston. At the time of the interviews, Karla had a job as a pharmaceutical technician in a drugstore with desires to further her education. She was the only one besides Antonia who was a member of the LDM. A year before our conversation, Karla was married to Martin, a member of the Magnolia congregation and a second-generation migrant. Antonia and Karla used to travel together every August to attend the Holy Supper in Guadalajara and of course met every day at the church for evening services. She emphasized in her conversations that the congregation was like her spiritual family.

Antonia lived and worked alone in Houston for many years, in order to support her children and to give them a better education. Joaquín stayed in Ciudad Juárez, and did not join the family until a few years before our interviews, when he traveled to Houston to attend Karla's wedding. It was Antonia who frequently visited her husband in Ciudad Juárez to keep her marriage alive. Joaquín never prohibited his wife from attending religious services; in fact, he himself started frequenting Sunday services around the time I interviewed Antonia in Magnolia.

Antonia's biography is very similar to many Latin American women who either leave their husbands or are abandoned by them and consequently become the breadwinners of their one-parent families. In this case, her church networks made it easier for Antonia to settle in a foreign country all by herself, and she was able to achieve education, jobs, and legal status for all her children. And maybe she did the same for her husband. She married an outsider from the church and in this sense, consciously or not, disobeyed its norms. Two of her children did not seem to be interested at all in Antonia's religion, although they both helped their mother with their earnings. Maria paid for her mother's travel every year to Guadalajara. Although Antonia never mentioned it, she seemed happy and satisfied with Karla's achievements in both the secular and the religious spheres. They all got along well despite the fact that they were a real hybrid and plural family. I did not see any pressure from Antonia toward Maria concerning her worldly life. Joaquín and Antonia went shopping together, walked to the park, and even went together to the temple sometimes. So Antonia was able to maintain her religion as well as her family. She was a very well-respected member within her religious community. Celebrating Karla's wedding in Houston's congregation instead of the big temple in Guadalajara was a good choice for Antonia's social status. She explained to me that when people marry in La Hermosa Provincia in massive collective weddings (especially during the Santa Cena week in August), the couples can get lost in the crowd. For somebody like Antonia, her daughter's wedding in their own local community would have certainly brought her higher status.

Second Case Study: Second Generation

Isabel was born in 1963 in Guadalajara. She was only twenty-three in 1986 when she migrated with her husband to Houston. She belonged to the fourth generation within LDM. In June 2000, I phoned her to arrange an interview, but she was leaving for Guadalajara to stay with her family for Father's Day. When she got back to Houston in July, she approached me at the entry of the church on her own initiative and asked me if I still wanted the interview. It was one of these lucky days that anthropologists seldom have in the field. We had a very pleasant chat, and Isabel was especially honest with her answers.

As a child, Isabel grew up within the confines of Hermosa Provincia. She was the third child of ten siblings. Her father, as well as the rest of the family, had always been in trade. She attended public schools, finished her middle education, and became a public school elementary teacher in Guadalajara. In those times, to become a teacher it was not necessary to have the equivalent of a high school education. Before she married, she replaced a teacher for a year and also worked in one kindergarten class in La Hermosa Provincia. At twenty-two she married Abelardo from an old family of the same religion and barrio, and together they went to try their luck in Houston in 1986. Abelardo worked very hard in the construction business, and they were able to buy a plot of land and built a couple of houses. At the time of the interviews, they were constructing a third house and were renting out one of their properties, which was next door to the temple. At the time they had four children, ages fourteen, twelve, nine, and eight. Isabel had lost her last child, so she was very afraid of getting pregnant again. However, Abelardo wanted to have more children as he came from a small family. Isabel used to complain about this, saying that he was not the one who had to look after the children.

When Isabel and Abelardo arrived in Houston in 1986, a married sister of Isabel, Esther, was already living there. In fact, it was Esther's husband who told Abelardo about the job in Houston. Isabel did not really need any help from the church as she had her sister there to support her. Isabel had never worked outside her home since she married. When she had spoken about getting a job like her sister's, Abelardo replied that she would have to earn enough money for him to stop working so he could take care of the children and do the housework. He also argued that she would arrive back home too tired and in a bad mood and would be unable to look after her family properly. Certainly, looking after four children, two of them in their teens, would have been very difficult and time consuming for Isabel and would have required being a full-time mother and housewife. Maybe from a feminist point of view, Abelardo should have worked less to have been able to share some of the child care responsibilities in order to give Isabel an equal opportunity to have a job outside the home.

However, we cannot simply assume that Abelardo acted out of a patriarchal attitude, nor can we confidently assert that his sole concern was to give his wife a more comfortable life. Isabel never complained about her situation during our conversations and seemed content to follow her family trading tradition, in her case selling salty snacks every evening when the services ended to make some pocket money. Presumably, she also received rent from the houses. Therefore, they had a comfortable income.

They traveled to Guadalajara at least four times a year, where they stayed in their own house between one and three weeks. Isabel, like many other Mexican migrants, learned how to drive in Houston. She was assigned a position as *encargada* of a group of sixty young married women (between fourteen and twenty-nine years old). She attended religious services twice a day and gave a sermon every three weeks in the women's meeting. Her social life was mostly reduced to church people and family. In contrast to Antonia's complicated life, Isabel's was very steady, though it was not one without struggle. As a child she had the means to attain some formal education, which allowed her to work before her marriage. Despite the fact that both women were raised as members of the same church, each one of them took a rather different path when they decided to marry. While Antonia had been on her own a great deal of her life, Isabel had kept her husband by her side, and apparently, she had never been in a position that might have led her to resist her husband's authority. There was no need for her to become insubordinate to Abelardo, no reasons for challenging or confronting him. He was always a good husband and father, the breadwinner of the family who abided by church norms. Perhaps it would have been counterproductive to fight against him, and for Isabel it was better to remain the way she was. When I asked her if she wanted to have more children (she had four already), Isabel hesitated a great deal with her answer and said, "Well, it is not that I do not like children, but I think they mean a lot of hard work." This statement only proved that she had internalized the implicit and explicit set of cultural norms regarding how to be a proper "woman" within both the LDM and her social context. In Houston, with its relatively liberal social and cultural context, women in general enjoy more freedom than in Mexico; however, personal circumstances can become determinant in allowing women believers to attain the same rights that men have, as these cases illustrate. Antonia and Isabel have responded to their own circumstances the best way they could. Although Antonia did not follow very orthodox methods, she managed to solve her problems in the end.

Third Case Study: Third Generation

I first talked to Amanda in May 1999 when I visited the Central Congregation in Houston for the first time. She was extraordinarily frank about her personal experiences and expectations in the United States. The following year, on June 12, she picked me up at the Central Congregation in Houston and took me to her home. There, the two of us had a long and quiet chat. She was very kind, giving up her few free hours off work during the week for an interview that I was eagerly anticipating. Amanda's oldest sister worked at the Public Relations Office of the church in Guadalajara. Amanda's family was relatively close to the higher echelons of the hierarchy of the church.

She was born in Mexico City in 1976. When she was eight years old her father died and her mother took Amanda and her three sisters to live in La Hermosa Provincia, Guadalajara. Amanda's mother worked as a nurse in a national health institution, never married again, and was able to raise four daughters on her own. Amanda and her sisters represent the fourth generation of her family as church members—her great-grandparents were the first to be converted to LDM. She spent the rest of her childhood in La Hermosa Provincia, where she attended public schools through high school. When she was seventeen, she met Ezequiel in Guadalajara, and a year later they married and went to live in Houston. Like Amanda, Ezequiel's family had belonged to the church for generations, was well-known in the LDM, and most of his relations were Mexican migrants. His parents were living in New Orleans, but he preferred Houston, where he had lived for five years before marrying Amanda. He was an electrician and was also studying computer engineering with a scholarship from the company where he worked.

Amanda had been in Houston for five years; she was twenty-three years old when I interviewed her. She recounted that the first year she lived in Houston was the most challenging time in her life. Newly married, she could not speak any English, did not have a phone at home to communicate with her family, and felt very depressed for a while. She used to think that she had made a mistake or was foolish to leave home; she did not know what to do. However, as she had done before, she recovered quickly from her culture shock and decided to fight through her difficult circumstances. I remembered very vividly even now, as I am writing this chapter many years after the fact, the strong emotion that accompanied Amanda when she narrated her story. In her own words she said, "I left my apartment, went to the nearest hotel a few blocks away, and asked for a job. I filled in an application form and was helped by somebody who could speak Spanish and English. And when I was called I even rejected a job as a cleaner, and was able to choose a different type of job. I became responsible for placing a rose and a chocolate in each room every afternoon."

Amanda turned down the first job that she was offered and said again in her own words, "I did not want to become anybody's servant." During our conversation Amanda emphasized that she did not want to be like "most of the Mexicans here [there in Houston], who only hang around with other Mexicans or Hispanics and do not mix with Anglo, African, and Chinese Americans." She wanted to have more multicultural connections than most Mexicans have. That is why she put all her energy into working and learning English. An example of the effort that Amanda and her husband had made toward becoming more "American" is an English message on their recording machine. Theirs was the only message in the English language that I ever heard among Luz del Mundo people.[18]

From April to the end of July 2000 Amanda worked fourteen hours a day. She took up two jobs (both in doughnut shops) with only one day off. Two years later she was able to speak fluent English, lived in a more multicultural neighborhood than those of her religious fellows, and mixed with middle-class white and Black people. Amanda and her husband were already buying the house where they lived. Her house was considered a much better place than those inhabited by most of the Mexican immigrants from the same church. Amanda seemed as if she was becoming part of the American mainstream faster than other Mexicans inside or outside LDM. She credited those achievements to her own strength and willpower.

Because of her working hours, Amanda was unable to attend religious services on a daily basis, as required by LDM. So she went to the temple on her own many times during the week just before she started her first job at five o'clock in the morning. There she prayed and sang for ten minutes and then drove to the doughnut shop. She stated that praying every morning made her feel better the rest of the day; other believers expressed similar sentiments. According to Amanda and other churchgoers, Samuel, the Servant of God and Apostle at that time, used to pray every morning in Guadalajara from four-thirty to five o'clock. Amanda thought that praying at the same time as the Apostle would translate into more blessings for her. She also attended the temple on Mondays in the afternoon on her days off. She had informed the minister of her working hours and therefore about not being able to attend religious services during the week. Amanda volunteered the information about this dialogue with her pastor, as I did not ask her anything concerning the church.

Amanda also had an arrangement with Ezequiel concerning the two jobs that she had taken. While Ezequiel was both working and studying to earn a degree in computing, he was just as busy as she was, except for the weekends. During weekends he went to see Amanda at her job and they had lunch together. As long as she and Ezequiel agreed on her work schedule, she would continue the work. In any case, she stressed that she was keeping both jobs only for a few months until they went to Guadalajara in August for the religious festivities. Just like Isabel's family, Amanda and Ezequiel travel three or four times a year to Guadalajara to attend religious festivities and visit their families. Amanda said that she was going to start a course in nursing in September of the same year of our interview, so she could get a better job afterward. In fact, Amanda often thought of getting a better salary in order to achieve a higher standard of living.

Ezequiel and Amanda fared well in both education and income. They were already planning to buy another house, which would be closer to the new temple that was being built for the Central Congregation. Once they had their new home, they planned to rent their first house, which was already paid for, in order to finance the second house. Amanda also had to pay monthly for her new car, which as she had said before leaving Guadalajara two years earlier, had been the main reason she was working so hard. As a couple, they had worked out a very precise division of labor. Ezequiel's money paid the bills, and they were able to acquire appliances for the house. A month before our interview took place, they had bought a washer and dryer. They also bought computing equipment that was used mainly by Ezequiel for his studies. It did not really surprise me to hear of Amanda's lifestyle and expectations as she had let me know about them when I interviewed her in 1999. She seemed to be taking advantage of her social capital to be able to integrate into American society for her own benefit.

CONCLUSION

One first and superficial glance at these three limited case studies allows us to see the diversity of choices that women with the same religious background can make in their lives. We can also note that, though the church can act as a constraining and coercive factor, individual women always find out how to pursue their own interests without completely cutting themselves off from the religious community. The cases presented are also illustrative of some important changes existing among the different age-generations of the three women. Those changes are not only the result of the women's agency or of the religious framework intensifying or halting these transformations but are obviously connected to the external world, to the social, economic, and political development of the two countries in which they live. Women's attitudes in the world have undergone great changes from the 1960s to the present. Antonia, who represents the oldest generation, finished only elementary school; Isabel managed to complete a teacher's degree; and Amanda, of the youngest generation, was able to attain a high school degree and was planning to further her studies. Obtaining a high degree of education depends not only on the age of the person but also on the economic possibilities of the social class to which he or she belongs.

On the other hand, it is true that most members in this church tend to wed at a rather early age (sometimes from fourteen or sixteen years old) in Mexico and in the United States. But it is also true that an increasing percentage of women now are not getting married until their late twenties or are continuing their studies even after marriage. Many young female members have expressed that they are very cautious when looking for feasible husbands because they want to be sure that their men will be liberal enough to permit them to study and/or work while married. This means that these men must be willing to share some of the nurturing tasks at home and outside with their wives. This did not happen in Isabel's marriage. I have tried to establish that even within a Pentecostal church that should be easily classified as patriarchal, women are capable of reinterpreting the religious values and norms. Domains outside of the religious sphere can have an important influence on women's worldviews and everyday experiences, decisions, and actions. Devout women, like men, interact with a plurality of social actors in the political, economic, educational, social, and cultural domains that affect their views and permit them to reorganize their own system of beliefs as well as their practices.

In terms of gender relations, the cases also corroborate a considerable degree of diversity among them. Viewed within a continuum, Isabel seems to be at one extreme of the pole, fulfilling perfectly well what is expected from a woman in the traditional framework. Amanda stands in the middle of the continuum, never completely challenging the system of male authority but neither totally submitting to it, and with a certain degree of arbitrariness—as is always the case when interpreting another human being's life from the social scientific point of view—we can locate Antonia at the other end of the spectrum, since she resisted and somehow even confronted both the religious norms and the broader male-dominated system. Isabel is a housewife and plays the female role model in her religious post as an *encargada* of sixty young married women. She has followed the normative rules of being a mother and wife, always taking care of her family with apparently few interests of her own. Antonia, on the other hand, was never as conventional as Isabel. As we saw in Antonia's story, she was able to act at different phases in her life story, contradicting the domestic work imposed by the normative system of both church and society. She followed her own advice and left her man and then became the main breadwinner and guide of her children. At the same time, she maintained for many years her relationship with her husband, and in doing this she "wielded and yielded" simultaneously as anthropologist Magdalena Villarreal has pointed out.[19] She never left the unconverted members of her family, again abiding by the rules of Western society but at the same time living against the ideal principles of the church in that she was not able to integrate them into her religion (which could have meant that she had not given herself completely to God). As with Amanda, she can be placed in the middle of the continuum because she did not resist the male-dominated system as Antonia did, but neither did she put up with all the rules (like Isabel did). She was very good at playing the double role of being at the same time a good Christian and a liberal modern woman.

Amanda, the youngest of the group, was capable of conciliating her religious sphere with the outside world. She took seriously the modern goals and dreams of the Western world. Her life had to be surrounded by certain commodities that were carriers of meanings that brought her social status and personal satisfaction. Amanda floated in between deep personal needs, both spiritual and material. Unlike Isabel, Amanda had many projects outside her domestic domain. Though she was still young and yet without children, she started something that she would not probably give up later on. She had learned how to fight for herself and had struggled to obtain her goals. However, it is paradoxical that Amanda acted and moved as a liberal and modern woman in the economic world, yet she did not question her religious background. She did not seem to perceive any threat in the systemic gender inequality that pervades the LDM Church. She did not recognize her church as a coercive institution because, just as with Isabel, the religious norms were not an obstacle for her in accomplishing her life projects. On the contrary, Amanda and many other young female believers credited their religion for their personal success.

The cases described in this chapter offer evidence of Mexican migrants taking advantage of their new cultural and economic environment in the United States. However, in Amanda's case this process is clearer than in the others; she seems to be very conscious of her actions in order to become part of the "American world" but without disengaging herself from her Mexican world. As anthropologist Ulf Hannerz suggests, she can leave when she wants and come back when it pleases her to either of the two worlds.[20] She wants to acquire enough skills to move naturally in the American world, and she has done all things possible for getting them. In other words, Amanda has achieved "a personal ability to make one's way into other cultures, through listening, looking, intuiting and reflecting."[21] Antonia and Isabel lacked some of Amanda's skills; they were not able to speak English and hence their everyday activities were relatively limited to the "locals" who lived on either side of the border; they tended to interact mostly with people of their own spiritual community or to a lesser degree with people belonging to their own panethnic group, that is, Hispanics. In other words, women like Isabel and maybe even Antonia can be better classified as "guardians of continuity" rather than as "agents of change."[22]

Amanda's case study distinguishes her not only from Isabel and Antonia but from numerous female and male Mexican migrant believers in Houston, particularly concerning her expressed wish to interact with people from diverse ethnicities and hence also diverse faiths, as she emphasized in her interviews. It is one of many of the unspoken church rules that believers should not establish close social connections with people outside of LMD because it could be dangerous for them to be influenced by their worldly lifestyle, leading to members deviating from their faith or even rejecting it. In fact, prohibiting or limiting members' social connections with people outside the church can have a negative effect in their life because it will conceivably reduce the possibilities to enlarge their social networks, which are very important in order to accumulate social and economic capital.

NOTES

1. Gross, *Feminism and Religion.*

2. Lagarriga Attias, "Mujer," 251–64; Lagarriga Attias, "Experiencia religiosa"; Lagarriga Attias, "Participación religiosa."

3. Ortíz Echániz, "El poder del trance"; Ortíz Echániz, *Religiosidad popular.*

4. Quezada, "Alumbrados," 581–86; Quezada, *Enfermedad y maleficio.*

5. The research was undertaken between 1999 and 2002 within the global Religious Ethnic New Immigrants Research Project (RENIR2) directed by Helen Rose Ebaugh of the Center for Immigration Research in the University of Houston and financed by the Pew Charitable Trust Foundation; Ebaugh and Chafetz, "Introduction," 1–14.

6. Ebaugh and Chafetz, "Agents," 1–37,

7. Eusebio Joaquín González was the civilian name of the founder of LDM before April 1926, when he had a revelation from God that commanded him to be called Aarón. In the first chapter of the book by Jason Dormady, the author explains thoroughly the church and the founder's history. Dormady, *Primitive Revolution*, 19–62.

8. The French sociologist refers to the concept of "sacred goods" in order to explain, for example, how within Catholicism the production and circulation of the Bible remained a monopoly of the priests during many centuries. Bourdieu, "Génesis y estructura."

9. *Hermosa Provincia* [Beautiful Province] is a municipal area in which members of the church are concentrated in some cities in the world. The first Hermosa Provincia was founded in the 1930s in Guadalajara, and it also became the site of the LDM's largest and most sacred temple. The relatively small group of privileged people who live in La Hermosa Provincia, or even close to it, are the elite of the LDM. It would be like being a Catholic living in the Vatican.

10. Hervieu-Léger, "Faces," 104.

11. See chapter 2 of this volume.

12. Adrián Calvillo Delgado, spokesperson for the church, explained that there was a total of five million believers in the world with two million alone in Mexico in 2014. The spokesperson also said that this faith has extended into fifty-eight countries. Bareño, "Luz del Mundo."

13. To be in charge means being responsible for an age group of members that can number from thirty to three hundred. The members are of the same sex as that of the person in charge. The group holds religious prayers and doctrinal studies three times a week for one hour or less (depending on the congregation). The person in charge selects doctrinal topics to be discussed and also is aware of the absences or faults of the participants. In case of sickness, pregnancy, financial or personal problems, the *encargada* or *encargado* will try to solve or help the member, unless it is something extremely serious that requires consultation with the pastor. The encargada is a sort of spiritual guide for every member of her group. She must know the activities, jobs, and possibilities of the people in her groups to be able to advise, help, support, or admonish when necessary.

14. The Holy Supper is the most important ritual of the year and takes place every August 14 in the Hermosa Provincia of Guadalajara and in thousands of temples of LDM around the world. For extended and very detailed information concerning this central ceremony, see Fortuny, "Santa Cena," 15–50.

15. Names have all been changed to maintain the individuals' anonymity.

16. *Pozole* is a typical dish from the state of Jalisco. It is made of corn and cooked with pork, beef, or chicken. It is served with sliced cabbage, onion, radish, *chile*, and toasted tortillas, or tostadas.

17. The Magnolia barrio has been inhabited by Mexican migrants since the 1980s. People of Mexican or Latin American origin are very visible in Magnolia, and it is very common to hear people speaking in Spanglish or Spanish.

18. I noticed that the majority of LDM's followers (unlike Amanda and Ezequiel) did not understand, nor could speak or read in English. In fact, the numerous services that I attended in Houston (from 1999 to 2002), and later on in Atlanta (in 2006), were usually in Spanish, even though the second generation of migrants or those who were born in the United States were able to speak and read very well in English; for these young people Spanish was their second language.

19. Villarreal, "Wielding and Yielding."

20. Hannerz, *Transnational Connections*, 103.

21. Ibid., 103.

22. Ibid., 28.

BIBLIOGRAPHY

Bareño Dominguez, Rosario. "La Luz del Mundo a nivel mundial" [The Light of the World Worldwide]. *El Occidental*, June 7, 2019. https://www.eloccidental .com.mx/local/luz-del-mundo-a-nivel -mundial-3734715.html.

Bourdieu, Pierre, "Génesis y Estructura del Campo Religioso" [Genesis and

218 *Oneness Pentecostalism*

Structure of the Religious Field].
Relaciones: Estudios de historia y sociedad 27, no. 108 (2006): 29–83.

Dormady, Jason. *Primitive Revolution: Restorationist Religion and the Idea of the Mexican Revolution, 1940–1968.* Albuquerque: University of New Mexico Press, 2011.

Ebaugh, Helen Rose, and Janet S. Chafetz. "Agents for Cultural Reproduction and Structural Change: The Ironic Role of Women in Immigrant Religious Institutions." Unpublished paper, 2000.

———. "Introduction." In *Religion Across Borders: Transnational Immigrant Networks,* edited by Helen Rose Ebaugh and Janet S. Chafetz, 1–14. Walnut Creek, CA: Altamira Press, 2002.

Fortuny, Patricia. "The Santa Cena of the Luz del Mundo Church: A Case of Contemporary Transnationalism." In *Religion Across Borders: Transnational Immigrant Networks,* edited by Helen Rose Ebaugh and Janet Saltzman Chafetz, 15–50. Walnut Creek, CA: Altamira Press, 2002.

Gross, M. Rita. *Feminism and Religion: An Introduction.* Boston: Beacon Press, 1996.

Hannerz, Ulf. *Transnational Connections: Culture, People, Places.* London: Routledge, 1996.

Hervieu-Léger, Danièle. "Faces of Catholic Transnationalism: In and Beyond France." In *Transnational Religion: Fading States,* edited by Suzanne Rudolph and James Piscatori, 104–18. Boulder, CO: Westview, 1997.

Lagarriga Attias, Isabel. "Experiencia religiosa y cambios de creencias en algunas mujeres mexicanas" [Religious Experience and Belief Changes in Some Mexican Women]. Paper presented at the 49th Congreso Internacional de Americanistas, Quito, Ecuador, July 7–12, 1997.

———. "La mujer en la heterodoxia en México" [The Heterodoxy of Woman in Mexico]. Primer Anuario de la Dirección de Etnología y Antropología Social, Lagarriga, Isabel (coord.), Colección Obra Diversa. Instituto Nacional de Antropología e Historia, México, 1995, 251–64.

———. "Participación religiosa: Viejas y nuevas formas de reivindicación femenina en México" [Religious Participation: Old and New Forms of Female Vindication in Mexico]. Paper presented at the 12th Congreso de Estado, Iglesia y Grupos Laicos, Jalapa, Veracruz, México, October 28–30, 1998.

Ortíz Echániz, Silvia. "El poder del trance en la participación femenina en el Espiritualismo Trinitario Mariano" [The Power of Trance in Female Participation within Marian Trinitarian Spiritualism]. Paper presented at the XX Mesa Redonda de la Sociedad Mexicana de Antropología, México, 1987.

———. *Una religiosidad popular: El Espiritualismo Trinitario Mariano* [A Popular Religiosity: Marian Trinitarian Spiritualism]. Colección científica. Mexico City: Instituto Nacional de Antropología e Historia, 1990.

Quezada, Noemí. "Alumbrados del siglo XVII: Análisis de casos" [The Enlightened of the 17th Century: Analysis of Cases]. *Religión en Mesoamérica, XII Mesa Redonda en Sociedad Mexicana de Antropología.* Mexico City, 581–86, 1972.

———. *Enfermedad y maleficio* [Sickness and Witchcraft]. Mexico City: Universidad Nacional Autónoma de México, 1989.

Villarreal, Magdalena. *Wielding and Yielding: Power Subordination and Gender Identity in the Context of a Mexican Development Project.* Wageningen, Netherlands: Wageningen Agricultural University, 1994.

CHAPTER 10

Liturgical Spaces in Mexican Oneness Pentecostalism
Architectural and Spatial Dimensions

Daniel Chiquete

In recent years, studies on Pentecostalism have produced significant writings that address various aspects of this Christian tradition. The diversity and complexity of North and Latin American Pentecostalism demand more specific and geographically delimited studies in order to understand aspects of this spirituality not readily apparent from more general studies. This chapter seeks to contribute to the understanding of an important site of Pentecostalism: the worship space. Here, I offer an interdisciplinary study of Pentecostal architecture in a region of northwestern Mexico and an interpretation of Pentecostal worship spaces. Special attention will be devoted to the interrelation between liturgy and the worship space, along with other factors that affect the spatial conformation. In the field research carried out for this study (including interviews), I analyzed more than thirty places of worship (temples) of Pentecostal churches in the state of Sinaloa, all of which exhibited different particularities of the region. Given the historical primacy and dominance in Sinaloa of the Iglesia Apostólica de la Fe en Cristo Jesús (IAFCJ), the analysis will revolve principally around this Oneness Pentecostal flagship denomination and its charismatic and Neo-Pentecostal spin-offs.

The community of believers that gathers to celebrate its faith in the liturgical act acquires form and reality in a specific space. Through the liturgy, each person relates to the community and to the space and establishes various types of relationships with both. In their interrelation, any change in one of the elements will be reflected in the other two. None of them can be comprehended in isolation.

According to the theology of the liturgy, the worship space should serve the purpose of making the worship celebration adequately visible, audible, clear, and meaningful; it should help reinforce the message without distorting it. The liturgy, in turn, should strive not only to use the space correctly but also to engage it, respect it, and include it as a valuable element of the celebration. Both should allow the celebrating community guidance, security of action, an atmosphere of worship, and a sense of well-being. The body of believers and the liturgical space are thus linked by practical and religious factors. The liturgy, as an expression and celebration of faith, is linked to the worship space in individual and communal perception in such a way that the celebration of worship, as a basic expression of faith, acquires a strong spatial connotation.[1]

THE RELIGIOUS SIGNIFICANCE OF ARCHITECTURE

Architecture, the result of multiple constantly intersecting viewings and counterviewings (aesthetic, technical, cultural, environmental, etc.), is one of the most complex of human creations. It aims to respond to individual and collective needs, both materially and spiritually. It relates to almost all human activities and needs; therefore, it is often replete with spiritual meanings. Humans, as essentially religious beings, express spirituality in almost all the acts of life, both in the individual and social sphere. The spaces created by religious actors implicitly reflect and carry this religious dimension.

Architecture is also a sign. It expresses the function and intention of each space and reveals much about its builders and users. Different liturgies generate, in turn, different architectural forms and liturgical spaces. For Erika Huschke, "The ecclesiastical spaces are parabolically established and express certain convictions about God, about the relationship of human beings with God, the relationships of human beings with each other, and what awaits us after death."[2]

In Pentecostalism the celebration of worship is both a religious and social occasion. The community and the meeting space are simultaneously spiritual and sociocultural realities. These dimensions must be considered, in order to understand the complex interrelation established between them. Believers become the *church* when they acquire corporeality and concreteness within a built space, which is inserted in a larger sociocultural space. The liturgical space is delimited and separated from the outside world but also gives concrete expression to the celebrant community as the body of Christ.

In Catholicism, unlike Protestantism, the temple is valued as a privileged space, as a determined historical place for the encounter of the community with God and for divine revelation through the sacraments and the priestly office. The temple and the liturgy, especially at the Eucharistic moment, directly mediate the presence of God and make possible communication between the community of believers and the sacred. Catholic theologian architect Juan Anaya Duarte affirms: "The destiny or function of the Christian temple is to be the sacred space where Christians, gathered in community/communion, receive the signs of God and they signify their response to him. Therefore, the temple must express that dialogue and signify that encounter of the ecclesial community with God. Furthermore, the temple is part of the dialogue with God."[3]

THE CONTEXT OF THE SPACES ANALYZED: THE STATE OF SINALOA

All religious life is experienced as mediated by an environment; this allows the celebrating community to establish different types and levels of relationships (integration, assimilation, confrontation, etc.). Architecture expresses part of this range of relationships with the environment. Thus, the interpretation of Pentecostal architecture must take into account the frame of reference where it exists. Pentecostalism is particularly sensitive to its context.

The state of Sinaloa is located on the coast of the Pacific Ocean in the northwest region of Mexico, across the gulf of California from the Baja California peninsula. Together with the states of Sonora, Baja California Sur, and Baja California Norte, it forms a broad geopolitical region called "Northwest Mexico," which is framed by the Pacific Ocean and the rugged Sierra Madre Occidental mountain range. The sea and the mountain plains are the principal elements that comprise this geographical space.[4]

Sinaloa lies beyond the area that anthropologists and ethnologists called Mesoamerica, which extends from northern Mexico to Costa Rica. The most important pre-Hispanic cultures of North and Central America developed in Mesoamerica. This partly explains the difference of its cultural background from that of other regions of the country. In the past, California, Arizona, and New Mexico belonged to this region, with which Sinaloa is still linked in various ways. One index of this: 68 percent of Sinaloans in the United States reside in California and 20 percent in Arizona.[5] This linked population also facilitates the flow of religious ideas between the two countries, including Pentecostalism.

The agricultural wealth of the state of Sinaloa spares the region from suffering the acute poverty of most regions of the country. The unfair distribution of wealth, however, produces social inequalities that generate social tensions. Sinaloa is also one of the states with the highest level of crime in the country (third highest), most of which is directly or indirectly linked to drug trafficking. This is where one of the most violent and best organized mafias in the country is based. Furthermore, drug use is one of the region's most dire social ills.[6]

Thus, social imbalances, drug trafficking, the geographic links between the center of the country and the southwestern United States, the migratory waves of peasants in search of better living conditions, the general consumption of drugs, among other problems, generate an environment of insecurity and violence conducive to the emergence of various religious manifestations, including various Pentecostal Movements.

Brief Historical Description of Worship Spaces in Mexican Pentecostalism

In a strict sense, a history of the liturgical spaces of Pentecostalism cannot be written. What can be attempted is a description of the spaces that have been used by some Pentecostal groups as worship spaces. These descriptions, at best, give us a reference on how they have been understood and used. As there is no reference work on the subject, what I will offer is a review of some of the most important works on the history of Pentecostalism and, from those, expand upon observations that the authors made regarding spaces of worship.

From Topeka and Los Angeles to the Consolidation in Mexico, 1900–1925

The origin of Pentecostalism is rooted in the reappearance/restoration of glossolalia and other ecstatic experiences that had disappeared from Christian practice. Most scholars agree that the reappearance/restoration of these experiences occurred at Charles Parham's Bethel Bible school in Topeka, Kansas. With some reservations, scholars have established January 1, 1901, as the date of this event. Originating in a school, Pentecostalism has since its beginning been detached from or very weakly linked to temples and traditional "holy" places. This school was at once a center of study and a place of prayer. The classrooms were converted into places of worship, where the gift of glossolalia was sought. A witness to these events, Howard D. Stanley, wrote in 1922: "near ten o'clock, while I was in one of the upstairs *rooms*, tongues spread like fire and reached the corner of the *room* (I saw them)" (emphasis added).[7] After some difficult years of rejection and conflict, Parham wrote: "When buildings were closed to us we preached in the streets."[8] Parham was invited in 1903 to preach to Galena, Kansas, and there "began preaching at the Arthur *home*, then they set up a large tent in an adjoining lot and from there they moved on to a larger *auditorium*."[9]

The Pentecostal Movement extended to Los Angeles, where the first glossolalic experience reportedly occurred on April 9, 1906, in one of the prayer meetings organized by William Seymour in a private home.[10] When Pentecostalism spread in this city, the space of the houses became insufficient for the meetings, and Seymour had to rent an old church on Azusa Street that, according to accounts of the time, was almost in ruins after the departure of the original Black Methodist congregation, its later use as a horse stable, and damage after an arsonist's fire.[11] This place would be converted into the Apostolic Faith Mission and would become the main launching point of Pentecostalism's worldwide expansion.

In summary, the early worship sites in this first stage of Pentecostalism were private houses, school halls, tents, and rented churches. From those founding experiences, Pentecostals assigned a value to the spaces based on their usefulness and use in the service of a community and not as places that bore a religious or spiritual value per se.[12] I will later show how this valorization persists in most Pentecostal groups, at least in the region under study.

Oneness Pentecostalism in Northern and Northwestern Mexico (1925–80)

The flagship Oneness Pentecostal denomination in Mexico is the Iglesia Apostólica de la Fe en Cristo Jesús (IAFCJ). The first Apostolic community was founded by Romana Carbajal de Valenzuela in 1914. She and her husband Genaro converted to Pentecostalism in Los Angeles, where they visited a Pentecostal community of Mexican immigrants who "held their meetings in a private *home*" in the aftermath of the Azusa Street Revival.[13] Two years later, Valenzuela returned to her native Chihuahua with the Pentecostal message. Her converts met in a private home in her hometown of Villa Aldama. Valenzuela convinced

Chihuahua City Methodist pastor Rubén Ortega to take charge of the small group. From the beginning, Ortega held services in private homes. A letter quoted by historian Manuel Gaxiola recollects the site of Ortega's later meetings in Chihuahua City: "Mr. Elías Hernández . . . and I attended several times the Pentecostal services that Mr. Ortega led in a private house in the Pacífico neighborhood."[14] Upon Ortega's return to the state capital, Miguel García Carbajal assumed the Villa Aldama pastorate. The town's barber, García, "decided that he would take as a model the church that appears in the Acts of the Apostles and that he would pastor it according to the instructions read in the Epistles. After a season of persecution, García moved southward to Torreón, Coahuila, where he established a sizeable congregation that anchored the movement's expansion throughout northeastern Mexico."[15]

The Apostolic Movement reached the state of Sinaloa in 1925. The construction of the railroad had begun in this state at the beginning of the twentieth century. The city of Guamúchil, located about sixty miles north of Culiacán, the capital city, was an initial outpost: "Some of the North Americans who were directing the construction began to worship in their tents."[16] In 1918, Miguel Gaxiola, who was not Pentecostal but openly sympathetic to Protestant ideas, gathered the people of the towns near Guamúchil and preached to them. Manuel Gaxiola, Miguel's grandson (and oft-cited author in this chapter), narrates, "My mother read the Bible aloud and Don Miguel explained it to her. He also prayed for the people."[17] These activities were carried out in the courtyards of the houses or in the town squares. The arrival of Apostolic repatriates from the United States watered the proto-evangélico seedbed and yielded a considerable harvest that would transform Sinaloa into a bulwark of Apostolicism.[18]

In 1932 the IAFCJ organized as a formal institution in Torreón, Coahuila, in close collaboration with the sister denomination Apostolic Assembly of the Faith in Christ Jesus (AAFCJ) in the United States.[19] The move led to important changes in the spaces, since from henceforth the communities were encouraged to build spaces for worship, as well as homes for pastors.[20] Economic booms, membership growth, and the institutionalization process became the main drivers for the construction of worship spaces in the following decades.

Thus, in the case of this flagship denomination, a historical process and developing understanding can be observed in terms of the relationship of the communities with the spaces for worship. Sacred places per se do not exist; rather, pragmatic criteria predominate in the use of space. I will return to this topic later.

Independent and Neo-Pentecostal Churches

The numerical growth of the IAFCJ accentuated the need to consolidate doctrine, church organization, and leadership strategies. Faced with this process of "institutionalization," some groups and local leaders reacted through the intensification of charismatic experiences such as the reception of the Holy Spirit, glossolalia, and the communication of prophetic messages. A 1973 revival in Guamúchil and Guasave quickly reached Culiacán and other cities. The national leadership resorted effectively to the available institutional disciplinary instruments; this, in turn, provoked internal ruptures. The Iglesia successfully consolidated its institutional control of the majority of the faithful, while the dissidents continued under the same doctrinal principles but detached themselves and reorganized into independent communities. The charismatic fervor waned over the months and years within both factions. The IAFCJ offshoots overlap, of course, in style and influence with other charismatic groups of Pentecostal and mainline provenance. As elsewhere in Latin America, the educational and economic level of Neo-Pentecostal groups is higher than that of the "classical" Pentecostal churches. Neo-Pentecostals are also characterized by their tendency to seek the spectacular in worship, with expectations of extraordinary signs of the presence of the Holy Spirit. The priority that these new churches give to music in their gatherings—with the participation of many musicians, praise teams, and dancers and the use of professional-quality sound equipment and musical instruments—has caused significant changes in the worship spaces. For example, the front areas have been greatly enlarged, taking on a performance stage appearance. The need for greater mobility and flexibility of the space has meant a gradual move away from the use of traditional heavy benches, which have been replaced by folding chairs. The rapid numerical growth of these congregations requires constant expansion of their meeting spaces. This growth has also influenced the exterior form of buildings due to the necessary adaptations undertaken and the loss of importance of the few symbolic elements that "classical" Pentecostalism had preserved from its Protestant roots, such as a certain "ecclesiastical" projection of doors and windows, the use of modest stained glass, the framing of the main entrance, among others.

This "postmodern" spirituality, focused more on the momentary, the spectacular, and individuality, is practiced by groups with greater financial resources, which makes possible the rental of expensive places. Accordingly, spaces such as restaurants, hotel meeting rooms, or cinemas are used as places for liturgical celebration. The relationship between community and worship space, still preserved in "classical" Pentecostalism, tends to further weaken in Neo-Pentecostal practice.

This section highlights the most important characteristics of the spaces for Pentecostal worship services. The intention is to establish the bases for our subsequent interpretation of these characteristics.

Predominance of Quadrangular Surfaces and Linearity of Shapes

Spaces, shapes, areas, and surfaces are determined by linearity and right angles. The most visible and important construction elements, such as doors, windows, stairs, and columns, are also linear. Such features predominate in some furniture and objects such as benches, advertising surfaces, pulpits, and tables, among others.

In terms of function, form, and appearance, the walls of these spaces do not differ from those used in other buildings in the region, such as those of a house, office, or school. The interior walls are minimally utilized since the aim is to avoid any visual obstructions or distractions. Both inside and outside, they are smooth and built with the traditional materials of the region. In the interiors, light colors, especially white, predominate. The buildings contain a fair number of large windows, which allows for sufficient lighting and ventilation in this hot semitropical region.

The volumetric and geometric shape of worship spaces is static and not dynamic. The typical volumetric shape is that of an elongated cube, where the longest axis is generally from the main access to the center of the back wall to the pulpit. The relationship between the length and width, which in various historical periods of religious architecture has been a minimum of 2:1 and frequently 3:1, 4:1, and even greater, rarely appears in Mexican Pentecostal spaces of worship. Of the more than thirty places of worship visited, with one or two exceptions, all correspond to the ratio 2:1 or 1:1.5. The importance of this ratio consists in the relationships that can be established between the people and between the people and the space. The greater the volumetric space, the more the relationships of its users tend to "hierarchize." Volumetric spaces close to the 1:1 ratio allow for a more "democratic" organization of the community, for example, in a semicircular or oval shape. This arrangement allows for closer eye contact and intimacy between a greater number of participants.

The general trend in Pentecostal worship spaces is toward simplicity and clarity. They have an internal structure organized into three basic areas in most cases, although there are other spaces that are organized into five. The three main areas are (1) the area where the community is located, (2) a slightly raised surface, where the pulpit is located and, in some communities, the music group and some seats for the ministers, and (3) an intermediate area, called by the majority the altar. The fivefold division occurs in some churches where the access area assumes certain threshold functions and in which at the back of the pulpit area, separated from it by a curtain, there is a room with a baptismal font, a frequent case in many IAFCJ temples (given the centrality of the baptismal ritual). In the worship spaces of the oldest and institutionalized IAFCJ churches, the entrances are formally and visually more marked/noted than in the independent and Neo-Pentecostal churches.

Dynamic Pentecostal liturgy calls for areas that allow the worshippers to move about and meet at various points in the service. The most important of these areas are the entrance, the small threshold (in some cases), the aisles, and the intermediate area or altar. Although loosely classified, all the areas of the Pentecostal place of worship function as areas of movement or meeting. Again, in this respect a certain difference is perceptible between the older "classical" Pentecostal and the newer Neo-Pentecostal ones. In the latter, they are significantly wider than in the former, although visually less distinct. In general, classical Pentecostal spaces favor meeting/encounter while Neo-Pentecostal ones favor moving about. In "classical" Pentecostalism spaces one celebrates more "in community," while in Neo-Pentecostalism the believer celebrates "alongside a community."

Pentecostal communities are concerned with having visually pleasing spaces for worship, but "aesthetics" are not a high priority. For the decoration or setting of their spaces, they resort to the traditional media of the region, the same ones that are used in homes, offices, and other secular spaces. They ensure that the spaces for worship are well painted; curtains and rugs are used in many; they hang colored banners with a Bible verse or other uplifting message and adorn the altar with flowers. In some cases they break with the predominant linearity by using elements of triangular or oval shapes in windows, facades, or access points. Lacking Catholicism's attention to visual catechism or sacramentality, they do not use any elements or objects that can be identified with that tradition's symbolism, such as bells, sculptures, crosses, candelabra, or candles. Some wooden furniture, such as benches or pulpits, can be considered as well-made crafts. In some churches the baptismal writing is painted on the wall or a fresco of an idyllic scene, such as an orchard. In two church entrances we also find a wall painting with a biblical motif. Human figures are never depicted. The name of the church and the institution's identifying logo are almost always present on the main facade, a feature made important by the 1992 Constitutional reforms over religion and the assignment of a new legal designation protecting religious property: Asociación Religiosa, or A.R.[21]

In older communities, pews, inherited from the Protestant and Catholic traditions, are preferably used, while the Neo-Pentecostal communities opt for the flexibility, lightness, and economy of folding chairs. This preference for the chair also facilitates different kinds of communal events, according to the needs or preferences for the use of space. After chairs and pews, the most important furniture and equipment is that related to music. For singing, the texts of the songs are projected on the front wall or on a movable screen. This frees the faithful from having to hold the old hymnals; they now have a broader vision of what is happening in their environment, with hands freed to clap, hug, or extend toward heaven. The importance of music in this liturgy is also reflected in the visible presence of musical instruments in the front space (or slightly to one of the sides), speakers, and other sound equipment. The pulpit is treated and placed differently in Pentecostal churches. IAFCJ pulpits are usually large and elaborate and are placed in the center of the frontal area. A large open Bible is placed on them but is not used during worship. The pulpits in independent and Neo-Pentecostals churches are much lighter, are not fixed in place, and do not hold a Bible.

Pentecostal churches' worship spaces are generally in direct contact with the street or sit very close to it (unlike their United States counterparts). Some of the older buildings are clearly distinguishable from the immediate neighborhood context, which is generally made up of houses. The distinction is due to their greater volume, and not because their shapes are significantly different or because they have some other distinctive feature. The more recently built churches are not clearly distinguishable from their immediate surroundings, neither by the use of color nor by the construction materials; indeed, many are not distinguishable at all. Thus, their integration into the immediate context is natural and simple. There is no explicit attempt at rupture or integration. They belong to the built environment almost naturally, at least from a visual point of view.

The Worship Service Space as Perceived by Pentecostal Pastors

Any attempt to interpret the worship spaces of Pentecostalism must take very seriously the perception of its builders and users, that is, Pentecostal believers themselves. In this section I will try to present some aspects of this perception, based on the analysis of a large number of interviews with pastors from the different Pentecostal churches in the region of study.[22] For the sake of clarity, I will divide the exposition into four subthemes, which correspond to those most repeated and emphasized by the pastors themselves: (1) Perspective on Liturgy and Worship, (2) Community as the Temple of God, (3) Pragmatic Valorization of the Worship Space, and (4) Explicit or Implicit Negation of Catholicism.

A Perspective on Liturgy and Worship

The liturgical space serves primarily for the celebration of worship and has been built or adapted for that purpose. The specific type of liturgy will largely define the form and organization of the celebration space. For Pentecostal pastors, the liturgy is a means to experience the presence of God, and space, therefore, is the setting of that experience. Pastor 1 (IAFCJ) maintains that "The worship of the IAFCJ is dynamic, revivalistic, joyous, and where the presence of God is experienced"; whereas for Pastor 2 (Centro Cristiano Agua Viva-CCAV), the ideal worship service is one in which "people leave edified, in which people receive, feed, renew themselves; in which they leave full of the presence of God."

Almost all interviewees agreed that the most important components of worship are praise and preaching, although they referred to these by different names. Other liturgical moments such as prayer, testimony, laying on of hands, and intercession were also mentioned as very important.

Pastor 3 (IAFCJ) emphasizes, "Worship has worship and the Word as fundamental elements." He explains further: "I think it is difficult to separate worship from the Word because worship somehow prepares, gives sensitivity to the believer to receive the message that God has for us." Similarly, Pastor 1 (IAFCJ) argues that "Good music, good praise, good worship, and a good message strengthen the church and, incidentally, visitors like it." Pastor 2 (CCAV) opines, "I feel that there are people who are touched by praise and also by preaching. I feel that people are affected by the whole service, the whole service motivates them." For Pastor 4 (Comunidad Cristiana de Culiacán—CCC), "We understand the celebration as a time of worship to minister to God through praise and adoration and a time to minister to the needs of the people through prayer, laying on of hands, of letting the Holy Spirit give us what he is going to do at that moment."

The pastors argued against a too-rigid liturgy, favoring more flexibility. But they also expressed their rejection of a disorderly worship service. For Pastor 5 (CCC), "I believe that the order of service should not be something firmly pre-established; I believe that we must give God, his Spirit, an opportunity to lead us." Importantly, almost all the pastors understand liturgy to be a moment of fiesta, victory, and communal meeting—albeit, with various degrees of emphasis. Pastor 5 (CCC) describes his church's worship as "A time of celebration, jubilation, shouting, joy, freedom, gratitude to God.... In our services there are dances, there are shouts of joy, there are palm branches, there are whistles, trumpets." According to Pastor 6 (CCC), "On Sunday we are happy for the testimonies that are poured out, for all that God did that week, because we pray, we greet each other, because we see each other again." Also for Pastor 7 (Centro Cristiano Casa de Vida—CCCV), "Worship is of paramount importance as a time for meeting, as a time of celebration and also as a time in the week where you see your brothers, your friends." Neo-Pentecostalism's characteristic bellicose discourse is exemplified by Pastor 4 (CCC): "I see victory in celebration. It is the victory of the week for the warriors who raise their spiritual weapons and bring in all those who have been conquered by the power of the Gospel."

Community as the Temple of God

Pentecostal pastors appreciate this theological metaphor, used by Paul to explain his ecclesiological understanding for use in the service of resolving community problems. All interviewees agreed: The temple is important, but the most important thing is the community, the true temple of God. According to Pastor 5 (CCC), "Right now the temple is us, because the veil of the temple has already been torn." The same pastor argues, "We are in charge of lifting up the name of the Lord and it will be lifted up with or without a building, with a sumptuous building or with an austere building.... God is pleased to dwell in us, we are his temple, we are the church." Pastor 3 (IAFCJ) declares, "It is not the temple or the building itself that makes the life of a church attractive, but rather the communion, the unity of the church, makes a temple attractive.... The Holy Spirit does not depend on a constructed building."

Pragmatic Valorization of the Worship Space

Understanding the religious imagination of a particular group is key to understanding its material production of, in this case, worship spaces, although other determinants, such as socioeconomic ones, also carry important weight. A pragmatic approach, such as that revealed in the interviews, forces us to keep this dimension in mind for the correct interpretation of the worship service spaces. Religious and pragmatic evaluations are often closely linked, as will be seen in some of the following quotes.

For pastors, the basic requirements of worship spaces are functionality and comfort. To this end, Pastor 7 (CCCV) expressed: "Basically what interests me, speaking of the building, is a place that allows us comfort and enough room. I think that an austere but comfortable place is enough." Pastor 6 (CCC) similarly opined, "We want something that is comfortable, that has a floor, that is spacious, air-conditioned, well ventilated and illuminated. That's enough."

This position is reinforced by two complementary convictions. The first is that any place can be used as a place of worship. For example, Pastor 6 (CCC) averred, "For me the church is where the congregants are. It can be a very large house, or a very large patio that has a canvas or tiled roof." Pastor 7 (CCCV) expressed a similar conviction: "I believe that the building, more than anything, is precisely that: a space that allows us to meet in comfort." Pastor 4 (CCC) even advocated for the use of tents: "I would like us to have huge tents for worship. I say tents because tents have an enormous opportunity to move and grow." The second conviction is that the presence of the worshipping community sanctifies any gathering place. According to Pastor 5 (CCC), "The temple, the altar, for me it is an ordinary place, as far as the temple, the auditorium, the building is concerned. But for me that place is very important when the ministering begins; at that point for me it is no longer an ordinary place. When the service begins, that place is well respected, but under normal conditions it is an ordinary place." Pastor 2 (CCAV), whose community must rent its meeting space, argued, "I believe that a hotel meeting room does not detract from devotion at all, for the purposes of worship. I prefer a temple, but as long as there is no temple we are comfortable in a hotel. It could be a warehouse, it could be a tent, we would be the same."

Explicit or Implicit Negation of Catholicism

Pentecostalism in Sinaloa maintains a position of rejecting Catholicism and seeks to deny any sense of it, at least on a symbolic level. Architecture, as a symbolic system, transmits institutional or group values. The negation of Catholicism is evident in the dismissal of its worship spaces. These positions were repeatedly expressed in the interviews. The careful reader can note the veiled references to Catholicism as another form of negation.

Pastor 5 (CCC) shared, "For Catholics the temple is something sacred, it is something they idolize. In the act of passing a Catholic church making a sign of the cross upon themselves, I believe that Catholics are paying homage to the structure and the building. But it is a public building, made by men's hands." Pastor 6 (CCC) commented, "It is not as important for us to have a temple like the traditional ones"; while Pastor 7 (CCCV) avowed, "We are not very interested in the issue of traditional aesthetics."

Pentecostal Architecture: Toward a Theo-Phenomenological Interpretation

Next, I assay an interpretation of Pentecostal architecture, building upon and expanding the previous discussion. Although it concerns a specific expression of Oneness Pentecostalism in a certain region of Mexico, I believe my interpretation has certain relevance for the wider field of Latin America, and for Latino/a migratory contexts in the United States.

Although the architecture of the temples of the IAFCJ of Sinaloa shares common features with those of other regions of Mexico, it also maintains distinctive ones, which is explained in part by the climatic characteristics of the region and the sociocultural and historical composition of its population. The state located to the south, Nayarit, has a wetter climate, with jungle topography, while Sonora's climate to the north, is more desert or semidesert; both neighbors experience less population movement. These general differences will also produce differentiated architectural models. We can extend this comparison to other regions, such as the center of the country, where Catholicism is much more deeply rooted and social relations are less communal and more individualized; this does not favor a deep rootedness of charismatic Christianity in urban areas. If we look toward the border regions with the United States, we can see that the evolution of Pentecostalism and its architectural models have gradually moved away from Mexican influences and have assumed those of movements that are more seeker-sensitive and receptive to independent charismatic and Neo-Pentecostal Movements with their respective liturgical, evangelistic, and building models.

THE DYNAMICS OF PENTECOSTAL LITURGY

Pentecostal liturgy derives its morphology and programs from the theological understanding and the sociocultural formation of its communities. One of its main characteristics is its dynamism, which is indispensable in the construction of worship spaces. These spaces are characterized by being homogeneous, spacious, and regular, that is, characteristics that produce a static sense. This spatial statis serves as a stabilizing sensory factor and is the most adequate to contain the dynamism of the Pentecostal liturgy. This liturgical dynamic is generated by the various bodily movements during the different liturgical moments, which take place throughout the worship space. This explains the breadth of the altar, the aisles, the access, the pulpit area, etc. For Pentecostals, worship must be "fluid" and under the sign of the "freedom of the Spirit of God." This translates into the near unimpeded use of static space.

The Centrality of the Human Body in Pentecostal Liturgy

The human body and its communicative and expressive possibilities play a central role in Pentecostal liturgy. For Pentecostalism, the human body is sanctified by the presence of the Holy Spirit and transformed into the spirit's dwelling place, into an instrument of praise and a channel of blessing. The Spirit is understood as a gift, albeit a gift that must be sought, requested, communicated, and expressed. All these acts are expressed in the liturgy through bodily movements that require adequate and sufficient spaces. This centrality accorded the human body I also consider to be one of the most valuable characteristics of Pentecostal spirituality. The simplicity and clarity of the Pentecostal liturgical space is a psychological, sociological, and liturgical necessity. A complex spatial structure would conflict with the dynamics of this liturgy. A simple space, on the other hand, provides an important compensatory effect of stability. The white color of the interiors helps both to highlight the outline of the people, the main protagonists of worship, as well as to accentuate the effect of visual clarity and stability.

The Relationship or Concurrence Between Preaching and Singing

Pentecostal worship has maintained a moderate balance between its liturgical moments. Preaching, prayer, testimony, song, and other processual elements follow upon and complement each other. However, the excessive prominence that music has acquired in recent years has become a factor of liturgical imbalance and, consequently, of the liturgical space also. Music struggles to become the predominant component of the worship service, relegating other elements to a secondary position. This displacement is reflected in the transformation of space. The presence of the musical group and its location in front of the community, or slightly to one side of the pulpit, requires the expansion of that area. Musical instruments, speakers, overhead projectors, and microphones become visually dominant, at times reducing the pulpit to a small isolated and visually almost insignificant piece of furniture. In the "classical" Pentecostal churches, as I have mentioned, the pulpits are usually still large, with a large Bible resting on many of them. I interpret this as symbolic of the refusal of the preaching function to relinquish the central place in the liturgy it has always held in Protestant traditions. It seems that with the accentuation of music and organized dance groups in Neo-Pentecostalism, the desacralization of space is accelerated and diverted in favor of the sacralization of the spectacle.[23]

THE STAGING AND SYMBOLIZATION OF THE WORSHIP SERVICE

The simple Pentecostal space is the setting where complex symbolic, spiritual, and psychological relationships unfold. This is a site for the staging of the salvific drama as well as of the social dramas that find expression and resolution in each service. As L. S. Campos states, "Pentecostalism, more than historic Protestantism, has maintained in its worship services a greater proximity between religion and spectacle, which makes it easier to analyze from the dramaturgical point of view."[24] In Pentecostal worship the most intense moments such as baptism with the Spirit, prayer for healing, exposition of testimony, etc., occur at the altar; this explains the altar's existence as a large central area framed by the community, the raised area (or ministerial area) along with the pulpit, and the musical group, among other elements. All symbolic forces are directed toward that defining space. With regard to the 1:1 or 1:1.5 ratio of most of these spaces, I consider it as the symbol of the "democratization" of the Pentecostal liturgy, and the Pentecostal understanding of the "universal priesthood of all believers." If everyone can receive the Holy Spirit and all space is homogeneously holy, the distance between clergy and laity tends to dissolve. To be sure, in some churches the special treatment of the pastoral or ministerial area is still common. I consider that the slight rise in the area where the pulpit is located obeys practical criteria, as some pastors explained, but it may also express a certain continued symbolization of pastoral power.

The Symbolic Negation of Catholicism

Just as silence in human language can be semantically loaded, so too in architectural vocabulary the absence of elements can imply a message. This is the case with Pentecostal architecture, which has renounced the reproduction of any material symbol identifiable with Catholicism. In Mexico Catholicism is apparent in architecture with the visually and formally rich Baroque style. The verbal rejection expressed by the pastors finds its correspondence in the material negation of architecture. The simple, rectangular shapes of Pentecostalism, for example, stand in opposition to the richly crafted, dynamic shapes of Catholic temples. I interpret the predominance of white and the profuse lighting of the interiors in this same manner. At the level of suspicion, I argue that Pentecostal temples' homogenization with the urban environment is a renunciation of the exercise of symbolic power over the city, a projection so characteristic of Catholic architecture.

SPACE AS A PLACE OF ENCOUNTER WITH THE HOLY SPIRIT

The search for the encounter with the Holy Spirit, in its various interpretations (baptism, blessing, illumination, healing, etc.), is one of the main objectives of Pentecostal worship. This meeting is understood as an individual event, but it has the most effective spiritual framework in the worshipping community. The believers, rapt in their inner experience, require a space without too many disturbing visual stimuli. For the Pentecostal believer, access to God is direct; it does not require any type of material mediation.[25] The atmosphere of worship is greatly appreciated and is handled by the community. Space, then, has little or no value in the pursuit of this goal. After some time, it will gain greater significance, since the religious experience will remain linked in memory, both individually and collectively, to the space where such experience is lived. It is expected that the encounter with the Holy Spirit will take place in the liturgical place, but not because that place has in itself a sacred quality of its own, but because there is the community and, therefore, the promised presence of God.[26]

The Process of Desacralization of Space

Pentecostal believers have a deep respect and affection for their place of worship, but this does not mean that they assign it a sacramental or salvific value of its own. In reality, a process of desacralization of the liturgical space is perceptible in their communities' understanding. This process is reflected in the formal and spatial changes of the architecture, for example, change in the shape and style of the main door and access. I have mentioned that in older IAFCJ churches the main entrances and doors are visually and formally accented, while in newer (Neo-Pentecostal) ones they are almost imperceptible in the whole facade. The more traditional communities understand that the temple is part of the invitation to the unconverted to enter the space of worship where they can "meet the Lord." In the newest churches, the predominant idea is that the church has the task of going out into the "world" to search for "the lost." Thus, the entrance becomes the exit and loses symbolic and formal relevance. It is also in the oldest churches where the modest thresholds can still be found, due to the fact that in them a certain sacred-profane tension is still perceptible, and this liminal "space of passage" is required between the street and the place of worship.[27]

Space as a Place of Community Encounter

The centuries-long discussion about whether the liturgical space is *domus Dei* or *domus ecclesiae* has never worried Pentecostals. Theirs have always been community spaces. Indeed, the current trend, especially among Neo-Pentecostals, is to build and view spaces as multipurpose rooms, which is another reason why they appear so minimally "ecclesiastical." These churches are characterized by their flexibility in use, largely helped by the change from heavy benches to light chairs. It is not uncommon for the space where worship is held to serve, on other occasions, as a conference room, cinema, theater or dance rehearsal room, party room, garage, or hostel. Pentecostals, though, are not alone in this understanding of liturgical space. Klemens Richter, one of the most important liturgists of Protestantism, representing many, affirms, "An ecclesiastical building is the house of God only insofar as it is the house of the community."[28]

THE REAL-WORLD CONDITIONS OF PENTECOSTAL COMMUNITIES

I would be remiss to fail to mention, at least as a side note, that despite the fact that Pentecostalism has reached increasingly broad sectors of the middle classes in recent years, it continues to be a Christian expression located mainly among economically vulnerable groups in society. The limited financial possibilities of many Pentecostal communities do not allow them to assay more technically and architecturally complex constructions. Related to this condition is the urban location of most of the Pentecostal places of worship, which are located in popular neighborhoods from whence most members come. These neighborhoods are characterized by a very modest architecture. Pentecostal construction projects reproduce or adapt to the surrounding conditions, producing an architecture that can best be described as popular.

PROTESTANT PRECURSORS AND MODELS

The dynamics of Pentecostal architecture can be understood, of course, in light of historical experience. The first decades of the Protestant Reformation did not see significant changes in the construction and use of places of worship vis á vis prior epochs. The common practice of the Middle Ages of using ecclesiastical spaces for multiple activities, such as teaching, storing food, community meetings, or conducting business transactions, continued. The main reformers commonly attributed a more utilitarian than religious value to the temples. Martin Luther, for example, wrote in a collection of sermons printed in 1526: "There is no other reason to build churches than that people come together to pray, hear preaching, and receive the sacraments." Equally well known is his statement made during the inaugural preaching of the Schlosskirche church, in Torgau, in 1544: "[In the churches] nothing else happens, other than our beloved Lord himself speaks to us through his holy Word and we, through our part, speak to him through prayer and praise."[29]

The first changes can be seen toward the end of the sixteenth century, but they became more evident in the seventeenth century. Protestant liturgy privileges preaching and the pulpit was elevated for both acoustic and theological reasons. The use of benches in churches was implemented, which also indicates the importance of the liturgical community in Protestantism. A seated community causes less noise and is better able to hear the preaching and see what is happening in the space. The baptistery was moved to the choir area so that it would be visible to the community. Another special result of the Reformation was the spatial arrangement of the altar, the pulpit, and the organ in an axial layout in the eastern part of the church, that is, also visible to the community gathered in the nave. Notably, the Reformation put into motion the idea of the centrality of the community in the liturgical celebration. The preaching, delivered in the community's language, became one of the most relevant moments, and the Eucharist loses its mystery, but the community gained in its understanding and participation of the ritual.

From the eighteenth century onward, the discussion of the ecclesiastical building as *domus Dei* or *domus ecclesiae* acquired theological relevance and continued during the following centuries without achieving a consensus either in Catholicism or in Protestantism. In general terms, it can be said that in Catholicism the trend is toward the *domus Dei*, while in Protestantism it is toward the *domus ecclesiae*, and in the Orthodox Church toward a balance. Pentecostalism offers a clear response: it is the *domus de la ecclesia* to meet its *Dei*.

FINAL WORD

The formal simplicity and pragmatic character of Pentecostal worship spaces in northwestern Mexico are the result of the specific understanding and experience of the communities that build and use them. They reflect the materialization of their theology and also a form of being-in-the-world. The historical processes of the transformation of Mexican Pentecostalism, such as its expansion, institutionalization, social ascent, or "modernization," have left their marks on the spaces. Pentecostals' understanding of their places of worship is grounded in scriptural understanding and traditions of the Protestant Reformation; so are its understanding, use, and experience of liturgical spaces.

I am aware that in contexts other than those analyzed here, whether as a general trend or as isolated cases, there are Pentecostal communities undertaking enormous construction projects with an extravagant expenditure of formal and technical resources, but I do not believe that it is nor will it represent the general trend in Latin American Pentecostalism. They do not represent or reflect the essence of this rich Christian tradition. I am also aware that the geographical limitation that I imposed on this study left out very valuable liturgical experiences and architectural examples. Nevertheless, as a pioneering work on the subject, it invites dialogue on this very important aspect of Oneness and other Pentecostal traditions.[30]

NOTES

This chapter is a modified version of a longer article originally published in Spanish as "El espacio litúrgico en el pentecostalismo mexicano: Acercamiento teológico a la arquitectura Pentecostal" [Liturgical Space in Mexican Pentecostalism: A Theological Approach to Pentecostal Architecture], *Estudos de Religião* 16, no. 22 (June 2002): 110–40. Translations of this chapter were provided by Lloyd D. Barba and Daniel Ramírez.

1. According to Leonildo Silveira Campos, "The spatial foundation of a group's religiosity becomes inevitable, no matter how strong the rejection this may invite. Over time, acts and places are identified, because of repetitive ritual reenactments, thus generating a memory linked to

physical space, a more durable element than emotions and events. . . . The meeting place, linked to the rites practiced, can be that something durable with conditions to guarantee the continuity of a religious expression in time and space." See Campos, *Teatro*, 152–53. [Editors' note: Quotations from non-English language sources have been translated.]

2. Huschke, *Kirchen erzählen vom Glauben*, 36.

3. Duarte, *Templo*, 96; chapter 2 offers a broad presentation of official Catholic teaching on the importance and meaning of the temple (61–93).

4. Ortega, *Breve historia*, 15–29; Rangel and Amador, *Historia y geografía*, 8–45, 156–75; Fisher, *Sinaloa*.

5. Lizárraga, *Nos llevó la Ventolera*, 146.

6. See Hoffmann, "Drogengeld," 39–43.

7. Quoted in Gaxiola, *La Serpiente y la paloma*, 108.

8. Quoted in ibid., 111.

9. Ibid., 111; emphasis added.

10. Hollenweger, *Pentecostalismo*, 9.

11. Robeck, *Azusa Street Mission*, 69–74.

12. Leonildo Silveira Campos observes: "The first Pentecostal preachers gave no importance to space but to the events that took place in them. It is possible that the aversion to luxurious architecture is also linked to the development of the idea that the abandonment of the old ecclesiastical setting would be the *sine qua non* for religious rebirth and that, the resurgence of a powerful Christian faith, similar to that of the first apostles, would only be possible outside the traditional schemes of expression of Christian religiosity, including architectural ones." Campos, *Teatro*, 118.

13. Gaxiola, *La serpiente y la paloma*, 143; emphasis added.

14. Ibid., 150.

15. Ibid., 151.

16. Ibid., 196.

17. Ibid., 196.

18. Ramírez, *Migrating Faith*, 89–94.

19. Gaxiola, *La serpiente y la paloma*, 214.

20. This obligation is clearly laid out in the church's charter. *Constitución y Principios Doctrinales de la IAFCJ*, 98–99, cap. 20, artículos 58 y 59.

21. [Editors' note: In 1992, during the Carlos Salinas administration, Mexico reformed the stringent anticlerical Articles 27 and 130 of the 1917 Constitution, a legacy of the Revolution and violent (Catholic) church-state conflicts of the late nineteenth and early twentieth centuries. The subsequent legislation (1992 and 2003) rescinded the harsh laws of the Cristero era and finally granted all churches legal personhood and ownership of temples and related properties, which had previously had been considered "patrimony of the Nation." By 2003, more than 6,119 "Asociaciones Religiosas" (A.R.) had registered with the government. The continuing guarantee of official protection, as well as the public projection of equal status, prompted many groups to eagerly display their AR number prominently on the facades of church buildings. Temples of the IAFCJ often display the denomination's logo and AR number. See "Ley de Asociaciones Religiosas."]

22. The interviews were conducted from February to March 2001. Random interviews with other church members, male and female, were also conducted. Their opinions are not included here, owing to methodological reasons. However, these do not differ significantly from those held by the pastors. For the sake of anonymity, the respondents are assigned numbers.

23. Ibarra, *Entre la espontaneidad*, 30–44.

24. Campos, *Teatro*, 68. See also Hartmut Becks: "The service can be viewed as a grand scenario: the stage and directions serve solely to effect in the visitor the sensorial experience of the invisible dimension of the transcendent." Becks, *Der Gottesdienst in der Erlebnisgesellschaft*, 184.

25. See Klemens Richter: "A place or space does not possess any sacred significance on its own, but rather acquires this and in the measure that (a community) establishes it as a place of encounter with the holy God." Richter, "Raumgestalt," 222.

26. Sternberg, "Suche nach einer neuen Sakralität?," 65: "The sacrality of the ecclesiastical building, in the Christian understanding, can only be derived from the holiness of the worshipping community. As long as the persons in this space celebrate and pray, the space has a different quality from other spaces. God is holy, and persons and their actions depend on Him. Everything else is 'holy' only in a derivative sense."

27. Eliade, *Sacred*, 25: "The threshold, the door shows the solution of continuity in space immediately and concretely; hence their great religious importance, for they are symbols and at the same time vehicles of passage from the one space to the other."

28. Richter, "Raumgestalt," 103. Richter also points out: "The ecclesiastical building should not be understood as a limited space of worship dedicated to God in the religious aspect, in such a way it is converted into a symbol of a special religious world, set off from the quotidian world" (104).

29. Quoted in Koch, "Die Wirkungsgeschichte der Reformation," 202.

30. See Rojas, *Entender el templo*, for a broad architectural analysis of Chilean Pentecostal temples.

BIBLIOGRAPHY

Becks, Hartmut. *Der Gottesdienst in der Erlebnisgesellschaft: Zur Bedeutung der kultursoziologischen Untersuchung Gerhard Schulzes für Theorie und Praxis des Gottesdienstes* [Worship in Living Society: The Importance of Gerhard Schule's Sociocultural Research for the Theory and Practice of Worship]. Waltrop: Hartmut Spenner, 1999.

Campos, Leonildo Silveira. *Teatro, templo e mercado: Organização e marketing de um empreendimento neopentecostal* [Theater, Temple and Market: Organization and Marketing in a Neopentecostal Enterprise]. 2nd ed. Petrópolis, São Paulo: São Bernardo do Campo, 1999.

Constitución y Principios Doctrinales de la IAFCJ [Constitution and Doctrinal Principles of the IAFCJ]. México, D.F.: Iglesia Apostólica de la Fe en Cristo Jesús, 1985.

Duarte, Juan Anaya. *El templo en la teología y la arquitectura* [The Temple in Theology and Architecture]. México, D.F.: Universidad Iberoamericana, 1996.

Eliade, Mircea. *The Sacred and the Profane: The Nature of Religion*. New York: Harcourt, 1959.

Fisher, Richard D. *Sinaloa, Mexico: From the Sea to the Sierra*. Tucson: Sunracer, 1989.

Gaxiola Gaxiola, Manuel. *La serpiente y la paloma: Historia, teología y análisis de la Iglesia Apostólica de la Fe en Cristo Jesús, 1914–1994* [The Serpent and the Dove: History, Theology and Analysis of the Apostolic Church of the Faith in Christ Jesus, 1914–1994]. 2nd ed, corregida y aumentada. México, D.F.: Libros Pyros, 1994. First published 1970 by author.

Hoffmann, K. D. "Drogengeld unterwandert den Staat: Mexiko ist zum wichtigsten Transitland für den illegalen Drogenhandel in die USA geworden" [Drug Money Undermines the State: Mexico Has Become the Most Important Transit Country for the Illegal Drug Trade to the USA]. *Der Überblick*, February 2000.

Hollenweger, Walter. *El Pentecostalismo: Historia y doctrinas* [Pentecostalism: History and Doctrines]. Buenos Aires: La Aurora, 1976.

Huschke, Erika. *Kirchen erzählen vom Glauben: Vom Kirchenbau zum Gemeindeaufbau* [Churches Narrate Faith: From Church Building to Congregation Building]. Hamburg: Waxmann, 1995.

Ibarra Silguero, Abraham. *Entre la espontaneidad y el profesionalismo: Análisis del fenómeno litúrgico-musical contemporáneo en América*

Latina [Between Spontaneity and Professionalism: Analysis of the Contemporary Liturgical-Musical Phenomenon in Latin America]. Coatzacoalcos, México: Buena Noticia, 2000.

Koch, Ernest. "Die Wirkungsgeschichte der Reformation für den Kirchenbau" [History of the Impact of the Reformation on Church Construction]. In *Lernort Kirchenraum: Erfahrungen—Einsichten— Anregungen* [Church Space as a Place of Learning: Experiences— Insights—Suggestions], edited by Roland Degen and Inge Hansen. Münster: Waxmann, 1998.

Ley de Asociaciones Religiosas y Culto Público y Su Reglamento [Law of Religious Associations and Public Worship and Their Regulation]. México, D.F., 2003. Subsecretaría de Población, Migración y Asuntos Religiosos, Secretaría de Gobernación.

Lizárraga Hernández, Arturo. *Nos llevó la Ventolera: El proceso de la emigración rural al extranjero en Sinaloa; Los casos de Cosalá, San Ignacio y El Verde* [The Wind Gust Carried Us: The Process of Foreign Rural Emigration from Sinaloa: The Cases of Cosalá, San Ignacio, and El Verde]. Culiacán: Universidad Autónoma de Sinaloa, 2004.

Ortega Noriega, Sergio. *Breve historia de Sinaloa* [Brief History of Sinaloa]. México, D.F.: FCE and El Colegio de México, 1999.

Ramírez, Daniel. *Migrating Faith: Pentecostalism in the United States and Mexico in the Twentieth Century*. Chapel Hill: University of North Carolina Press, 2015.

Rangel, María Eugenia de Lara, y Rubén Octavio Amador Zamora, *Historia y geografía de Sinaloa* [History and Geography of Sinaloa]. México, D.F.: Nuevo México, 2000.

Richter, Klemens. "Raumgestalt und Glaubensgehalt: Der liturgische Raum prägt den Glauben" [Spatial Design and Faith Content: The Liturgical Space Shapes Faith]. *Kunst und Kirche* 56 (1993): 102–7.

Robeck, Cecil M. *The Azusa Street Mission and Revival: The Birth of the Global Pentecostal Movement*. Nashville: Thomas Nelson, 2006.

Rojas, Rodrigo Vidal. *Entender el templo pentecostal: Elementos, fundamentos, significados* [Understanding the Pentecostal Temple: Elements, Bases, Meanings]. Concepción, Chile: Centro Evangélico de Estudios Pentecostales, 2012.

Sternberg, Thomas. "Suche nach einer neuen Sakralität? Über den Kirchenraum und seine Bedeutung" [Looking for a New Sacredness? Concerning Church Space and Its Meaning]. In *Raumerfahrungen: Raum und Transzendenz; Beiträge zum Gespräch zwischen Theologie, Philosophie und Architektur* [Spatial Experiences: Space and Transcendence; Contributions to the Conversation Between Theology, Philosophy and Architecture], edited by Dirk Ansorge, Cristoph Ingenhoven, and Jürgen Overdiek, 62–81. Münster: LIT Verlag, 1999.

Conclusion

Navigating New Paths to Old Landmarks

Lloyd D. Barba, Andrea Shan Johnson, and Daniel Ramírez

This volume has served to introduce and analyze a significant and growing religious movement in North America. Often lost among the multitude of broader Pentecostal denominations, Oneness Pentecostals have long deserved recognition and separate study. Variously referenced as "Apostolic" or "Jesus' name" in popular and scholarly parlance, Oneness Pentecostals' recent incursions into the public square, like those of other Pentecostals and Charismatics, have garnered notable press attention. To be sure, however, the activism of some African American and Latino groups predates this period. This first published volume on the movement's diverse history may help to contextualize these diverse and staggered paths of engagement. To conclude, we consider eight key themes that emerge from this volume, all of which deserve deeper and more nuanced study.

OUTSIDERS AND INSIDERS

First, as a movement of religious outsiders in every sense of the word and from its very beginning, Oneness Pentecostalism provides an especially rich venue for interpretation. The chapters by Ramírez, Barba, Sailes, Coleby Delgado, Johnson, and Fortuny analyze this diversity along the lines of race, ethnicity, class, gender, and even geographic location. While the various groups under study share a general theological disposition, they are not necessarily alike in their practice and self-understanding. This has led the constituencies of the various denominations on decidedly different social and political paths, a subject of future study. Also, as R. Laurence Moore has suggested, outsiders' agency has often proved constitutive to insider identity.[1]

This is clearly the case in the early schism over notions of the godhead; the outcome of the conflict was the consolidation of an ultra-Trinitarian flagship denomination, the Assemblies of God, which then eased the AG's eventual imbedding within the general universe of American Evangelicalism. Within the Apostolic movement, perennial schisms have also helped to shape and sharpen insider (and outsider) identities. Understanding schism as both doctrinal and sociological breaking points sheds light on imagined social identities. More remains to be fully fleshed out regarding important competing expressions such as the Mexico-based transnational Iglesia Evangélica Cristiana Espiritual and the Salinas, California–based Church of Jesus of the Americas, the leading Oneness group in the heavily indigenous southern Mexican state of Oaxaca. We could also include other African American–led denominations such as the Church of Our Lord Jesus Christ, the Pentecostal Church Apostolic Faith, and Bible Way Church of Our Lord Jesus Christ Worldwide (BWCOLJC); the more recently formed International Bibleway Church of Jesus Christ (an excision of BWCOLJC) and Worldwide Pentecostal Fellowship (an excision of the United Pentecostal Church International); and others such as the Branhamite and Latter-Rain movements, and even Oneness practitioners of snake-handling.

THEOLOGY

Second, Oneness Pentecostals are often understood as having chosen the Finished Work path of salvation and then further split from the like-minded on that issue when they adopted a Oneness theology and soteriology. As the chapters by Reed and Segraves demonstrate, the theological underpinnings are more complex and even include aspects of ancient Eastern Christian theology. Indeed, the prescient work by Manuel Gaxiola points to the movement's "unfinished" theological labor. And while it remains beyond the purview of this book, a smaller stream of Wesleyan Oneness Pentecostalism—the Birmingham-based Apostolic Overcoming Holiness Church (AOH)—begs historical recovery and analysis, as does the wider Black Apostolic Movement's overlap with Church of God in Christ orbits. The decentering of the Oneness Movement's origin story also invites an examination of Wesleyan roots and continuities in Mexican and

Mexican-American Apostolicism, as well as robust (and even more heterodox) offshoots like the Luz del Mundo of Mexico, whose founder's vision in 1926 claimed a full renewal of the primitive church and his role (and that of his progeny) as the apostle of that restoration.

PENTECOSTAL STUDIES

Third, the general study of Pentecostalism has often neglected to deeply nuance its important divide of the early twentieth century, and even more so, to acknowledge the similarities and unique differences evident in the Oneness strand of the movement. In *Heaven Below*, historian Grant Wacker focused on early American Pentecostals'—Trinitarian and Oneness—shared social history.[2] While Robert Mapes Anderson, in *Vision of the Disinherited*, included Oneness leaders in his study of early Pentecostalism, the "New Issue" did not factor into his larger argument about social mobility and immobility.[3] Yet, belief mattered. Indeed, sectarian introversion may help to explain white Apostolics' staggered socioeconomic and political developments compared to more mainstream Trinitarian Pentecostals. Through this volume's chapters we can see how at times Oneness Pentecostals operated much as other Pentecostals, yet a thorough examination of their history illustrates ways in which previously underrepresented groups were significant in the movement. As Coleby Delgado and Johnson show, women in ministry experienced much of the same frustrations as women in ministry in the larger Pentecostal Movement, yet Oneness women took part in doctrinal debates and managed, despite much opposition, to carve out space for their callings. As the chapter by Barba illustrates, Pentecostals in the Okie migration were influenced by their migratory experience, which uniquely influenced a regional expression of the Oneness Movement. Similarly, the book's several chapters invite further— comparative and interdisciplinary—theological, historical, social scientific, and cultural studies of a movement of such intense journalistic interest today.

EVANGELICALISM AND POLITICAL ENGAGEMENT

Fourth, a close examination of Oneness Pentecostalism offers a nuanced view of Evangelicalism's historical and current trends. Indeed, as noted by Russell Spittler and Donald Dayton, the acritical application of Evangelical typology to Pentecostalism has often proved an uncomfortable fit.[4] Many within the sectarian Oneness Movement would agree and spurn the "Evangelical" label—the "denominal" world was often decried in the white Apostolic pulpit.

Also, Swiss sociologist Lalive d'Epinay's conclusion that apolitical Chilean Pentecostals were uselessly disengaged from their society's pressing questions (of the late 1960s) was clumsily applied to Pentecostals everywhere, including in North America.[5] As a result, the current political incursions have caught many observers by surprise. To be sure, American politics in the final quarter of the twentieth century began to make for strange bedfellows around the issues of abortion, family, marriage, and nationalism. Even more recent political shifts lend credence to the notion that "Evangelical" finds more points of agreement and better coheres if conceptualized as a political identity, rather than as a religious one; as a result, sectarian distinctives are deemphasized.[6] White Oneness Pentecostals' relatively late and perhaps cautious incursion into the political arena demonstrates this point precisely (e.g., National Apostolic Christian Leadership Conference), while some African American and Latino Apostolics' engagement with the great social and political matters of the day reflect their embeddedness in distinct historical moments and settings. Black Apostolics long maintained a prophetic witness against racism, even as their white Oneness counterparts remained apathetic, or, worse, opposed federal legislation to tackle racism. The chapters by Barba and Sailes demonstrate the potential of the movement to find a home in a particular version of secular politics and complement Ramírez's earlier work on Apostolic leadership in Mexican agrarian communes and solidarity and sanctuary for repatriated and undocumented immigrants and refugees in the United States.[7] Much historical recovery work remains to be done, however, including, say, on AOH protagonism in Alabama civil rights history. The new studies will offer, of course, important challenges to received paradigms of apolitical, sectarian withdrawal and to new prescriptions for and temptations toward political engagement.

RACE AND ETHNICITY

Fifth, this work shows both the triumphs and failures of the movement as it crossed—beginning with the Azusa Street Revival—many of the racial, geographic, and gendered boundaries of the day. Indeed Oneness Pentecostalism was the final branch of US Pentecostalism to succumb to Jim Crow's encroaching shadow. The influence of Black PAW leader G. T. Haywood on the movement as a whole serves as a reminder of this interracial heyday and of the potential that was lost as segregationists held sway. But not entirely.[8] Sailes's chapter offers important insights into the clear-eyed and forceful leadership of Black Apostolics in the heyday of Chicago civil rights activism. Coleby Delgado's chapter demonstrates the way in which African American women in ministry often bore a double burden in their identities, while Ramirez's work on hymnody demonstrates how shared music can retain distinct meanings, depending on location, and how original Latino compositions often reflected the existential reality of migratory and borderlands experience against a backdrop of intensified xenophobia and still-hegemonic Catholicism.

Future studies on Oneness Pentecostalism and race and ethnicity ought to also examine how various denominations responded to racial tensions in the United States, including the civil rights movement and anti-immigration measures. Consider for example, Rev. Smallwood Williams, founder of the Washington, DC–based Bible Way Church, who in 1947 held a "proper" (celebratory) funeral for the recently deceased Theodore Bilbo, former governor and senator of Mississippi, a staunch segregationist and KKK member. Apparently, Williams had prophesied Bilbo's demise (for that same year). Over two thousand people attended this "funeral."[9] The recovery of such a datum and many others would offer a fuller and more precise picture of Oneness Pentecostalism and would allow for comparisons between Black and historically white organizations as these sought to make sense of and pragmatically adjust to the end of segregation brought on by the Civil Rights Act of 1964 and other measures, and even to sort out racialized polity arrangements.

CLASS

Sixth, Oneness Pentecostals were often seen as being from working-class roots, an image they were not quick to shed; indeed, their songs often proudly alluded to this. The chapter by Barba demonstrates the ways in which this played out for Okies in the Central Valley of California. The chapter by Sailes shows how concerns about the urban working class led to community activism on the part of the Braziers in Chicago. Similarly, Ramírez has examined Apostolicism's success in reaching and taking deep root in peasant and proletarian niches in Mexico and its labor diaspora, niches clumsily overlooked by mainline Protestant precursors.[10] An examination of the working-class roots of the movement should be continued. For example, many snake-handling groups, with heavily working-class congregations, hold Oneness theological views but may prefer fellowship with non-Oneness snake-handling groups of similar class location over those with similar theology. The recent move by some Oneness Pentecostals toward political involvement and leadership reflects sociological developments as much as theological ones. In this, they do not differ greatly from other groups whose socioeconomic ascendancy and increased literacy have propelled them toward the center of cultural and political life. Pilgrims and settlers in American Zion can view the immediate and cosmic stakes very differently. One suggestive index for future study: the eclipse of world-renouncing themes (e.g., "This World Is Not My Home") in the new global worship repertoires (e.g., Hillsong, Bethel, etc.) adopted by Oneness Pentecostals.

GENDER

Seventh, Pentecostals were noted for their acceptance of women in the pulpit and as leading agents of evangelism. As the chapters by Johnson, Coleby Delgado, and Sailes indicate, this trend carried over to both Black and white groups. This often meant that women were afforded a place behind the pulpit, although they could be deplatformed when their churches wanted to establish male-centered leadership. In this they were not unlike many of their Holiness brethren and sisters, but these chapters provide helpful comparisons. There is some question, however, about the long-term stability of this trend. Many denominations saw the number of women on their ministerial rolls decrease over time. The impact of Cold War conformity and entrenchment in the household, as well as the desire of 1950s and 1960s activists to establish a place for Black men, no doubt had an impact on the church. As an example of such containment trends, Louisiana United Pentecostal Church International women fully weighed in on behalf of the state's opposition to a revival of a call for support of the Equal Rights Amendment in the 1970s.[11] In addition, Latinas often faced more restrictions within their denominations, an ironic development, given their catalytic role as movement founders (e.g., Mexico's Iglesia Apostólica's matriarch Romana Carbajal de Valenzuela) and ordained deaconesses and their impressive industry in developing the economic engines that drove foreign missions and temple construction projects throughout the twentieth century.[12] The irony is complex. In 1975, the Iglesia Apostólica commemorated Romana Carbajal de Valenzuela to mark the first International Women's Year declared by the United Nations Educational, Scientific and Cultural Organization (UNESCO).[13] Clearly, more comparative work contextualizing these trends is key for future study.

GLOBAL MOVEMENT

Finally, Oneness Pentecostals were embedded in a larger global movement. As the chapters by Gaxiola, Reed, Segraves, Ramírez, Fortuny, and Chiquete demonstrate, the movement was not comprised chiefly of white North Americans. Rather, the movement developed simultaneously among African Americans, immigrants of European ancestry (often traversing the Canada-US border), and others, especially Mexicans and other Latinos. All of these migrants brought their preexisting expressions of Christianity with them and influenced the movement. In recent years, the movement, like many other Evangelical ones, has shown significant increase in the global South and in global South–driven growth in the United States through migration. Future research should include examinations of the role of missions and the ways in which the missionized and their progeny have adapted *sui generis* versions of Oneness Pentecostalism. The apostle-led and Guadalajara-based Luz del Mundo church exemplifies this pattern, including, especially, its recent practice of "reverse missions."

NEW PATHS

The question of origins and routes undergirds many of this volume's discussions. The travel metaphor is apt for a movement still finding its way forward. When the revivalists of 1913 boarded the electric railcars to Arroyo Seco, they probably hoped to regain something of the glory days of the Azusa Street Revival events. It is doubtful that any of them anticipated an experience that would eventually split the burgeoning movement over the godhead question. Nevertheless, their retrospective view of the outcome confirmed their conviction that they had moved in a true direction toward apostolicity. For their antagonists, of course, Oneness folks had run the gospel car off the rails. When Romana Carbajal de Valenzuela rode a train to take the news of the new Pentecost to her native Chihuahua, the intrepid evangelist had no way of knowing the outcome: that today Apostolics would represent up to one-half of Mexican and Mexican American Pentecostals. Many other pioneers similarly walked or rode by faith. The Oneness Pentecostal Movement that resulted from those origins now can be found in a diversity of forms and places. Much of the history of this movement remains yet to be written. Future scholars are sure to find fruitful work in this area. This volume seeks to begin that task.

NOTES

1. Moore, *Religious Outsiders*.
2. Wacker, *Heaven Below*.
3. Anderson, *Vision of the Disinherited*.

4. Spittler, "Are Pentecostals and Charismatics Fundamentalists?"; Dayton, "Limits of Evangelicalism," 36–56.

5. D'Epinay, *Haven of the Masses*.
6. Martí, *American Blindspot*, 251.
7. Ramírez, *Migrating Faith*.
8. French, *Early Interracial*.
9. Harvey, *Through the Storm*, 107–8.

10. Ramírez, *Migrating Faith*.
11. Mitchell, "Spirit Filled Women," 164–66.
12. Barba, "Farmworker Frames, 716–17.
13. Ramírez, *Migrating Faith*, 72.

BIBLIOGRAPHY

Anderson, Robert Mapes. *Vision of the Disinherited: The Making of Modern Pentecostalism*. New York: Oxford University Press, 1979.

Barba, Lloyd. "Farmworker Frames: Apostólico Counter Narratives in California's Valleys." *Journal of the American Academy of Religion* 86, no. 3 (September 2018): 691–723.

Dayton, Donald W. "The Limits of Evangelicalism: The Pentecostal Tradition." In *The Variety of American Evangelicalism*, edited by Donald W. Dayton and Robert K. Johnston, 36–56. Knoxville: University of Tennessee Press, 1991.

Epinay, Lalive d'. *Haven of the Masses: A Study of the Pentecostal Movement in Chile*. London: Lutterworth Press, 1969.

French, Talmadge. *Early Interracial Oneness Pentecostalism: G. T. Haywood and the Pentecostal Assemblies of the World (1901–1931)*. Eugene, OR: Pickwick, 2014.

Harvey, Paul. *Through the Storm, Through the Night: A History of African American Christianity*. Lanham, MD: Rowman & Littlefield, 2011.

Martí, Gerardo. *American Blindspot: Race, Class, Religion, and the Trump Presidency*. Lanham, MD: Rowman & Littlefield, 2020.

Mitchell, Glenda Bridges. "Spirit Filled Women: Louisiana's United Pentecostal Church International and Modern American Culture." PhD diss., University of Georgia, 2003.

Moore, R. Laurence. *Religious Outsiders and the Making of Americans*. New York: Oxford University Press, 1986.

Ramírez, Daniel. *Migrating Faith: Pentecostalism in the United States and Mexico*. Chapel Hill: University of North Carolina Press, 2015.

Spittler, Russel. "Are Pentecostals and Charismatics Fundamentalists? A Review of American Uses of These Categories." In *Charismatic Christianity as a Global Culture*, edited by Karla Poewe, 103–16. Columbia: University of South Carolina Press, 1994.

Wacker, Grant. *Heaven Below: Early Pentecostals and American Culture*. Cambridge: Harvard University Press, 2001.

Lloyd D. Barba (PhD, University of Michigan) is Assistant Professor in the Department of Religion at Amherst College. He is the author of *Sowing the Sacred: Mexican Pentecostal Farmworkers in California* and numerous articles on Pentecostal history, the US Sanctuary Movement, and religious migration. He currently serves as the cochair of the History of Christianity Unit of the American Academy of Religion.

Daniel Chiquete (PhD in History from the Universidad Autónoma de Sinaloa, PhD in Theology from the University of Hamburg, and Bachelor in Architecture) is a Mexican scholar and cofounder and current continental director of the Red Latinoamericana de Estudios Pentecostales (RELEP—the Latin-American Network of Pentecostal Studies). He is a teacher at the Instituto Tecnológico y de Estudios Superiores de Monterrey. He has previous taught at the Universidad Bíblica Latinoamericana (Costa Rica) and was Director of Studies (Studienleiter) at the Missionsakademie of the University of Hamburg. He is the author of several books and articles on Pentecostalism, Architecture, and History.

Dara Coleby Delgado (PhD, University of Dayton) is Assistant Professor of Religious Studies and Black Studies at Allegheny College. Coleby Delgado was a 2018–19 AAUW Dissertation Fellow and has contributed to various academic journals, edited volumes, and popular news outlets. Coleby Delgado's research interest in Pentecostalism, gender, and race comes together in her forthcoming book on Bishop Ida Bell Robinson, founder of the Mount Sinai Holy Church of America, Inc.; that book project is also with Penn State University Press and part of the Studies in the Holiness and Pentecostal Movements series.

Patricia Fortuny-Loret de Mola (PhD, University College, London) is Research Professor at the Centro de Investigaciones y Estudios Superiores en Antropología Social or CIESAS Peninsular (Center for Research and Study in Social Anthropology) in Merida, Yucatan, Mexico. Her extensive publication record of books and articles (in both English and Spanish) covers numerous topics on religious diversity, pluralism, and international migration. Her publications on the Mexico-based denomination La Luz Del Mundo (Light of the World) have distinguished her as a leading authority on this rapidly growing global movement. She is a regular commenter for Mexican and US media on matters pertaining to minority religious groups in North America.

Daniel Ramírez (PhD, Duke University) is Associate Professor of Religion at Claremont Graduate University and former President of the American Society of Church History. He is a specialist in the history of transnational Pentecostalism. His award-winning book *Migrating Faith* was the first to document the ways in which reverse missions helped spread Pentecostalism through North America.

David A. Reed (PhD, Boston University) is Professor Emeritus of Pastoral Theology and Research Professor at Wycliffe College, University of Toronto. He is author of the award-winning volume *"In Jesus' Name": The History and Beliefs of Oneness Pentecostals*, as well as numerous articles and chapters on Pentecostal and charismatic history and theology.

Rosa Sailes (EdD, National-Louis University; MA, McCormick Theological Seminary) is an independent scholar and the founder and director of the Chicago-based EZRA Project. She is the author and editor of various books on Pentecostalism and ministry.

Daniel Segraves (PhD, Regent University) is Professor Emeritus at Urshan Graduate School of Theology. Segraves is the author of *Andrew D. Urshan: A Theological Biography* and numerous books and articles on Oneness Pentecostalism.

Andrea Shan Johnson (PhD, University of Missouri) is Associate Professor of History at California State University, Dominguez Hills. She is a specialist in the history of religion and social movements in the twentieth century and has published several journal articles on Pentecostal history. She serves as the current chair of the History Interest Group of the Society for Pentecostal Studies and cochair of the Pentecostal-Charismatic Movements Unit of the American Academy of Religion.

Milton Keynes UK
Ingram Content Group UK Ltd.
UKHW041323111024
2132UKWH00035B/178